Gettysburg Eddie Plank

ALSO BY DAVE HELLER

*Ken Williams: A Slugger
in Ruth's Shadow* (McFarland, 2017)

Gettysburg Eddie Plank

A Pitcher's Journey to the Hall of Fame

Dave Heller

McFarland & Company, Inc., Publishers
Jefferson, North Carolina

Library of Congress Cataloguing-in-Publication Data

Names: Heller, Dave, 1968– author.
Title: Gettysburg Eddie Plank : a pitcher's journey to the Hall of Fame / Dave Heller.
Description: Jefferson, North Carolina : McFarland & Company, Inc., Publishers, 2021 | Includes bibliographical references and index.
Identifiers: LCCN 2021039768 | ISBN 9781476684543 (paperback : acid free paper) ∞
 ISBN 9781476642482 (ebook)
Subjects: LCSH: Plank, Eddie, 1875-1926. | Baseball players—Pennsylvania—Gettysburg—Biography. | Baseball players—United States—Biography. | Pitchers (Baseball)—Pennsylvania—Gettysburg—History. | Pitchers (Baseball)—United States—History. | Major League Baseball (Organization) | National Baseball Hall of Fame and Museum. | BISAC: SPORTS & RECREATION / Baseball / History
Classification: LCC GV865.P62 H45 2021 | DDC 796.357092 [B]—dc23
LC record available at https://lccn.loc.gov/2021039768

British Library cataloguing data are available
ISBN (print) 978-1-4766-8454-3
ISBN (ebook) 978-1-4766-4248-2

© 2021 Dave Heller. All rights reserved

No part of this book may be reproduced or transmitted in any form or by any means, electronic or mechanical, including photocopying or recording, or by any information storage and retrieval system, without permission in writing from the publisher.

Front cover: Philadelphia Athletics pitcher Eddie Plank. circa 1910 (Photograph by Louis Van Oeyen)

Printed in the United States of America

McFarland & Company, Inc., Publishers
 Box 611, Jefferson, North Carolina 28640
 www.mcfarlandpub.com

For my brother, Steve.

Baseball—watching and playing,
both on the field and at home
(we had to have owned
every tabletop game of our era)—
bridged the gap and brought us together.

Table of Contents

Acknowledgments   ix
Preface   1

1. Baseball Beginnings   5
2. From College (Sort of) Straight to the Pros   14
3. Quickly Making a Name for Himself   25
4. A Champion   32
5. The Crossfire   42
6. The Workhorse   48
7. Hitting 300 One Final Time   61
8. The Gettysburg Guide   75
9. A Death in the Family   84
10. California, Cuba and Everywhere in Between   97
11. Catching Ire   108
12. 36 and Stronger Than Ever   118
13. Slowing Down   132
14. The Pinnacle and the Mathewson Myth   143
15. Holding Out and Helping Out   155
16. Making a Federal Case   166
17. One Year with the Feds   177
18. Meet Me in St. Louis (Again)   188
19. A Disappearing Act   197
20. Industrial Work   205

21. End of the Line	213
22. Legacy	221
Chapter Notes	231
Bibliography	239
Index	243

Acknowledgments

Producing a book is largely a solitary project—the idea, the research, the writing, and so on. But it definitely takes more than one person to get said book published.

After I got word that my book on Ken Williams had been published by McFarland, I mentioned to my editor, Gary Mitchem, that I had an idea taking shape on a new project. Gary said he would love to hear about this new manuscript. It was all the push I needed to go forward full steam.

McFarland is such a great repository for telling baseball's history, and I am very grateful to Gary and his staff for not once but twice turning one of my ideas into a book which others can hold in their hands and read.

It's hard to describe the feeling when someone tells you they've read one of your books, and trust me, I never take it for granted.

I also never take for granted the people who didn't know me but still offered their help.

Roughly 30 minutes after I wrote the National Baseball Hall of Fame and Museum's research department inquiring about a clip file for Eddie Plank, I surprisingly received everything in a PDF file. Fortunately, they already had scanned it all, and instead of making arrangements to have it mailed to me, I was able to peruse articles on Plank not long after sending my email. Talk about service.

By the way, I've been to the Hall of Fame a few times and even was allowed to comb through articles and magazines in their research library for another book. I thank them for their help throughout the years and, of course, can't make a high enough recommendation to visit.

John Heiser at the Gettysburg National Park pointed me in the right direction in trying to determine if Eddie in fact ever was a tour guide there, and I thank Frederick Hawthorne and Steve Slaughter of the Association of Gettysburg Licensed Battlefield Guides for providing me the information.

Amy Lucadamo of the Gettysburg College archives department helped explain Eddie's time at the college and what certain designations meant in subsequent yearbooks. Over a year later, I contacted Amy again about possibly getting use of some photos, and she quickly got me the authorization. So when you see those pictures in the book, you can thank Amy, too.

As a former boss of mine once said, the internet is the greatest resource human beings have ever had at their fingertips. He said that two decades ago, but the sentiment remains. Not only could I email everyone mentioned above, but also thanks to scanning of newspapers there are incredible resources one can access right from home, including the Library of Congress' Chronicling America and newspapers.com.

My local library, Whitefish Bay Public Library through the Milwaukee County Library system, allowed me to access census records and Eddie's draft card.

My mom, Elaine Lyon, is probably the one responsible for books being in my life. She is a former librarian—if I want to know which libraries own my books, I have a good source—and I know she's proud each time I get something published. In fact, on the day I am writing this, she told me she can't wait to read this book (it'll have been around another year before she's reading these words) and trust me, my mom reading a baseball book is not her usual genre. Now, if it were about Syracuse basketball, maybe.

My brother and I always joke about my dad—there's a lot of material there, but in this case it's how he ended up with two sports-crazed sons, while he has never had any real interest in sports beyond casual viewing in his later years. One thing about my dad: he's from Philadelphia (if you're ever with him in another city, something will remind him of Philly). When I told him I was publishing on Eddie Plank, who pitched mostly for the Philadelphia Athletics, I got a story about where he was when he heard the Athletics were leaving town for Kansas City. Most parents (myself included), tell and retell the same old stories. This one, though, I had never heard. In fact, it was probably the first time the Athletics had ever been discussed between the two of us. So, in some way I feel like this book of mine intertwines with my dad more than previous ones. At the very least, it will remind him of Philly.

When I wrote my first book, my boys, Laben and Kieran, were just that—boys, aged four and one. Now my boys are men, aged 22 and 19. When your kids are young, you try to teach and inspire them. What I've learned is the tables kind of turn as they get older. Of course, I'm still trying to guide them, but watching all they've accomplished academically, athletically, socially, etc., they've ended up inspiring me as I continue to chase my dream of writing books. And here we are.

I always seem to mention my wife, Shelly, last. Maybe I should be putting her first. There's not enough space in this book to put down everything she's done—and does—for me. It all enables me to do what I love, sitting

Acknowledgments

in front of a computer for hours on end, researching and writing about a baseball player she's never heard of before. But always encouraging, always proud, always behind me 100 percent. I'm a pretty lucky guy.

I'm also lucky that you took the time to read this as well as my book. Like I said, I don't take you for granted, either. Thank you and I hope you enjoy the story of Eddie Plank.

Preface

There have been twenty-four 300-game winners in the history of Major League Baseball.

How much do we know about each of these rare pitchers?

Twelve played after World War II, when newspaper coverage expanded, games were broadcast on radio and television, and for some, highlights were a regular part of daily viewing.

There are six who pitched only or primarily in the 19th century, which many likely know little or nothing about. After all, it was a time when the game's rules were tweaked annually. Four balls for a walk, for example, wasn't established until 1889, and until 1893 pitchers threw from 50 feet away, not 60 feet, 6 inches. For these men, pitching 300 or 400 innings was not out of the ordinary, and some appeared nearly every day for their teams.

Of the remaining six, five are likely recognized even by the casual baseball fan. Walter Johnson, Christy Mathewson, and Lefty Grove are three of the game's icons. There's a famous movie about the life of Grover Cleveland Alexander. Cy Young, of course, has an award named after him.

That leaves Eddie Plank.

Plank has the 13th-most wins in MLB history, with 326, and is fifth in shutouts with 69. This despite being 36th in starts (529) and 28th in innings (4,495⅔).

But those are all just numbers. What do we know about Plank and his career? For me, it wasn't much. Sure, I was familiar enough with Plank to know that he was left-handed, from Gettysburg, and a member Connie Mack's early powerhouse Athletics teams that featured the $100,000 infield. But honestly, not much more than that.

The more I looked around, I wondered: did anyone?

Yes, there was a lot of information out there, but much of it could be contradicted.

Perhaps the most famous quote about Plank was attributed to his former teammate and friend Eddie Collins. In 1943, sportswriter Harry

Grayson published syndicated articles on various former players. In the article on Plank, Collins said, "Not the fastest, not the trickiest, and not the possessor of the most 'stuff,' but just the *greatest*."[1] Further research, however, showed that this quote originated in 1922 in an article for the August issue of *Illustrated World* titled "The Man Who Did Not Flash," by William Fleming French. This doesn't take away from Collins' quote, but knowing this was said in 1922 perhaps lends a different weight to it than if it was said over 20 years later.

In 1938, Collins claimed, "Eddie Plank, that great southpaw, was never used by Connie in Cleveland."[2] League Park certainly wasn't where he made his most frequent appearances, but with the Athletics, Plank did pitch in 24 games with 19 starts there.

Mack *would* often hold his pitchers for certain games. For a few years he liked Plank pitching in series openers. And, of course, if teams had heavy left-handed hitters in their lineup, he would prefer Plank to pitch (Detroit, for example). But Plank had at least 459 innings, 52 starts, and 68 appearances against the other seven American League teams in his career. There was no fear in pitching Plank against any team, at any locale.

In MLB Network's *Prime 9* series on the best left-handed pitchers in history, which aired in 2010, it was mentioned that Plank was not a strikeout pitcher.[3] Also false. By modern standards, yes—but in 12 of his 17 seasons he finished in the top 10 in the league in strikeouts per nine innings, including four times in the top four.

Plank was also commonly known to have a very deliberate style of pitching, which was true, but perhaps not to the extent that has been presented—that will be delved into in greater detail in forthcoming pages. But it was this slowness to his game which has also led to it being said that people, other than in Philadelphia, wouldn't show up to games if it was known Plank would be slabbing the rubber that day.

This myth is likely attributed to a quote from a May 1952 issue of *Baseball Digest* in which Fred Bendel of the *Newark News* said, "No commuters would come out to see the St. Louis Feds play if they thought Plank was going to pitch, because they knew they would all miss their regular trains home."[4]

Plank pitched one year in the Federal League, in 1915, and pitched all of three times at Newark. The first time was in a May 2 doubleheader which a reported 16,000 attended. The second was on June 17 in relief, and the final occasion was a start on August 14, with 7,000 in the stands. He also pitched just twice in Brooklyn; one game drew 5,000 while the other was unreported.

There's the case of Frank Foreman, who made many claims relating to Plank to anyone who would listen or write about it. According to Foreman, he was not only responsible for Plank going to the Athletics but also taught the pitcher his famous crossfire and predicted great success in the major leagues. One of Foreman's claims is possible, the others blatant lies.

It's not the only falsehood told about Plank. Yes, there was plenty that was written that was true, and still other stories that straddle the line between fact and myth.

There are instances in which Plank made definitive statements, but not nearly enough. Such was early 20th-century sports writing, and Plank himself preferred not to say much or toot his own horn, especially early in his career.

Many questions could have been answered, as a book—"Reminiscences of the Life of Eddie Plank"—had been in the planning stages before his untimely and unexpected death put the kibosh on it.

Thus, some mysteries and myths remain. I've done my best to tackle each one, attempted to further the truths, expose the falsehoods, and give the best evidence in those stories that lie in between. In the end, I hope to have created a more accurate portrait of Eddie Plank, a true Hall of Famer.

◆ 1 ◆

Baseball Beginnings

Connie Mack was not above giving a player a tryout, even in a regulation American League game, and this was a good example.

It was 1901, the first year of the American League as a major league, and Mack had put together on paper what appeared to be a very competitive team for his Philadelphia Athletics.

Like his fellow brethren in the upstart league, Mack purloined several players from the National League to come over to the AL, regardless of their contract status. His lineup on May 13 for the Athletics' game in Baltimore included a few contract jumpers: outfielder Phil Geier, who played in 30 games with Cincinnati in 1900, former Brooklyn third baseman Lave Cross, and the prize haul for the American League, second baseman Nap Lajoie, a .345 hitter over five years with his previous team in the National League—Philadelphia; a crosstown theft which the bereaved team would not let go of lightly.

Mack rounded out his lineup with three players who appeared in the American League in 1900, the circuit's last as a minor league. Socks Seybold, a power-hitting first baseman, and Mike "Doc" Powers, a veteran catcher who appeared in 97 NL games in the 19th century, came over from Indianapolis, one of the teams which was disbanded from the AL in favor of bigger cities, such as Philadelphia. Outfielder Dave Fultz, who like Powers had seen limited action in the National League from 1898 to 1899, had played for Mack in 1900 in Milwaukee and joined the manager with the Athletics, despite his previous team's ascension into the new 1901 major league, the American League.

But 2½ weeks into that inaugural season, the Athletics had won just five of their 13 games and were losers of four of their last five. Despite Mack's collection of quality players, there were still holes to fill. Mack couldn't find a shortstop and had on occasion used Fultz there, although that was more of an emergency plan than a solution. Harry Lochhead, bought from Detroit a couple of weeks earlier, manned the position in this game but would be off the roster and out of Major League Baseball days later.

Then there was the pitching. Mack had signed three hurlers from Philadelphia's National League club—Bill Bernhard, Chick Fraser, and Wiley Piatt. However, in 1900 the Phillies had the worst pitching staff in the NL—their 4.12 ERA was the only one in the league above 4—and Bernhard (4.77 ERA) and Piatt (4.65 ERA) were a big reason why. Fraser at least had led that team in ERA (3.14) and tied for the most wins (15). As we'll see later, he also played a big part in the career of our story's protagonist.

But as Mack and every baseball front office from the 19th century to modern day knows, it's hard to find good pitching. In the loose rules of 1901, Mack could bring in a pitcher, give him a tryout, and if he didn't work out, send him along his way without owing a dime. A week and a half earlier, he had sent to the mound a young pitcher from Philadelphia, Pete Loos, to give the ailing arms on his team a rest. Loos had pitched for the Athletics in an exhibition game, but even in the advent of the American League, he wasn't up to the task of a regular-season contest. After walking five batters, including four to open the second inning, the tryout was over, and Bernhard had to finish out the game—he proceeded to allow 19 hits in a 23–12 loss to Boston.

What Mack exactly saw in the pitcher he sent out to start the May 13 game in Baltimore is not known. Mack did have a proclivity for left-handed hurlers, though. He figured out early that most of the best hitters in the game hit from that side of the plate, and left-handed hitters often had trouble hitting left-handed pitchers. If Mack could find a lefty pitcher who could also get out right-handed batters with regularity, well, then he would have something special. The majority of Mack's successful Athletics teams had at least two quality left-handed starting pitchers, which was quite out of the ordinary for the time. At the turn of the 20th century, the vast majority of teams carried just one left-hander—if any.

Piatt was left-handed, as was another Athletics pitcher, Billy Milligan, although the latter had been ineffective in the early going of the season and was left back in Philadelphia as the team embarked on a month-long road trip.

Against Baltimore, Mack sent out a left-handed pitcher he recently signed—Charles Baker. Baker had made his major league debut two weeks earlier, on April 28, for Cleveland. His appearance that day did not go well. It was just Cleveland's fourth game of the season and the final contest of a four-game series in Chicago. Cleveland lost, 13–1, with Baker pitching all eight innings and allowing an incredible 23 hits as well as six walks.

Mack either didn't know or didn't care about that performance. Cleveland sold Baker to St. Joseph of the Western League, but Baker would not honor his contract and instead jumped to the Athletics, where he was to face the Orioles.

Against Baltimore, Baker's control was shaky at the start. He walked the first three men in the first inning, all of whom scored without a hit. Baker wasn't as bad as in his start in Cleveland—he would allow just six hits with six walks—but Baltimore scored 11 times, and after six innings Mack had seen enough.

It was the last time Baker played in the major leagues, while his replacement, another left-hander getting a tryout by Mack, would be playing in his first game as a professional. It was obvious that the new, lanky pitcher was not a regular on the Philadelphia squad. While his teammates bore the uniform of the Athletics—with a blue "A" sewn on the jersey top over the player's heart—the pitcher was wearing his collegiate outfit, complete with the school's name—Gettysburg—emblazoned across the middle of his chest. For the fans in the stands, it was likely the only thing they knew about this new pitcher, and it was an appropriate introduction as in the years to come it would be hard to think—or read—about Eddie Plank without Gettysburg being mentioned.

. . .

Eddie Plank would one day be a favored son of Gettysburg, his exploits on the field and his time spent off it tracked in the local newspapers. Residents would gather around a scoreboard for the latest updates from his World Series starts and read—often on the front page—of his comings and goings from town or the latest gossip regarding his off-season workouts and contract squabbles. Writers from around the country would refer to him using such nicknames as "Gettysburg Eddie," "The Gettysburg Guide," and "The Gettysburg Gatling."

Truth be told, however, Plank wasn't really from Gettysburg. He was born four miles north, in Straban Township, the fifth of six children born to David and Martha Plank. David L. Plank and Martha McCreary were married in 1870, when both were 21 years old. Martha McCreary was from nearby Hunterstown, one of two daughters of Jesse, a tailor, and Jane McCreary; the family lived in a house constructed in 1860, mostly of log.

David Plank was the fifth of six children, like his famous son, of John and Mary Plank. However, three of the first four Plank children died at an early age. John, born in 1831, died when he was barely 10 months old. Charlotte was born in 1833 but died at age seven in 1841, while Alverta was 4½ when she died in March 1847. David Plank was born in 1849, and he was followed in April 1852 by Anna (who broke the jinx of Plank daughters, living until 1924).

The Gettysburg team circa 1900. It is believed this picture was taken after they defeated McSherrystown in 1900 and became the champions of York and Adams counties. Eddie Plank is seated on the far left (courtesy of Special Collections/Musselman Library, Gettysburg College, Gettysburg, PA).

However, five months after the birth of Anna, John Plank died. With two young siblings and a widowed mother to care for, John Edward Plank took over the family farm, located on Harrisburg Road. It was here on July 1, 1863, when a Confederate army division, led by Gen. Jubal Early, marched past in the early afternoon as they approached their conflict during the Battle of Gettysburg.

When David Plank married seven years after the famous battle, he took over the farm with his mother, now 57, also residing there. The farm was 130 acres of tilled land and produced a variety of goods. According to the 1880 census, Plank had six horses, six milking cows, over 20 swine, and nearly three dozen chickens and roosters. The farm also had oats, rye, wheat, Irish and sweet potatoes, an acre of both apple and peach trees, and even enough bees to manufacture 30 pounds of honey.

There was plenty to do on this farm and, as it turned out, Eddie would come to enjoy the farming life, so much so that eventually he would take over the farm. In his later years, after marrying and moving off the farm, he openly talked about wanting to return to that life.

1. Baseball Beginnings

By 1880, the Planks also had a full house. Besides David and Martha, Mary, now 68, was listed as a border. There were five children—Mattie, 10; Luther, 9 (incorrectly listed as 7 on the census); Howard, 7; Eddie, 5 (incorrectly reported at times as being born in 1876, Eddie's birth year was 1875, which he confirmed in legal documents such as his draft card); and Grace, who was born in April of that year. Another boy, Ira, would join the clan in 1882.

David Plank was a proponent of education—in the mid–1890s he served as a school director, helping decide such things as school tax levies, when terms should start and how to enforce, or not enforce, district lines—and all of his children went to school at an early age (he was also a lifelong Democrat, something his second-youngest son would inherit). In the 1880 census, for example, Mattie, Luther, and Howard were all listed as having attended school in the previous year.

Eddie Plank was no exception, and like his brothers and sisters he attended Good Intent school. While it was, like many of its era, a one-room schoolhouse, at Good Intent students sat on chairs with desks, instead of benches like many of their peers around the country.

Good Intent also had as a teacher named Robert King Major. And Major happened to like, and play, baseball. Eddie Plank's life was about to change.

. . .

Abner Doubleday, incorrectly credited with creating baseball, fought in the Civil War, and there's a statue of him on the Gettysburg battlefield on Reynolds Avenue. While Doubleday might not have had anything to do with baseball, soldiers during the Civil War would at times play the game during breaks at forts, rest periods during battles, and at prisoner of war camps.

The game, which had been largely played in New York and New England, spread throughout the country, to the south (as Confederate soldiers picked up the game and nuances) and west. More teams began to be formed, and nearby towns would challenge each other to games. Gettysburg, Pennsylvania, was no exception.

Robert K. Major wanted to have one of those teams. Somewhere along the line, the teacher at the one-room schoolhouse Good Intent had played baseball—but apparently knew no one else in the Straban Township area who had a similar experience. Fortunately, as a teacher, he had access to a plethora of potential ballplayers—his students. Thus the Good Intent baseball team was formed in 1895.

In recalling the formation of the club, an article posted shortly after Major's death in 1934 claimed, "with the exception of Major, none of them [the other players] ever had had any experience in playing the great national game."[1]

Included in that group of players were three of the Plank brothers. Luther played catcher, Howard was the shortstop, while Eddie "was selected as pitcher because of his ability to throw a ball hard and accurately."[2]

How Plank developed his powerful left arm is one of those stories which has been recited as fact over the years. However, all the information comes from tales told after the pitcher's death, and therefore has no corroboration from the pitcher.

It was first reported by the *Gettysburg Times* that Plank "spent many weary hours pitching against an old haystack, developing his speed and curves."[3] This is a story the paper repeated some 60 years later with the additional detail that Plank "also found it easy to knock birds off fences with a rock."[4]

However, just a few years after the original haystack story, an article in the same paper claimed David Plank "frequently would scold [Eddie] after his powerful pitching against the barn door, shattering it on several occasions." In Ira Plank's obituary in 1951, the barn door theory—and not throwing against a haystack—was mentioned.

Likely, Major gave those interested quick pointers and saw that Plank naturally could throw hard. After all, in later years Plank made it seem as though he didn't put much effort in his pursuit of the game. In 1910, he told author Joseph B. Bowles:

> As I told you, I was born in Gettysburg, and I played some baseball around there in an amateur way, and without giving the game much thought. You see I had other things to do, and down in Gettysburg we regard baseball as a Fourth of July and Saturday amusement rather than a business. Honestly, I had never even read the scores or knew who played in the big leagues until I was 20 years old. Gettysburg looked big enough to me, and when I could play ball I played because I liked the running and the throwing and everything else, I didn't know a squeeze play from third base, hardly.[5]

Plank might not have known the game, but he took to it quickly. The first public notice of the team was in August, when it was reported, "Robert Majors [sic], the popular young Republican of Straban township, has organized the 'Good Intent' base ball club and they are ready to meet all local teams."[6]

It didn't take long for Good Intent to find its first opponent. On August 2, the team played Hunterstown—the hometown of the Planks' mother—and easily won, 25–2, in a contest which lasted only five innings. "The features of the game," said the *Gettysburg Compiler*, "were the pitching and catching of the Plank brothers."[7]

Inexperienced or not, Robert Major had built a powerhouse team. While it was later reported that Good Intent didn't lose a game until the

1. Baseball Beginnings

summer of 1896, the team did fall to New Oxford in one of the three match-ups played in 1895. Eddie Plank was certainly one of the reasons for such a successful year. In one game played in Straban Township, Plank "had the Arendtsville boys completely at his mercy"[8] in a 15–7 win, striking out 13 in the process.

Some future stories about Plank asserted that he played baseball with Good Intent while wearing his farmer's clothes, and this is why he picked up the nickname "Farmer" (although this would not be his most common sobriquet).

However, this couldn't be further from the truth (and, as we will see, there was another occasion in which it was claimed Plank pitched in his work clothes). Upon founding the team, Major asked a Gettysburg tailor, John D. Lippy, Sr., to fashion the uniforms using a gray wool which Major supplied. Eddie Plank might have been a farmer, but when playing baseball he looked like anything but.

Things weren't much different for the Good Intent team in 1896. Two games against the Gettysburg College freshmen produced 14–10 and 24–16 wins. We know Eddie Plank pitched in the first game, allowing 10 hits as well as getting a hit of his own at the plate. As spring came to a close, Good Intent beat Fairfield, 17–4, and Idaville twice, 10–6 and 19–0.

While newspapers stopped giving accounts of these games other than the final score, Plank was gaining notice. It was rumored that the last-place York White Roses, who would win just eight of 31 games in the Pennsylvania State League before the circuit folded in mid–June, could try and bring aboard Eddie and Luther.

"The pitcher is a left-hander, with a deceptive drop and cool head, while the catcher is very quick and sure," reported the *Harrisburg Telegraph*. "Both young men are big and strong, and do their share in the batting line. They might help our sister town out of the mire of defeat."[9]

Just one year after being introduced to the game, it was already being talked about as if Eddie Plank could get paid to play. Actually, however, he already was. Good Intent was an amateur team—Plank himself later described it as such—however, he was paid, on at least one occasion, $5 to play. During a banquet in 1913, "William Hersh Esq. sprung one of the hits of the evening when he produced a receipt signed by Eddie Plank for $5.00 for 'one week's service on the Gettysburg base ball team.' It was given to John L. Hill, treasurer of the town team in 1896."[10]

If Plank was also playing for the team in Gettysburg in 1896, and not just Straban Township's Good Intent, it was never noted in the newspapers, although he could have been assuming another name to prevent a conflict.

In 1897–1898, the local newspapers didn't write about baseball much, with the occasional report on area college teams. It's because of this we know Plank was still pitching, but not for Good Intent. On April 30, 1898, Gettysburg College defeated the town team, for which Plank toiled, 6–4. Plank allowed just five hits in the loss, walking two and striking out six. At the plate he had a single and stole a base.

In 1899, Plank was back with the Gettysburg town team, and here again was the supposed origin for his nickname of "Farmer." Of course, as with many things relating to Plank, this story appeared well after the fact. In 1921 a pair of former teammates spoke to the *Pittsburgh Post-Gazette* and gave what they claimed was the root of the moniker.

According to Robin Wolf and W. S. Grenoble, Gettysburg had a big series with the neighboring town of McSherrystown. However, as the Gettysburg team was about to embark on its trip for the first contest, its star pitcher, "Speed" Stimmel, was a no-show as he had fallen sick. Team founder and manager Morris Musselman (known as "Doc," Musselman was a pharmacist and baseball lover who in 1898–1899 offered free sodas at his drugstore for any Gettysburg College baseball players who hit a home run) remembered there was a pitcher of some accord for another local team— this of course turned out to be Eddie Plank—and the skipper quickly headed to the Plank farm, where he found the erstwhile pitcher, according to this tale, "pitching hay in a field."[11]

After a quick consultation with Eddie and convincing of David Plank, who "pointedly expressed his opinion of the foolishness of his son forsaking his dollar-a-day job to go gallivanting over the country with a 'passel o' ball throwers,'"[12] Eddie was on his way with Musselman and helped Gettysburg beat McSherrystown "despite the fact that the crowd continually yelled 'farmer' at him, besides hurling many worse epithets of a derisive and caustic nature."[13]

Beyond that, it's doubtful that David Plank would pay his son to work on the family farm (although there's a good chance Plank indeed was pitching hay that day before the game), the truth of the matter is, as we've shown, that not only did Eddie Plank pitch for the Gettysburg town team in 1898, but also in the June 13 edition of the *Gettysburg Star and Sentinel*, 2½ weeks before the McSherrystown game, Plank was listed among the members of the town team.

Given access to use Gettysburg College's Nixon Field for their games, the town team played its initial game of 1899 on June 24, a 10–1 win over Carlisle in which Plank allowed just two hits. Also announced was a seven-game series with McSherrystown, "the winner of the series to claim the championship of Adams county."[14]

As Plank's teammates said decades later, Gettysburg did win that opener over McSherrystown. Robin Wolf hit the game's first pitch for a home run, and behind an offensive assault which featured 16 hits and the left arm of Plank, Gettysburg rolled, 16–6. Plank "allowed a few scattered hits"[15] and, depending who you asked, he struck out 19 (*Gettysburg Compiler*), 20 (*Gettysburg Star and Sentinel*) or possibly even 21 (W. S. Grenoble). The *Compiler* understatedly said, "Plank is improving in form and promises to be a sure winner."[16]

Plank impressed the reporter from the *Hanover Record*—McSherrystown being just on the outskirts of Hanover—especially since, yes, the pitcher had been working on his farm earlier in the day. As relayed by the *Gettysburg Compiler*, the paper observed: "The game was featureless, except for Plank's marvelous pitching. Though speedy, he was steady, and had no difficulty in locating the plate. Plank has not pitched more than a half a dozen games in his life and is an Adams county rustic. The reporter learned incidentally that he unloaded two huge wagon loads of hay in the morning, and it surely did not seem to affect his arm, for from appearances he could have pitched another nine innings."[17] The image of Plank doing farm work apparently stuck in Hanover as a year later the paper would refer to him as "famously known as 'Farmer' Plank."[18]

Inferior competition had no chance against Plank. He tossed a two-hit, 17–0 shutout against the Paxtang Club of Harrisburg in the first game of a July 4 doubleheader and a couple of weeks later blanked the Athletics of York, 16–0, striking out 16. The *York Gazette* reported:

> The newspaper in the vicinity as well as those in some of the large cities have been telling stories of young Plank's remarkable pitching abilities and the easy manner in which he disposed of hard hitting Athletics in the game yesterday is positive proof that the people and the newspapers who speak of him of being naught did not go wrong in their assertions. The several hundred local enthusiasts who saw him work yesterday are convinced that he's a wonder—about the warmest manipulator of a base ball ever seen in York.[19]

Not all of Plank's games were wins for Gettysburg, however, as the team lost its series with McSherrystown, four to two, although Plank struck out 17 in a 4–3 loss in 10 innings and fanned eight in a 2–0 defeat. He gave up just three hits in Gettysburg's other win in the series, 5–4.

Plank's prowess had him in demand. It was reported that "a Harrisburg team" (perhaps Paxtang, which saw his ability first-hand) "has made overtures to get Plank but he prefers to say in Adams county and pitch hay."[20] What this Harrisburg team didn't realize was that Plank was at heart a hometown boy. Even during his major league playing days, he would often make trips back home to Gettysburg during off-days and always had a desire to play with a team located close to his boyhood home. As an amateur, that didn't give him many options, having already played for Good Intent and the Gettysburg town team. But there was still one team left to play for, and surely his father would approve of this one.

2

From College (Sort of) Straight to the Pros

In 1899, Gettysburg College was searching for a coach for its baseball and track teams. In April, the school hired William F. Dill, who had a background in both sports at Harvard, where he had learned under the guidance of trainer Jim Lathrop. When he wasn't coaching the collegiate sports, Dill also played a little baseball himself with the Gettysburg town team.

Dill lasted only one season as Gettysburg's baseball coach, but he is the obvious connection between the college and Eddie Plank, who in January 1900 was one of the new players listed who were getting in some winter work in preparation for the baseball season.

David Plank might have been happy to see his son at Gettysburg College, but there's some question as to whether Eddie Plank ever attended classes. Eddie was actually part of Gettysburg Academy, which was a prep school. He is listed in the Gettysburg yearbooks of 1901 and 1902 (Plank pitched for Gettysburg College in 1900 and 1901; the yearbooks are titled for the graduating year of Gettysburg's *junior* class) as a "middler" rather than the advanced grade of a "sub-freshmen." Those sub-freshmen who graduated went to college.

Whether or not Plank actually went to classes or was just enrolled is unknown, although Amy Lucadamo, an archivist with the college, said neither Eddie nor his brother Ira, who would also attend the college and was listed among the "sub-freshmen" in the 1902 and 1903 yearbooks, "was ever enrolled in the College proper and the records point to neither graduating from the Academy."[1]

With Dill gone, Harry Lantz was appointed captain and de facto coach. In February, the school hired Frank Foreman, who had pitched for a number of teams in various major leagues, mainly from 1889 to 1896, to help coach. Foreman arrived in the middle of March and left four weeks later to continue his professional career.

2. From College (Sort of) Straight to the Pros

The Gettysburg College team is listed as circa 1902 but most likely this is from 1901, as Eddie Plank (top row, second from left) was in the major leagues in 1902 and the picture includes future Boston Red Sox pitcher George Winter (top row, second from right), who joined the team in 1901 (courtesy of Special Collections/Musselman Library, Gettysburg College, Gettysburg, PA).

Foreman had an immediate effect on the team and Plank. It was reported that "practice which had heretofore been at random is now conducted systematically under his direction.... Those who are developing rapidly are Plank, the star pitcher of Gettysburg's town team of last season."[2]

Enrolled at the academy, Plank could still pitch for the college's varsity team under the rules of the day, and when the final roster was set, he was listed as one of the team's pitchers. He drew the opening start of the season, going the distance and allowing just three hits while striking out either 11 or 15 (the box score of the game in *The Gettysburgian* said 11, the story 15) in a 14–8 win over Franklin & Marshall on April 7. Gettysburg committed seven errors in the game, helping account for many of the runs allowed.

Shoddy defense would be a trend for the entire season. In a 6–5 loss at Nixon Field to Syracuse, Plank allowed five hits and two walks with seven strikeouts "and should have won the game easily but for errors at critical moments."[3]

Plank's baseball career to this point had consisted of pitching in town games and a few starts for Gettysburg College. Nevertheless, he had impressed someone, as in late April he was offered a contract by Richmond of the Virginia League. Plank accepted but wouldn't report until the end of the collegiate season in June.

Gettysburg was glad to have him. With Plank on the mound, the college was hard to beat (compared to the other pitcher on the staff, someone named Ketterman). Plank defeated Susquehanna twice, Dickinson College, Bucknell, and Carlisle that spring.

Two days after beating Carlisle in the home finale on June 9, Plank boarded a train for Richmond. Unbeknownst to him, however, Richmond was having issues staying afloat. Already one team in the Virginia League, Petersburg, had disbanded—on the same day Plank left his Gettysburg home—after a 6–5 loss at Portsmouth, dropping its record to 8–27. The loss of that team was expected to have a domino effect on the league, "and it is thought that this will necessitate the dropping of the Richmond team, which is now being run by the players on a co-operative basis."[4]

The Richmond Bluebirds had been in the Atlantic League through 1899 and had been successful, with a 63–25 record. However, the league disbanded on June 14 of that year. Now the team was facing the same fate a year later, although not of its own accord. On June 12, the leaders of the Virginia League met and decided to reorganize. The six-team circuit became a four-team league. With Petersburg having made the league go from six to five teams, dropping a club being operated by the players was an easy decision (not to mention that Richmond didn't have a seat at the league table).

The Richmond players found out their fate in the middle of their game on June 12. Incredibly, they kept on playing, although after receiving the news they "made no attempt to win after this."[5] Leading 2–0, the Bluebirds allowed eight runs in the fourth inning—not-so-coincidentally the same inning they heard of their disbandment—and lost, 9–2. Even more amazing—the team played the next day as well, falling 8–2 to Newport News in a game which was "listless and devoid of interest."[6]

With his services no longer needed for a team that didn't exist, Plank was back in Pennsylvania on June 16, leading the Actives of Lancaster to its first win of the season, 2–0 over old foe McSherrystown. Plank was overpowering, allowing one baserunner (a hit) and striking out nine. Plank perhaps had other professional options.

The *Gettysburg Compiler* reported that Plank would "probably play with the Hamilton, Ontario, Canada team."[7] Harry Lantz, the captain of the Gettysburg College team, was heading up to the International League team and might have put in a good word about his teammate to the minor league club. Years later, veteran baseball scribe Ernest J. Lanigan wrote in *The Sporting News* that "Somewhere on the tablets of my memory is a thought

2. From College (Sort of) Straight to the Pros

that in the summer of 1900 I read a squib that the New York Nationals were going to give a trial to a rising young left-hander from Gettysburg College named Plank, Manager George Stacey Davis having heard good accounts of him."[8]

Offers or not, Plank remained in Gettysburg. He pitched for rival McSherrystown on June 25 in a 6–2 win over Chambersburg. However, soon after a group in Gettysburg wanted a team of its own and after getting some funding from residents and businesses—roughly $200 was expected to be raised—Gettysburg had its own team, ready to play games once again at the college's Nixon Field. Noted local baseball enthusiast Morris Musselman would manage the team.

They would likely boast the best 1–2 pitching punch in all of amateur or semi-pro baseball. In addition to Plank, Gettysburg signed Frank Foreman. The former coach for the college was looking for work after pitching briefly for Springfield of the Eastern League. His addition pushed Plank to the outfield when Foreman took to the box.

Plank wasn't losing pitching time due to ineffectiveness. He struck out 19 batters from York's Penn Park team in one game and 13 in another and beat tough teams like McSherrystown and the Actives of Lancaster. But the addition of Foreman gave Gettysburg some marquee value—not to mention a stiff booking fee, as Chester manager Jess Frysinger found out. The *Chester Times* reported:

> When Manager Frysinger first mentioned about booking the Gettysburg club to play in Chester on a Saturday many people thought it was a job, especially as their car fare alone amounts to nearly $80, but as the Gettysburg club has proved itself to be one of the fastest in that part of the State, they were booked to play here next Saturday. It will cost Manager Frysinger more money to bring this club here on Saturday next than any other club received in this city for years, barring the Brooklyn League Club, but when a club is worth the money the Chester Manager does not hesitate to book them.... The Gettysburg club should draw the largest crowd of the season on Saturday.[9]

Plank, dubbed a "famous left-handed college pitcher,"[10] pitched against Chester on August 18, but the game was called due to rain after four innings. Plank and Foreman split the starts after the arrival of the latter, but Foreman would leave, signing with Buffalo of the American League (at the time, a minor league). But when Gettysburg and McSherrystown met in a decisive seventh game of their Adams and York counties championship series, it was George Winter, soon to be a teammate of Plank's at the college, who got the start. Gettysburg prevailed, 7–3, with Plank, batting second in the lineup and playing center field, scoring a run. When the team returned home from York, the site of the deciding contest, they were welcomed by a band and a crowd estimated at 500.

It wasn't yet time to go back to the farm for Plank, however. He and one of his teammates, William Clay, were recruited to play for a team in Cambridge, Maryland. Cambridge was part of the Triple League, an organization of three clubs along Maryland's Eastern Shore. Along with Cambridge there were Easton and Salisbury.

Cambridge got off to a hot start in the league, jumping out to first place, but lost four of five before Plank's arrival. The left-hander, though, couldn't help the Cambridge cause as it lost its three remaining games by scores of 8–4, 4–0, and 8–5, with Plank pitching the first and third games. Errors and poor efforts on the basepaths seemed to be Cambridge's undoing. In the final game, it held a 5–4 lead going into the ninth inning against first-place Easton (Salisbury, which finished 8–7, had quit the league the day before after being unsatisfied with the results of previously protested games), but Plank walked three men in the ninth and Easton tallied four runs to send Cambridge to its 10th defeat in 14 games. Easton, at 9–4, was crowned league champion.

While the results might not have gone Plank's way, the Triple League games drew 500 or more fans for each contest. If Plank wasn't bitten by the baseball bug previously, he certainly was now. It was no surprise when Plank returned to the Gettysburg College baseball team in 1901—but he also had an arrangement for when the college season ended, signing with the Chester town team, which was managed by Jess Frysinger. While Chester's season began May 11, an agreement was made that Plank wouldn't begin his tenure with the club until June, when the college's season had finished.

Plank returned to Gettysburg not only as a star pitcher but also as one of its better hitters. Beginning in spring training, when the team traveled to Virginia, he would routinely be placed third or fourth in the lineup. When he wasn't pitching—George Winter had joined the team—Plank was stationed in right field.

On May 3, for example, he made a "sensational catch in right,"[11] drove home a run with a double, and scored in a 9–1 win over Dickinson at Nixon Field. Two days later in Lewisburg, he tossed a five-hitter while striking out seven in beating Bucknell, 4–1. Back in right field the next day, he banged out a pair of hits, although Winter and Gettysburg lost, 11–6.

Gettysburg played Carlisle—a team consisting of Native Americans, including Plank's future teammate Chief Bender—on May 8. Using a "seemingly exhaustless supply of curves and speedy balls,"[12] Plank allowed just one hit, which came in the ninth inning, and fanned 16. It was a truly dominating performance, and one Plank later attributed to his age. In 1901, Plank was 25 and facing players who likely ranged in age from 17–21.

"I was big and strong and fast and wild and inexperienced, and

2. From College (Sort of) Straight to the Pros 19

everything else that goes to make up a college pitcher," Plank told author Joseph B. Bowles in 1910 of his time at Gettysburg College. "I simply shut my eyes and cut loose and most of those who didn't strike out got bases on balls, and I have suspected since that a lot of them struck out just to escape from standing up there to bat. Seriously I think the real reason for my start was that I was older, stronger and better developed than the average college man. That made me stand out among them and it attracted the attention of professional clubs."[13] Someone was paying attention to Plank's performances.

In 1900, Charley Myers, an employee at the Western Maryland Railroad Company, was interested in the wireless telegraph. The technology had been around just a few years, and none were located near Myers' town of Gettysburg. He took it upon himself to learn about the telegraph, built his own, then tested it to success.

A few days after Plank pitched his masterpiece against Carlisle, Myers received a telegram intended for the pitcher from Connie Mack, the manager of the Philadelphia team in the American League. Myers went to his friend Allie Holtzworth, who owned a stable of horses. The pair hooked up a buggy and raced to the Plank farm just outside town. Plank would later say, "his heart was almost leaping from behind his tongue"[14] as he read the note from Mack. He quickly packed and boarded a train for Baltimore, where Philadelphia had begun a four-game series.

How did Mack find out about Plank and why did he offer him a tryout? As to the first part, there are many theories and no true answer, despite writings to the contrary over the years.

In 1911, William S. Farnsworth of the *New York Evening Journal* wrote, "In 1901, Connie Mack supposedly saw [Chief] Bender (Dickinson) and Plank (Gettysburg) play and they pitched 15-inning scoreless tie with Bender pitching a 1-hitter, and Mack signed both."[15] This statement was patently false as not only did Plank and Bender not pitch against each other, but also Gettysburg and Dickinson did not play a 15-inning game ending in a 1–1 tie, and Bender didn't join Mack's Philadelphia team until 1904.

One explanation, briefly put forth in 1921 by *The Sporting News*, posited, "Connie Mack, heeding the advice of his friend, Musselman, gave Plank a tryout,"[16] referring to Morris Musselman, the druggist and Gettysburg baseball enthusiast. Musselman certainly knew Plank's ability, having managed the town team. But there's no evidence that Musselman and Mack were acquainted, never mind friends, and a relationship seems hard to fathom with Mack not known to have visited Gettysburg prior to Plank's tenure on his team.

A theory which perhaps has some plausibility, though scant on evidence, is that Jess Frysinger, the Chester manager recommended Plank to Mack. In 1905, *Sporting Life* claimed Frysinger was the catalyst for several players making it to the majors, including Harry Barton, Chief Bender, Louis Bruce, Bris Lord and, of course, Eddie Plank, all signed by Mack, not to mention Joe Cassidy (Washington), Sherry Magee (Philadelphia NL), Tom Needham (Boston NL), Homer Smoot (St. Louis NL), Happy Townsend (Washington), and Rube Vinson (Cleveland). Mack and Frysinger definitely had a business relationship. Frysinger secured exhibition games with Mack's team in Wilmington, Delaware, in September and October of 1902, and Harrisburg, Pennsylvania, in September 1903, and a year later Mack sent one of his pitchers, Ed Pinnance, to Wilmington AA, which was managed by Frysinger. And then there was tipping Mack off about Bender, for whom Frysinger was "well reimbursed ... and has received a check for a liberal amount from the champions' manager [Mack]."[17]

The person claiming to be responsible who gained the most notoriety, though, was Frank Foreman (who ironically would pitch for Frysinger's team in Holyoke, Massachusetts, in 1905). The story appears to have originated in 1911 in a story which appeared in several newspapers and was reprinted through at least 1913. In part, it read:

> One of his [Foreman's] closest personal friends was Connie Mack. They had been in the National League together and a deep-seated friendship existed between the pair. One night while the Athletics were in Boston Foreman went to the hotel and saw Mack. "Con," he said, "there's a lefthander down at the college where your humble servant has been coaching that you want to get. His name is Plank. I'm staking you to this information because somebody is going to grab him." Connie flew downstairs. He grabbed a telegraph blank and wired terms to Plank, telling him if he was willing to accept to join the club in Washington."[18]

Foreman perpetuated this tale throughout his life. In an interview with the *Baltimore Sun* in 1940 as he approached his 77th birthday, Foreman recounted how he at first tried to get Baltimore to sign Plank—Foreman was from that city and lived there all his life, when he wasn't playing baseball—but when they didn't show interest, he went to Connie Mack.

Mack would also back Foreman's story in 1938, saying, "Frank Foreman, an old pitcher who had finished his career with Indianapolis in the Western League, was coaching at Gettysburg in 1901. I needed pitchers badly and Frank told me I'd make no mistake if I'd grab two good ones he had then, Eddie Plank and George Winters [sic]. I took Plank on Foreman's advice and Winters [sic] signed with Boston, where for a long time he pitched really good ball."[19]

All of these comments were made a decade or more after Plank's arrival, and in the case of the articles on Foreman in 1940 and Mack in

1938, we're relying on the memories of men who were in their late 70s. Some of Foreman's other comments in the article can now be proven to be half-truths or just plain wrong. The 1911 article noted that Foreman was a coach at Gettysburg—he was not in this role in 1901—and it is doubtful that Foreman and Mack were "close friends." Foreman's brother John, a left-handed pitcher, had been with Pittsburgh of the National League in 1895–1896, a team Mack managed as well as playing some catcher. Frank Foreman and Mack never had reason to associate other than on opposite sides of the diamond for a couple of seasons in the Western League. Mack also incorrectly stated that Foreman was coaching at the college in 1901, and there's some doubt as to how Foreman would have known of George Winter.

However, Foreman was indeed in Boston as the article stated when the Red Sox—Foreman pitched one game for Boston, then was used as a base coach before he was released a few weeks later—played Mack's Athletics on May 8–9, the series before Philadelphia left for Baltimore (of course, this also calls into question why Foreman would give tips about a pitcher to a team—or teams—other than his own).

Plank, unfortunately, was never quoted publicly on the subject (although Foreman insisted that late in Plank's life, the pitcher gave him all the credit). However, we do know that Mack sent the telegram, Plank received it and, despite being "rather shaky about making such a jump,"[20] he boarded a train and met the Philadelphia Athletics in Baltimore on a tryout basis.

. . .

Headed by league czar Ban Johnson, the American League made the jump from minor league in 1901 (formerly known as the Western League, the circuit changed its name in 1900). The AL looked to challenge the National League, which had been in existence since 1876, placing teams in several eastern cities where the NL already had a foothold, such as Boston and Philadelphia.

Mack, who managed Milwaukee in the Western/American League in its minor league stretch, was tabbed to lead the Philadelphia franchise. To give his team credibility, Mack did three important things. First, he had Columbia Park built for his team on a lot he had been leasing in the northern part of Philadelphia. Second, he quickly made a connection with the baseball fans of Philadelphia—and even around the country—by naming the team the Athletics. Philadelphia previously had a club with that nickname, and it just happened to have won the only pennant in the city's history, taking the American Association crown in 1883. It was a popular choice with the fans, and even in newspapers and periodicals, such as *The*

Sporting News, around the country, in stories, standings and box scores, Mack's team would be listed as "Athletics" instead of by the city (i.e., Boston, Chicago, etc.), as every other major-league franchise was treated. Finally, like the other American League teams, he signed National League players to come play for him and had the biggest coup with convincing Nap Lajoie to join the Athletics. The 26-year-old second baseman had already established himself as one of the, if not *the*, premier hitters and sluggers in the game. Mack also inked 20-year-old pitcher Christy Mathewson, who had put up stellar numbers in the minors before getting hit around in his brief major league time in 1900, but Mathewson reneged on the deal and instead went back to the National League's New York Giants, where he quickly became ace of the staff.

Mack certainly could have used Mathewson (any team would). The Athletics struggled out of the gate, losing their first two games against Washington at Columbia Park, 5–1 and 11–5. In Philadelphia's first 13 games it allowed five or more runs 11 times. Poor pitching and below-average defense were to blame, although Lajoie had proven to be the real deal and then some. He had a hit in 12 of the first 13 games—and in the lone contest he went without one he was ejected in the first inning—and had a preposterous 30 hits in his first 50 at-bats (a .600 batting average).

Philadelphia's Opening Day first baseman, Charlie Carr, had already been released, as was Fred Ketchum, who started five games in the outfield, and Pat Crisham, who was signed but never played. Mack kept trying and going back to Dave Fultz at shortstop, but he was better suited for the outfield. Pete Loos had already been given a brief tryout as pitcher and dismissed, while a catcher, Morgan Murphy, was signed as was pitcher Charles "Bock" Baker. They joined the Athletics as they departed for a road trip, while left-handed pitcher Billy Milligan was left behind.

"Mack is leaving no stone unturned in his efforts to strengthen the weak spots," wrote the Philadelphia correspondent in *The Sporting News*. "As in the case of the local National League club, it is the pitching corps that causes worry.... [Wiley] Platt and [Bill] Bernhard are away off. Milligan is inexperienced in his present company, and [Chick] Fraser, who has been doing good work with a lame back, may at any time join the list of inefficients."[21]

Losses in Boston by scores of 12–4 and 9–3 dropped the Athletics' record to 4–8, with a final game of the series rained out. On May 11, the Athletics beat Baltimore in their series opener, 7–6, scoring four runs in the eighth inning and then throwing out Chappie Snodgrass at home, trying to score after an error by right fielder Jack Hayden, to end the game. This is the team Eddie Plank was joining, and it was not exactly a picture of a steady club in a league trying to find its way in its inaugural season.

2. From College (Sort of) Straight to the Pros

When Plank joined the Athletics he most likely was given a quick look-over by Connie Mack. The common image of Mack is as an old man, with a wrinkled face, wearing his suit with a starched-collar shirt. In 1901, Mack was wearing a suit with a starched-collar suit, but he was 38 years old and only five years removed from finishing up his 11-year major-league career as a catcher. At 38, Mack often donned the tools of the trade to catch Philadelphia pitchers or, as he traveled around the country scouting, potential prospects.

Mack apparently liked what he saw—or just needed a fresh arm—for on May 13 he sent Charles Baker to start against Baltimore. After walking the first three batters he faced, Baker was generally "hit hard"[22] and in six innings allowed 11 runs. Trailing 11–4, it was as good a time as any for Mack to give a tryout to his other new left-hander.

And make no mistake, Eddie Plank was trying out. He had no signed contract and went to the box wearing his gray Gettysburg College uniform. With the word "Gettysburg" emblazoned in the front and a hat with two stripes, he was clearly not yet on the Athletics, whose players had a uniform brandished with a blue "A," but his outfit was also in stark contrast to the Baltimore team, whose black uniforms included an orange belt, socks and a big "O" on the left chest, a look about which *The Sporting News* commented, "The whole effect is horrible. Never since the old days when a League club came out of St. Louis attired in pale blue suits and yellow stockings has such a uniform been seen."[23]

If its attire was considered ugly, Baltimore's lineup had to be considered deadly, especially for someone like Plank, who had never even pitched in the minor leagues. Most of the Orioles' starting lineup had been pilfered from the National League—catcher Wilbert Robinson, second baseman Jimmy Williams, shortstop Bill Keister, third baseman (and manager) John McGraw, left fielder Mike Donlin, right fielder Cy Seymour and pitcher Joe McGinnity, who led the NL with 28 wins in both 1899 and 1900.

Fewer than 2,800 fans saw Plank make his major league debut, coming into the game with recently signed catcher Morgan Murphy (in his early days of managing, Mack liked to change his entire pitcher-catcher battery) in the seventh inning. The first batter Plank faced was first baseman Frank Foutz. In perhaps a bit of nervousness, he walked Foutz, who worked his way around the bases and scored. Plank allowed two more runs in the eighth inning on a triple by Keister and a Williams double.

Plank pitched only two innings and allowed three runs in an eventual 14–5 Athletics loss, but the local Baltimore scribes were impressed. From the *Baltimore Morning Herald*: "The collegian showed much promise, and when he got limbered up had the Orioles guessing. Plank has plenty of speed and a good drop curve that will prove effective when under control.... Plank has the earmarks of a good one."[24]

Mack saw something in the youngster—well, at 25, Plank was only 13 years younger than his manager—and told the *Baltimore Sun* that he planned on giving Plank a contract. (Baker, though, was let go and never pitched in the majors again.) Mack offered Plank a $1,000 contract. For comparison's sake, on the other end of the wage scale, Lajoie was making $4,000. But before Plank began his career with Philadelphia, he had one more point of business left in Gettysburg.

Two days after pitching for Mack's Athletics, Plank was once again in his Gettysburg College uniform, pitching for the school against Dickinson College in a game played in Carlisle. Gettysburg won, 4–2, with Plank allowing three hits and striking out 10 in a complete-game victory. The win, though, caused some bitter feelings as Dickinson felt that Plank should not have been allowed to pitch, what with him joining Philadelphia (it is unknown if he had yet signed that contract). Shortly after the game, Dickinson decided to end its relationship with Gettysburg and canceled all athletic events with the school for several reasons, but in part due to "the refusal to allow Plank to be disqualified in the base-ball game at Carlisle."[25]

Plank left Gettysburg on May 15 to join the Athletics in Washington, D.C. He would be missed. A large throng showed up at the train station, including many students, to bid Plank farewell. The student paper offered a parting sendoff: "Eddie was a conscientious student and very popular among his college friends. On the diamond his presence always diffused confidence among the players and our late achievements are attributable to him in no slight degree. Every undergraduate regrets that the College has had to part with him but all are one minded in wishing him all kinds of success."[26]

Eddie Plank, major league pitcher, hometown hero, would fulfill those wishes.

3

Quickly Making a Name for Himself

Eddie Plank left Gettysburg for Washington, D.C., to join the Philadelphia Athletics on May 17. The next day he made the first of his 529 major league starts—he would be in the top-10 all-time in that category until the 1930s and No. 11 until just after World War II.

For Plank's first start, the Athletics had something of a makeshift lineup—Nap Lajoie, normally the second baseman, played shortstop, outfielder Dave Fultz was at second base, and catcher Doc Powers was at first. Also, in a season of player turnover, several players in the lineup would not be with Philadelphia come season's end. But this lineup provided Plank with plenty of offense, scoring two runs in the first inning and four in the second to stake the rookie pitcher to an early lead. Plank had just one bad inning—allowing four runs in the sixth—and picked up his first victory, 11–6, allowing just six hits and striking out five, with some credit given to his catcher, Morgan Murphy, whose "coaching was a decided help."[1] Control was still an issue, and he walked four. Plank, who hit .340 for Gettysburg that season, also notched his first major league hits with two singles.

Plank also had to endure never-ending taunts from the visiting crowd and opposing players. This was not uncommon for that time period, especially if fans thought they could shake the confidence of a young hurler. But Plank "showed remarkable coolness"[2] and "never once left his feet this afternoon, despite the efforts of opposing players and the spectators to rattle him."[3]

The fans at American League Park also derided Plank over his slow, deliberate pitching style. "He is the slowest man, with the possible exception of [Boston Americans pitcher George 'Nig'] Cuppy, on the diamond, but still he seems to get there, and that is the main requirement in a twirler,"[4] opined the *Washington Post*. Frantically chewing gum, Plank had a delivery described as "deliberate, rhythmical, and nonchalant to an extraordinary degree,"[5] and slow enough that fans would start counting as he went into his windup until he actually threw the pitch.

Plank was praised in the early reviews of his work. "One winning game does not stamp a pitcher to be out of the ordinary, but unless all signs fall the Athletics have secured an A1 pitcher in this youngster," said the *Philadelphia Inquirer*. "He has plenty of speed, superb control, and mixes his slow ones with his fast ones in a way that will prove embarrassing to any set of hitters."[6]

Plank stumbled in his next start in Chicago on May 23. Philadelphia tallied five times in the top of the third inning, but Chicago knocked Plank out of the box with seven runs in the bottom frame. But Plank went on a hot stretch, starting on a chilly day in Milwaukee on May 27, settling down after giving up three early runs and allowing just four hits in an 8–3 Athletics victory. He followed that up with another four-hitter in Cleveland in the first game of a May 30 doubleheader sweep, resulting in a 3–1 win. "Plank, the new left-hander, has done exceptionally well at the start, winning three of the four games in which he has pitched," noted *The Sporting News*. "It is to be hoped he can make good throughout the season, and partly make up for some of the many disappointments Manager Mack has so far had to contend with."[7]

Plank pitched in his fifth straight road game on June 3, this time in Detroit. Again, his style of pitching was noted by the local press ("Plank's delivery is about as slow as Cuppy's, and there will be few games in which he takes part finished inside of two hours."[8]) but also his resilience in the face of a hostile crowd in beating Detroit 2–1, allowing the lone run in the seventh inning and finishing with just six hits allowed along with three walks and five strikeouts. "Young Plank had his nerve tested in the last two innings and proved that he was made of the right kind of stuff and that he is not an aeronaut," observed the *Detroit Free-Press*. "The 3,200 spectators tried in every manner possible to rattle the young pitcher, but he finished the game in fine style and ended the eighth inning with a remarkable play [catching a line drive off the bat of outfielder Jimmy Barrett]."[9]

The Detroit correspondent writing for the *Philadelphia Times* said of Plank, "This youngster certainly looks very promising, and his work to-day was the best of any left-hander seen here this season"[10] while the *Detroit Free-Press* sagely surmised, "Mack has landed a prize in Plank."[11]

Plank's win was the ninth straight for the Athletics and, although they lost the next two games in Detroit, the streak buoyed the hopes of the fan base. Over 10,000 turned out to Columbia Park on June 8 to witness the return to Philadelphia of the Athletics, who hadn't played at home in a month (May 7). The overflow crowd not only saw the home debut of Plank but also new first baseman Harry Davis. The Philadelphia native had been

3. Quickly Making a Name for Himself

working for the Pennsylvania railroad in Philadelphia when Mack convinced him to play baseball once again—Davis appeared in the National League from 1895 to 1899 and toiled for Providence of the Eastern League in 1900—and he joined the team in Chicago on May 22. Davis and outfielder Jack Hayden, who was from nearby Bryn Mawr, both were given floral arrangements from the fans prior to the contest.

But this would be Plank's day. When he took to the box to open the game, the large throng chanted his name "and compelled the youngster to acknowledge the cheers by raising his cap."[12] Despite pitching in front of the largest crowd he had ever seen, he handcuffed Detroit once again, this time on four hits with six strikeouts and no walks as the Athletics easily won, 6–1, the only run Plank allowing coming in the eighth with the game out of hand. The fans, who cheered him before he even threw his first pitch, kept it up throughout the game. In an apt description for his career, the *Philadelphia Times* noted, "Plank pitched a phenomenal game throughout, at no time showing any nervousness before the big crowd, and he was as steady as a clock."[13]

The local press was effusive in its praise and quickly compared him to Christy Mathewson, the former Bucknell pitcher now making a name for himself in the National League with New York after nearly signing with the Athletics. "Matthewson [sic] is all right but it begins to look as if Plank were still better. At any rate Connie Mack would not trade Plank for Matthewson [sic],"[14] said the *Philadelphia North American*.

Then there was this from the *Philadelphia Press*:

> There is lots to Plank, in size as well as ability. He is a regular giant for a youngster, and if there is anything he can't do with a baseball it will take an Edison or a Marconi to discover it. Plank had all kind of curves with speed enough to burn the atmosphere between the rubber and the plate and the way the horsehide had of escaping the bats of the Tigers suggested the work of a wizard. Over in New York they are naming cigars and soda after Matthewson [sic]; here in Philadelphia the fans will be inviting Plank to visit the State House, Carpenters' Hall and other famous Revolutionary relics if he keeps on his winning ways.[15]

That's a lot to put on a pitcher making just his seventh major league appearance. The team he beat in two straight starts, Detroit, was impressed as well, albeit not with the hyperbole of the Philadelphia writers. Third baseman James "Doc" Casey said Plank "has remarkable control of the ball, and is wonderfully steady,"[16] while manager George Stallings noted that Plank "has more speed than Piatt or any of the other left-handers."[17]

The Athletics lost their next three games, and the players—well, the hitters—complained to Mack that an advertisement on the center-field fence was obstructing their view of pitches. With a newly painted green fence behind him, Plank tossed his first career shutout, and his only one of 1901, giving up just two singles to left field in a 6–0 win over Milwaukee. The crowd at Columbia Park wasn't quite like Plank's last outing, with the attendance listed as 2,667. But those who did attend saw only two Milwaukee runners reach second base and the Athletics turn three double plays. Philadelphia pounded out 10 hits in the victory. "If the boys will keep on hitting as well as they did to-day I will have the fence painted a different color every day,"[18] Mack said after the game.

There was more praise for Plank, this time from the *Philadelphia Evening Telegram*, and again a comparison to Mathewson:

> There is no more used in smothering the truth than there is in trying to drown a cat in a tin cup. That man Plank is the greatest thing that ever happened and can shed a few rays of sunlight on any of them, not excepting the great and only Mathewson ... Mattie is all to the good, all right, but just part your eyebrows and gaze in rapture on the sweet boy that Connie Mack dug up from the battlefield of Gettysburg. The secret of Plank's pitching is no secret at all. He has a good, strong arm, a powerful constitution to back it, and neither drinks, smokes, chews nor swears, nor eats canned pickles, cornstarch pudding and buttermilk in the same breath. Added to this, he used to work ten hours a day in a pretzel factory, and knows how to twist things. There is no mayonnaise dressing on Plank, and we'll be plankety-planked if he isn't the warmest baby that ever came down Ridge road in a go-cart.[19]

The part about the pretzel factory was a pure fabrication, but Plank, like Mathewson, was often held up as a clean-living ballplayer over his career, and this is the first instance of such a characterization. Newspaper writers of the day would often take an angle and run with it, bending the truth where needed or just continuing the stereotype—Mathewson in particular would be presented with a squeaky-clean image so much throughout his career that it followed him for years after his death, if it still doesn't. The truth is, of course, that everyone has good and bad, but with some of the drinkers, rowdies and philanders in baseball, players like Plank and Mathewson probably did look like angels in comparison.

Despite all the laudatory articles, Plank was still learning to pitch as a professional. He lost his next three starts to Cleveland, Chicago and Baltimore, allowing 14 hits and nine runs, 10 hits and six runs and, again, 14 hits and nine runs. In the third of those games, around 400 people from Gettysburg made the trip to Baltimore—the $1 train ride left at 7:15 a.m.—adorned with yellow badges with black lettering which read "'The Athletics will win' Eddie Plank will pitch,"[20] signs with various rooting slogans, and a gold watch and chain, the latter of which was presented to the pitcher by umpire Al Mannassau when he came to bat in the third inning (he promptly singled, which might have been the only positive thing about his game that day).

3. Quickly Making a Name for Himself

Plank's outing four days later in Washington, D.C., didn't fare much better. It was a hot day—reported to be 103 in the shade—but it wasn't the temperature which did Plank in after just two innings. While he did walk five batters in his short stint, he was hit by a pitch in the second inning and then collided with Washington catcher Bill "Boileryard" Clarke at the plate trying to score. The teams played to a 13–13 tie, with the game called after nine innings due to the hot weather.

The Athletics lost again the next day, running their winless streak to 11 games (0–10–1). Back in Philadelphia, the losing skid came to an end July 3 with a 9–7 win over Washington, and Plank made it back-to-back victories as the Athletics topped the Nationals, 6–5, in the first game of a scheduled July 4 doubleheader (Game 2 would be postponed due to a rainstorm), striking out a season-high seven batters. Plank held a 6–2 lead in the ninth, allowed three runs and had the tying run on base with two outs but got infielder John Farrell to pop out to Lajoie to end the game.

However, Philadelphia lost two of three to visiting Baltimore, with Plank going the distance in an 8–7 loss on July 8. Perhaps he was blinded by the Orioles' uniforms, described as "garish"[21] by the *Baltimore Morning Herald*, whose fashion review stated, "The shirts and trousers are black, the stockings are yellow and black, the sweaters are a dark blue and the shirts are decorated with a flaming yellow 'O.' The effect is certainly loud enough to be heard a distance."[22]

Following a loss to former Gettysburg teammate George Winter, now with Boston (Connie Mack reportedly eschewed Plank's suggestion to sign the diminutive right-hander), in a game shortened by rain after five innings, Plank got into a pitching groove.

Again, facing Winter, Plank nearly blanked Boston at home on July 15, settling for a 6–1 win in which he allowed seven hits and struck out four. The lone run scored in the top of the ninth inning when with two outs and the bases loaded, Plank dropped a toss from first baseman Harry Davis. He followed that up four days later with a 3–1 win in Milwaukee, again allowing seven hits with just one walk.

It was another one-run effort for Plank in his next start, July 22 in Chicago, only this time he had to go 12 innings to secure a 2–1 win. The only run Plank allowed came in the third inning when Joe Dolan, the latest in a long line to play shortstop for the Athletics in 1901, dropped an infield popup with a runner on third base. After Plank went the distance and gave up seven hits with the lone run, the *Chicago Tribune* declared, "Plank [is] the find of the season for the Athletics."[23]

Plank allowed seven hits yet again but fell 4–3 in Detroit on July 25 in a game played in front of just 1,000 fans in a rare morning game, held early not to conflict with a parade celebrating the 200th anniversary of the city's founding.

Plank won four of his next five games—with the only loss coming in Washington on a field which was caked in mud after two days of rain—beating Boston twice, Cleveland, and Washington. In his second win over Boston, 6–1, in the second game of a doubleheader on August 12, Plank didn't allow a hit until there were two outs in the seventh inning and once again lost his shutout in the ninth. The win was Plank's 12th consecutive complete game.

Connie Mack, while bemoaning the fact that his team would be in the pennant hunt if Christy Mathewson had stayed under contract to Philadelphia, praised Plank's (who was now often being referred to as Hank Plank) recent work. "Plank has developed into one of the best youngsters in the league and has been a great help to me, and I think he will be even better next season," Mack said. "He is a wonder and will be right up among the winners at the end of this season."[24] He wasn't the only one taking notice.

The war between the American League and National League for players had no off-season. For example, there was the case of Morris Steelman. The catcher had been with Brooklyn, playing one game before being sent back to Hartford in the minor leagues. However, an injury necessitated his recall to the National League club. But before playing for Brooklyn again, Steelman wanted a raise, as his contract with Hartford actually paid him more money. Brooklyn, as relayed by manager Ned Hanlon, refused to up the ante. So Steelman called Connie Mack, made a deal with the Athletics, and was quickly inserted into the Philadelphia lineup on August 21. In other words, anyone was fair game.

At the end of July, when Philadelphia was in Cleveland, the Athletics were staying at a hotel called the Weddell House. A man claiming to be part of the Pittsburgh organization told Plank to name his price and come and join the National League club. Plank admitted as much after hearing that Cleveland pitcher Earl Moore and second baseman Erve Beck had been approached by an envoy of Cincinnati owner John T. Brush in an effort to get both players to jump. Athletics catcher Mike "Doc" Powers was also being wooed by Pittsburgh.

A report in the August 22 *Philadelphia Times* stated that "[t]hree clubs tried to get Pitcher Plank, and he was offered $2,400 by one club."[25] Plank turned down all offers as did teammate Lave Cross, who reportedly had $3,500 dangled by Brooklyn. The same report said the American League was going to sign a number of National League players in the off-season for 1902, including Philadelphia slugging outfielder Ed Delahanty, Philadelphia pitchers Harry Wolverton and Bill Duggleby, and Chicago outfielders Danny Green and Topsy Hartsel. All those players jumped to the American

3. Quickly Making a Name for Himself

League for the following season, further strengthening the veracity of the report surrounding Plank.

While Plank spurned the National League, he wouldn't be pitching for the Athletics for a while, either. Getting the start against Winter again on August 14 in Philadelphia, Plank had to exit the game after being hit in the head while batting in the fifth inning. He wouldn't pitch again until September 1 and ended the season by winning just three of his last nine starts.

Plank finished his first season in the major leagues pitching in 33 games, all but one as a starter, with 28 complete games. He was ninth in the American League in wins with his 17–13 record, 10th in ERA (3.31), sixth in hits per nine innings (8.8) and seventh in strikeouts per nine (3.1). He also led the league in wild pitches, with 13, and walked 2.3 batters per nine innings, a rate he wouldn't top for another decade.

After pitching in a couple of exhibition games with some of the Athletics players, Plank, as would become customary, returned home to Gettysburg. He also signed his contract for the next season without a fuss and early, on December 1. This would not become customary.

4

A Champion

After finishing in fourth place with a 72–64 record in the American League's debut season, Athletics manager Connie Mack went about looking to strengthen his club for 1902. He once again targeted his crosstown National League neighbors.

Mack continued the so-called baseball war by pilfering starting pitcher Bill Duggleby, who was 20–12 with a 2.88 ERA for the Phillies in 1901, veteran third baseman Monte Cross, who had played for Mack in 1895 when the latter was managing Pittsburgh's National League club, and young outfielder Elmer Flick, who in his first four seasons in the major leagues with Philadelphia owned a .338 batting average. In addition, Topsy Hartsel, a five-foot-five, left-handed-hitting outfielder, was signed away from the NL's Chicago franchise, where he batted .335 in 1901.

The Phillies and their owner, James Rogers, were still steamed over Mack signing three of his players the previous season, including star Napoleon Lajoie, and went to court to prevent the latest trio from playing for the Athletics. After the Athletics received a favorable ruling from the Court of Common Pleas, the Pennsylvania Supreme Court, by a unanimous vote, ruled that Lajoie and pitchers Bill Bernhard and Chick Fraser could only play in the state of Pennsylvania for the Phillies.

Lajoie, who led the American League in nearly every offensive category in the inaugural season, including batting average (.426), runs (145), doubles (48), home runs (14) and RBI (125), played in just one game for the Athletics in 1902, the opening game, and even at that he left after the eighth inning once he heard of the court's ruling. Bernhard started that game, also his only one with the Athletics, an 8–1 win.

Bernhard, Fraser, and Duggleby (who made two starts for the Athletics) all returned to Philadelphia's National League club. It took until the end of May, but Lajoie eventually signed with Cleveland, where he joined Flick. Worried about also being sidelined by an injunction from the courts, even though none had yet been filed involving him, Flick eventually decided he

4. A Champion

wanted out of Philadelphia. His wish was granted, and he signed with his hometown team in mid–May. Mack was quickly down a starting second baseman and outfielder, both of whom would make the Hall of Fame, and three starting pitchers.

There were suitors for other Athletics players as well. It was reported that New York's National League team was interested in Lave Cross, Monte Cross, Hartsel, and Plank, among others, and during spring training Boston tried to lure Plank to the NL. Plank remained loyal to Mack and the Athletics, as did the others. Lave Cross, who had jumped from Brooklyn to the Athletics in 1901, made no qualms that he had no desire to return to the National League.

"No, I am satisfied with Connie Mack's treatment since I joined his team, and I would rather play in Philadelphia than any other city," he said after being asked if he would jump back for a $5,000 contract. "The National League should have boosted the salaries when they had a chance of retaining their players, and while their bigger figures may tempt a few men, I believe most of them will remain in the American League. We are treated as men, and not slaves, and don't care to put another halter around our necks."[1]

After losing his players, Mack made some additions, purchasing pitcher Bert Husting from Boston of the American League and signing catcher Ossee Schrecongost—referred to as Schreck in the papers due to his long last name—who had been released by Cleveland.

Two of Mack's bigger moves came later in the summer, but early in 1902 a lot being depended on the left arm of Eddie Plank. And he was still learning how to pitch at the big-league level.

Plank lost his first three starts of the 1902 season. Pitching in Baltimore on April 24, the Athletics' second game, he allowed six runs in the first inning. He was fine after that opening inning but lost 6–2. Five days later in Washington, he gave up one run in the first inning and three in the second in a 7–2 defeat.

On May 2, Plank was on the slab for the Athletics' home opener against Washington, which was without slugger Ed Delahanty, pitcher Al Orth, and third baseman Harry Wolverton, all of whom jumped from the National League's Philadelphia team before the season and, like the three Athletics players, were not allowed to play in the state for any team other than the Phillies. Rather than risk arrest, they were housed outside of Philadelphia and didn't play. As a result, against Plank, Washington had to use two pitchers—Bill Carrick and Watty Lee—in the outfield.

No matter. Nearly 12,000 fans showed up, sporting signs in defense of Lajoie (such as "They Can Stop the Big Fellow but They Can't Stop Us" and "The Court Can't Restrain Us"[2]), who also was one of many players to receive floral bouquets. Lajoie would be cajoled out of the dugout by applauding spectators yelling "Larry!" Plank did not get such treatment from the home faithful. He allowed five runs in the first inning—Flick losing a ball in the sun didn't help—on six hits, two of them doubles. It got so bad that "Take him out!"[3] echoed from the stands. Mack stuck with Plank and the Athletics took a 6–5 lead, but Carrick's two-run triple in the eighth inning was the deciding factor for Washington. It was Plank's third straight complete-game loss, and he had allowed 32 hits in 25 innings. On the bright side, he walked none and struck out eight Washington batters.

That boded well for Plank as he took the mound four days later, once again facing Washington. This time he allowed just four hits, with only one runner reaching second base, as the Athletics cruised to an 11–0 win, prompting one paper to remark, "Plank today was in the best form he has ever exhibited in his professional career."[4]

That game turned out to be an exception, however. Plank lost his next three starts, all to Boston over an eight-day stretch. He was pounded for 12 hits in losing, 8–2, then 13 hits in a 6–3 defeat, both at home. In Boston, he battled Cy Young but fell, 2–1, allowing the go-ahead run in the bottom of the eighth inning.

With the Athletics bereft of pitchers, Plank was used often. Besides Plank, Mack could only rely on Husting and Snake Wiltse for regular work.

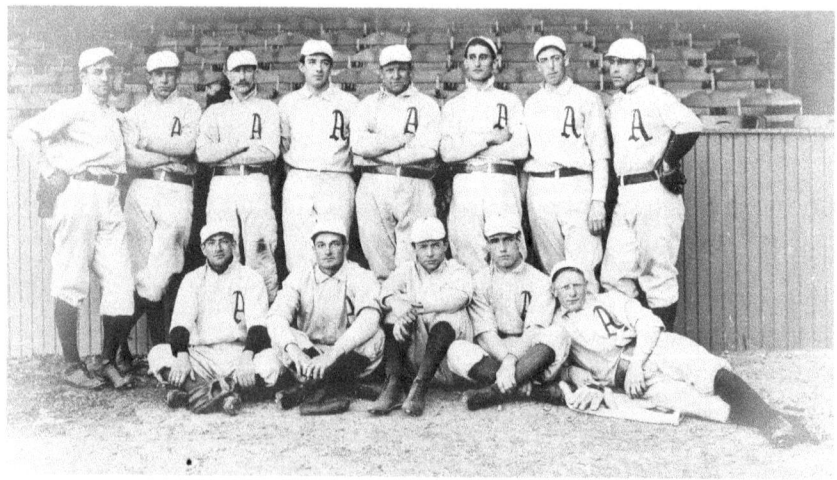

The 1902 Philadelphia Athletics, winners of the American League pennant. Top row (left to right): Bert Husting, Farmer Steelman, Monte Cross, Edward B. Kenna, Socks Seybold, Snake Wiltse, Eddie Plank, and Dave Fultz. Bottom row: Luis Castro, Lave Cross, Harry Davis, Doc Powers, and Topsy Hartsel (Library of Congress).

4. A Champion

He tried out a young right-hander named Ed Kenna, but after allowing 15 runs and 11 walks in 17 innings—and having Baltimore take advantage of his slow delivery by stealing six bases—he was released and was never heard from again in the majors. Thus, with just two days' rest, Plank was sent out by Mack again, and he nearly shut out Cleveland (without Flick, left at home, and yet to sign Lajoie) before allowing a two-out, two-run home run to third baseman Bill Bradley.

The next day, May 24, Plank was used in relief in a game which went extra innings after the Athletics tied it with five runs in the bottom of the ninth. Plank pitched a scoreless 10th but gave up six runs in the 11th on seven hits (five singles, two doubles) in a 15–11 loss. On May 28, it was Plank's turn again (the team had played just one game since his relief appearance) and he beat Detroit, 11–4, on a frigid day in front of a sparse crowd. Somehow, the Athletics were 16–11 and tied for first place.

After allowing 11 runs in a loss to St. Louis in his next start, Plank won three straight—topping Chicago, 9–7, on June 3 despite tiring late and allowing five runs in the ninth, winning in Detroit, 3–2, with both runs coming on home runs to light hitters Kid Elberfeld and Joe Yeager (their only home runs in 1902; the Athletics also hit two homers, and all four went over the left-field fence, so wind likely was a factor), and 4–3 in Cleveland, although he served up a three-run homer to his former teammate, Lajoie. Plank's next win wouldn't come for six weeks.

Between victories, three events occurred which changed the Athletics franchise's fortunes in both the short- and long-term. One was indirectly, when John McGraw, who feuded with American League umpires as well as league president Ban Johnson, followed suit of many players and jumped leagues. The Baltimore manager had skipped the series between his team in Philadelphia in early July and 10 days later left the AL entirely, headed to the National League's New York Giants to helm that team, taking several players with him, including first baseman Dan McGann, catcher Roger Bresnahan, and pitcher Joe McGinnity.

Connie Mack and McGraw sniped at each other as the ordeal took place, with the new Giants manager saying of Mack and his Athletics, "White elephants. [Owner] Mr. B.F. Shibe has a white elephant on his hands." To his credit, Mack embraced the insult, and soon there would be banners at Columbia Park adorned with white elephants. Mack eventually had white elephants painted on the outfield fence, and the Athletics basically adopted the animal as its mascot, found over 100 years later on the uniform of the modern-day Athletics incarnation in Oakland. However, it also added to the rivalry of future meetings between the two teams, both in exhibitions and postseason.

More directly, Mack needed to fill some holes in his lineup. First, he headed to Los Angeles, where Rube Waddell was pitching. The left-handed Waddell was enigmatic, eccentric, and erratic—he could leave a team with his whereabouts unknown for days—but he also was an electric pitcher. He was hard to handle but was thought to be worth the trouble due to all his talent (some things haven't changed over the years). Mack managed Waddell briefly in Milwaukee in 1900 and felt he could control the pitcher. Waddell had stints in the National League with Louisville, Pittsburgh, and Chicago from 1897 to 1901 with a modicum of success. He would come into his own under Mack in Philadelphia and was an immediate boon to the Athletics in 1902. Despite arriving in midseason, he pitched 33 games, with 27 starts, toiling 276⅓ innings.

Next, Mack knew he had to fill his hole at second base. After Lajoie's one game, Mack tried moving Dave Fultz back to second base, but especially after Flick left, he was needed in the outfield. Lou Castro, 25 years old and a native of Columbia, was given a shot next, despite having no major league experience. He hit .245 and made 14 errors in 36 games. In mid-June, Cleveland released Frank Bonner while the Athletics were in town, and Mack quickly snatched him up and put him in the starting lineup. Bonner had gotten himself exiled from Cleveland due to a drinking problem. Mack warned Bonner he would have to curtail his drinking with the Athletics, but after 11 games Bonner was suspended by Mack for two weeks for failing to live up to his end of the deal, and he was subsequently released. Bonner hit just .182 and committed four errors in his brief stay with Philadelphia.

Mack dug deep into the minors and signed Danny Murphy from a team in Norwich, Connecticut. Murphy played sparingly with the New York Giants in 1900 and 1901 (94 at-bats in 27 games), but he was destroying the low-level Class D Connecticut State League, batting .462 over 49 games. In his first game with the Athletics on July 8, a day after he had been purchased by Mack, Murphy went 6-for-6.

By this point, the Athletics had slipped to fourth place, and after a pair of losses on July 10 and 11 to Boston were 7½ games behind first-place Chicago. But Mack now had two key pieces in building a winner in Murphy and Waddell, and a third, the pitcher from Gettysburg signed a year earlier, was about to find his form.

Plank picked up just his seventh win of the season and first since June 11 when he allowed only four hits to Detroit in a home win on July 23. Backed by a Harry Davis home run, the Athletics won, 5–2, and were suddenly just one game out of first place. Philadelphia dropped back in the standings, going 3–8 with a tie in its next 12 games—Plank picking up two of those victories—as the Athletics slipped to 4½ games in back of Chicago, and in fourth place, after Detroit beat Plank, 4–3, on August 9. Plank was

4. A Champion

not supposed to pitch that day, but Waddell had left the team, albeit (as was often the case) just temporarily.

The Athletics and Tigers faced each other the next eight games, two more in Detroit and then three straight doubleheaders in Philadelphia. The Athletics won them all. When Plank beat the Tigers, 5–2, in the second game of the final twin bill on August 15, Philadelphia, which started the day in third place, leapfrogged the teams ahead of it and led the American League by one-half game.

Philadelphia extended its winning streak to 10 games, with Plank winning game No. 10 on August 18 against Chicago, striking out seven in a 12–5, complete-game win. It wasn't even that close. The Athletics ran around the bases, stealing eight, and after fanning the side in the eighth inning, armed with a large lead, Plank let up and allowed three runs in the ninth.

Plank won Mack a box of cigars a few days later. Mack and St. Louis manager Jimmy McAleer made a wager before their game on August 21, and Plank not only bested the Brown Stockings, 12–5, but also had two hits, including a double, and scored two runs.

There wasn't much that could stop the Athletics. The National League tried to poach their star pitchers but to no avail. Cincinnati contacted several American League pitchers, including Plank and Waddell, who were told, according to the *Detroit Free Press*, to "name their price if their services were in the market."[5] None signed with Cincinnati. Brooklyn made a pitch for Waddell as well, offering him more money to join its club. But Waddell, unsure of what to do, wanted some advice—so he asked Mack. Brooklyn's offer was rebuffed.

While traveling to Detroit from St. Louis after a doubleheader on September 1, the train the Athletics were taking went off the rails. The *Philadelphia Inquirer* described the wreckage:

> There in a ditch that runs parallel to the track lay one of the two engines used in hauling the heavy coaches, while the first engine and the engine of a huge freight train were locked together with their pilots five feet in the air. The engine that went over the embankment was a mass of splinters and twisted iron and the other two which remained on the track were useless. The long freight train broke in the middle and two of the big box cars were thrown at right angles with and across the track.[6]

The Athletics were fortunate that their cars were not affected, and they all escaped unharmed, albeit they ended up in Detroit seven hours late.

No matter. The Athletics, behind Waddell, who had pitched the first game of the doubleheader the day before, beat Detroit, 5–2, and won the next two games as well. Plank relieved Husting after one inning in the second affair and went eight innings in a 5–3 win.

The Athletics took two of three in Cleveland and were in first place by two games. Despite the slim lead, Philadelphians could smell a pennant. When the team returned home, an estimated 7,500 people, despite a downpour of rain which postponed that day's game, greeted them at the Broad Street Station when their train arrived. The next day, over 17,000 turned out to see the Athletics sweep a doubleheader from Baltimore. Philadelphia's National League team, which was also in town and hosting Pittsburgh, drew all of 172 fans. The next day, 11,295 turned out for another Athletics doubleheader sweep of Baltimore—Plank winning the first game, 9–1, allowing seven hits and striking out five in a complete game—while the Phillies' attendance was just 402 patrons. The Athletics were outclassing their city-mates as well as the rest of the American League, now holding a 3½-game advantage.

"Player for player, there are four teams in the American League which outclass the Athletics, but under the management of Mack teamwork has enabled them to get and hold first place to the most remarkable pennant race in the game's history,"[7] said *The Sporting News*.

The Athletics traveled next to Boston, which was in third place, four games behind Philadelphia. After losing the first game, the Athletics swept a doubleheader on September 15, Plank winning the opener, 6–4, in front of an overflow crowd of over 16,000. The *Boston Globe* summed up the pennant chances of their home team with a headline on a front-page gallery of pictures, "Scenes at the Waterloo of the Boston Americans."[8]

The Athletics' juggernaut kept moving on—and Philadelphians were turning out in droves to see them. A three-game home sweep of Washington was followed by taking three of four from Boston. Plank won two of those games—entering in the first inning in relief in a 6–2 win over Washington on September 18 and finishing the game and topping Boston, 7–2, on September 20 in front of nearly 24,000 spectators, with people standing 10 to 15 deep around the entire field. The *Boston Post* labeled it a "Niagara of humanity."[9] American League president Ban Johnson was at the game as well and sat with the Athletics on their bench. After all, everyone likes a winner. After the game, a Dr. Frank Kain gave Mack and the team a flag to be used once the team won the pennant. It was blue with stars and stripes adorned in each corner and a white elephant encompassing the rest.

The flag was waving soon enough as the Athletics won three straight against Baltimore, with Plank winning his final start of the year, his 20th victory of the season, 4–3 on September 23, allowing six hits and no walks with six strikeouts. The Athletics played a meaningless doubleheader in Washington on September 27, losing both games, then paid to have another doubleheader scheduled for Monday canceled. The reason: Philadelphia had a big celebration planned for their pennant-winning team that day. "It would not be fair to keep the Athletics over until Monday and cause a postponement of the celebration which has been arranged for, and I am only too glad to help the champions along," said Washington president Fred Postal. "If there is any man in the business who deserves to win the coveted prize, it is Connie Mack."[10]

Plank finished the year with a 20–15 record and 3.30 ERA in 36 games, 32 of which he started (completing 31 of those), toiling exactly 300 innings. Despite his late signing, Waddell went 24–7 with a 2.05 ERA. Murphy (.313) and Schrecongost (.324) also proved their worth as mid-season acquisitions. Third baseman Lave Cross led the team with a .342 average (fifth in the American League) and 108 RBI (third in the AL despite hitting no home runs), while outfielder Socks Seybold hit .316 with an AL-best 16 homers. First baseman Harry Davis (.307, 92 RBI) and outfielders Dave Fultz (.302, 44 steals) and Topsy Hartsel (.283, league-leading 47 steals) contributed to an offense which averaged 5.66 runs per game—more than a half-run better than anyone else in the American League. (Plank helped as well, batting a career-high .292 with six doubles, a triple, 16 RBI and four steals.)

Having not seen a champion in their city since 1883, Philadelphia went all-out to fete the Athletics. First was a benefit game against the amateur Wilmington A.A., a team which had beaten both Boston and Philadelphia of the National League in exhibitions. Rain held the crowd down some, but still drew around 11,000 (a Boston at Philadelphia NL game on the same day had a crowd of 101), with the players splitting $5,000 from proceeds of ticket sales and an auction of box seats. Newly adorned on the center-field fence was a

Ban Johnson was the founder of the American League, which Plank joined in its inaugural 1901 season, but also a member of the National Commission which ruled that the pitcher wasn't a free agent after the Federal League's collapse and was still the property of the St. Louis Browns (Library of Congress).

painting of a, yes, white elephant, holding a pennant in its trunk which read "Champions of 1902." The Athletics won, 11–8, Plank starting and Waddell finishing with a flair. In the ninth inning, he called his teammates into the infield just beyond the mound, then with two outs sent all but catcher Schrecongost to the bench as he struck out the final batter on three pitches.

A parade was held for the team which featured the players, of course, as well as numerous area baseball teams (including the Philadelphia Giants, an African American club), three cars filled with self-proclaimed Connie Mack fans, a band, and cyclists. "It is doubtful if there was ever a larger crowd on the streets to see any public demonstration,"[11] claimed one newspaper report. The team was honored with a banquet at the Bingham House Hotel, with each player given a watch fob engraved with both their name and the inscription "Champion Athletics, 1902." Connie Mack had a little extra included—four diamonds were put in his fob as well.

What came next for the Athletics was not a meeting with Pittsburgh, winners of the National League, however. At one point during the season, Pittsburgh owner Barney Dreyfuss issued a challenge to the American League, saying he would wager $5,000 that his club could beat any from the American League. Later, there were rumblings of a matchup between the winners of the two leagues, but Pittsburgh secretary Harry Pulliam put the kibosh on such a possibility when his team was in Philadelphia on September 11, the same day the Athletics took a doubleheader from Baltimore and appeared to be on their way to winning the American League.

Pulliam had a list of problems with such a potential meeting. First, Pittsburgh had a deal to play a conglomeration of players headed by Joe Cantillon, who umpired in the AL in 1901 and the NL in 1902, dubbed the "All-Americans," beginning October 7. Monte Cross, Harry Davis, and Rube Waddell of the Athletics were among those signed up to play on a scheduled four-city, seven-game tour. Interestingly, Pulliam mentioned this first. He then mentioned how Ban Johnson and Charles Somers, owner of Cleveland, came to Pittsburgh earlier in the season and tried to get players to jump to the American League. Pittsburgh suspended catcher Jack O'Connor on August 20 for attempting to assist Johnson and Somers. Finally, Pulliam objected to a transaction involving catcher Harry Smith in which he claimed Pittsburgh paid Mack $500 late in 1900 to obtain the player from Milwaukee, where Mack was managing at the time, only to have Mack turn around and sign Smith for the Athletics for the 1901 season (he would play just 11 games for Philadelphia and jump to Pittsburgh in 1902).

But really, one reason stood out among the three. "It was the Pittsburgh Club which first suggested the post-season series, and I went to Chicago last June and had a conference with Ban Johnson on the matter.

Everything was all right until Johnson visited Pittsburg and stole our players," Pulliam told reporters. "That ended it."[12]

Instead of a postseason series between league champions—that would have to wait one more year—the Athletics went on a barnstorming trip around Pennsylvania, playing various teams until mid–October. Eddie Plank returned to Gettysburg for the winter, a few dollars richer, carrying a gold watch fob and now known as a champion.

♦ 5 ♦

The Crossfire

> *[Plank] has achieved a national reputation in a remarkably short space of time, as two years ago he was unknown in the professional world.*[1]—*1903 Reach Guide*

In Eddie Plank's last 16 games of the 1902 season, he went 14–2, allowing four runs or more just five times. It wasn't just that he was finding his groove as a major league pitcher; he was perfecting his pitching style. How Plank delivered the ball to the plate had changed since his time at Gettysburg College or when he first joined the Athletics. He was now pitching with a crossfire delivery.

In later years, Frank Foreman claimed to have taught Plank the delivery at Gettysburg. In 1940, Foreman asserted, "Plank always pitched the way I'd taught him and late in his career he gave me credit for it. His cross-fire ball really was something to see."[2] There were also stories of Foreman seeing Plank throw the crossfire, then declaring he would make the pitcher a star. None of these were true.

Plank himself told the origin of his crossfire delivery in 1909, and he credited a couple of his teammates, not Foreman. "When I joined the Athletics I had never seen this delivery," he recalled. "Chick Fraser and my dear friend, Doc Powers, to whom I owe more than ever could have been repaid, explained it to me. I caught the idea. I found I could control the ball, and it has been my pitching mainstay ever since."[3]

Fraser, a right-hander, was with the Athletics only during Plank's first season, in 1901. Bert Husting, also a right-handed pitcher who joined Philadelphia early in 1902, was said to have "an effective cross-fire"[4] delivery. The first mention of Plank using the crossfire came from the *Detroit Free-Press* in June 1902, which reported, "Plank is using a cross-fire delivery this season. He learned this from Pete [sic] Husting, who is a postmaster in that style of delivery."[5]

Also given credit over the years for helping Plank was Matt Kilroy, a

5. The Crossfire

Philadelphia native who pitched 10 years in the majors, from 1886 to 1894 and in 1898. A friend of Connie Mack's, Kilroy, like Plank a lefty, operated a saloon in Philadelphia during Plank's time with the Athletics and was asked by the manager to tutor his young pitcher.

The crossfire was first believed to be used by Silver King in the 1880s and 1890s. The delivery consisted of more than just throwing a pitch side-arm—although some pitchers who just threw sidearm have also been described as using a crossfire, this is not the truest definition. *New York Herald* writer O.P. Caylor described King's delivery: "It consists of standing on the extreme end of the pitcher's plate, stepping away still farther from the direct line towards the batsman and sending the ball across the home base at an angle, which, although small, is very bothersome to the man with the bat."[6]

While King was right-handed, the theory was the same for the left-handed Plank. In 1913, the *New York Times* depicted Plank's style for its readers, noting that the pitcher "extends his right foot almost on a line toward first base and shoots the ball over the plate at a different angle ... He has mastered this style of pitching as no other left-hander has been able to do."[7]

It took time for Plank to become a crossfire expert. Connie Mack later noted that Plank "worked hour after hour to perfect control of that cross fire, and it made him."[8] Plank said the key for him was learning control. In 1902, he walked three or more batters five times in his first 15 appearances but in just four games thereafter. This coincides with his late-season hot streak and is likely when he started perfecting the crossfire.

"The cross-fire never goes squarely over the plate. That's why it is so hard to hit," Plank said of his success with his mode of delivering a pitch.

> It comes shooting past the eyes so quickly that it takes a lightning-fast swing to get anything more out of it than a chop hit, which cannot go very far. The ball is likely to be so close to the hands that there will be a little force to the drive. I am speaking now of its use against left-handed hitters, and this is where it will be found to give the best results. But right-handers don't find themselves comfortable while dealing with the cross-fire. It shoots so close that it will nearly always take a man a shade out of his natural position, and once you can do that, you will come pretty close to getting him on your staff.[9]

Decades later, a teammate backed up the pitcher's impeccable ability to guide the ball where he wanted with his crossfire. "Plank was the most remarkable left-handed pitcher I ever saw," said Jack Coombs, who pitched with Plank on the Athletics from 1906 to 1914 and later toiled for Brooklyn (1915–1918) and Detroit (1920). "Never did he pitch the ball over the center of the plate unless he absolutely had to. His crossfire delivery was very effective and he had it in perfect control."[10]

A writer for the *Los Angeles Evening Express* tried to explain Plank's delivery and accuracy after watching him pitch in a 1909 exhibition, leaving the reader a lot to imagine but at the same time understanding why Plank could be so difficult to hit: "The general impression of his delivery is that he starts the ball away off there somewhere and that it is going to travel somewhere else, but you seldom can guess just where that somewhere is."[11]

That control of the baseball, hitting the corners, and not putting a pitch in a hitter's sweet spot were pivotal—and something few, if any, other pitchers could do. "He was very studious out there. He used to pitch to spots," said Smoky Joe Wood, who won 117 games and had a 1.99 for the Boston Red Sox from 1908 to 1915. "They didn't do that much in those days. But Eddie Plank did."[12] New York Giants great Christy Mathewson toyed with the crossfire in 1901 but gave it up because of his lack of control. Joe Bush, later Plank's teammate on the Athletics, who pitched in the majors from 1912 to 1928, said Mathewson wasn't the only one with this problem. Plank was the exception. Bush reminisced about his former teammate in a 1929 article for the *Saturday Evening Post*:

> Eddie Plank was one of the cagiest men ever to grace the mound. His famous crossfire ball had the opposing batters standing on their heads! He was the only one who could control this unusual delivery. Eddie ... threw this ball from an angle instead of directly at the batter. He would step off the mound to his left with a big stride and from this point pitch the ball directly to the plate. It was unorthodox. Batters could not follow the ball from this angle as easily as they could when the pitch came straight from the hill. The ball, curving as it did, put the hitters in a bad position to meet it squarely, and they were forced to change quickly their stance when Plank would cross them and suddenly shoot this ball at them. Consequently they were off balance and had great difficulty hitting him. All batters fouled his pitches a lot. A peculiar feature of this delivery was that it lessened the fair or safe batting area for the hitters. Instead of having the entire diamond before them, the batters were forced to change their positions at the plate, cutting their hitting space to about one-half the field.... Right-handers would invariably hit between second and first bases, and the left-handed would bat the ball, if they hit it at all, to right field."[13]

Late in his legendary career, Ty Cobb recalled facing Plank. "His cross-fire was one of the most deceptive deliveries that I ever have seen," Cobb said. "Often I wonder why other pitchers did not work to develop a cross-fire like that used by Plank. Believe me, it was deadly."[14] Cobb didn't make his debut until 1905, but surely American League hitters in 1903 had similar thoughts.

In his first two years in the American League, Plank was a pretty dependable pitcher for the Athletics. By the end of the 1903 season, he would be considered one of the most reliable hurlers in all of baseball. During spring training in Jacksonville, Florida, manager Connie Mack

5. The Crossfire

noted, "pitching was our weak point last season. But I rather think I have two good men in this bunch, and perhaps four."[15] He was correct on the former.

Plank and Rube Waddell formed one of the best tandems in major league history; certainly, it would be hard to find a tougher 1–2 punch of left-handers. Both would turn in excellent seasons, with their names littered all over the AL leaderboards. They were helped out in part by the American League's decision to follow the National League's lead and count foul balls as strikes, except when the batter already had two strikes on him. Previously, a foul ball was just a "no pitch"—neither ball nor strike. Waddell fanned a major league-high 302 batters or 8.4 per nine innings, an increase of 1.6 from the previous year, when he also led the league. Plank whiffed 176, good for third in the league, while his 4.7 K/9 was sixth in the AL and 1.5 greater than his mark in 1902. Plank also finished second in the league in wins (23), 10th in ERA (2.38) and second in WAR for pitchers (7.1). Waddell was first in the latter category with an 8.4.

But the problem for Mack was that he couldn't develop two other dependable pitchers. He relied on two rookies—Charles Albert "Chief" Bender, who wouldn't turn 19 until early May, and 22-year-old Weldon Henley. Bender eventually became a Hall of Fame pitcher, but in 1903 he had the usual ups-and-downs of a young, first-year pitcher and went 17–14 with a 3.07 ERA—the league average ERA was 2.96—in 36 games (with 33 starts). Henley made 29 appearances with 21 starts and was 12–10 with a 3.91 ERA. Meanwhile, Plank and Waddell carried the load, starting 78 of Philadelphia's 135 games (not to mention pitching in exhibitions during the season). Plank led the league in both games pitched (43) and starts (40) and was second in innings (336; Boston's Cy Young led with 341⅔). Waddell also topped 300 innings (324).

After opening the season with back-to-back losses to Boston, including a tough 2–1 defeat to Cy Young in which neither pitcher walked a batter, Plank won twice in the Hub City with just one day's rest between starts. On April 30 he went the distance to beat George Winter, 12–2, and on May 1 took on Young again and blanked Boston on five hits, while striking out six, 3–0. In the latter game, Plank led off the ninth inning by smacking a Young offering all the way to the fence in right-center field and circling the bases for his first (of three) career home runs, all of which would be of the inside-the-park variety.

Plank won his next three starts as well. After he won in New York, 6–1 on May 6, the *Philadelphia Record* declared him in a headline as the "Athletics' Reliable Pitcher."[16] A week later, on a frigid day in Chicago, he tossed a three-hitter, allowing just one hit in eight innings before he "eased up"[17] in the ninth, in recording his second shutout of the year, 6–0. He won

The Athletics play at Washington's American League Park on May 6, 1905. The crowd was estimated at 10,000; note the fans on the field down the right-field line and in front of the left-field fence. Eddie Plank pitched and won this game, 2–1, allowing four hits, all singles, and striking out nine (Library of Congress).

his first three starts of June and, after beating St. Louis, 2–1, allowing three hits while walking no one and fanning six, on June 15, the Athletics were tied with Boston for first place. The Athletics moved into the lead by themselves, but only for a few days. By June 23, Boston was atop the standings and never relinquished the lead. The Athletics remained in striking distance for most of the summer, but by mid–August had slipped to eight games back.

With Boston running away with the American League pennant in September, Plank kept taking the slab. While Waddell left the team at times for various reasons (once, he was affronted that Lave Cross called him on his conditioning habits and he disappeared for days), Plank kept his turn in the rotation, often going on just two days' rest but never seeming to tire. He won his last four games, allowing seven runs in 38⅓ innings while striking out 30, including nine in each of his final two appearances.

In his last outing, the penultimate game of the season, he "pitched one of the best games he has shown this season"[18] as the Athletics won at home against Cleveland, 4–3, in 10 innings, to clinch second place in the American League. Plank bore down late in the contest. In the eighth inning, after a Bill Bradley looping hit with one out, he intentionally walked Nap Lajoie (who had homered and singled twice) before fanning both Charlie Hickman and Jack Thoney "amidst the wildest applause."[19] In the 10th, with a runner on second base and one out, Plank decided to walk both Bradley *and* Lajoie. He again struck out Hickman and got Thoney to pop out to catcher Doc Powers. The outs elicited an even bigger reaction than the eighth-inning strikeouts, as "Plank was cheered to the echo, with the crowd almost going wild with enthusiasm."[20] To top it all off, Plank reached on an error to open the bottom of the 10th and, after being bunted to second base, scored on a two-out single by Harry Davis.

The applause for Plank was well-warranted and earned. Philadelphia fans as well as the American League were learning what kind of player he was on the field and the type of person he was off it. Despite Waddell, also a left-handed pitcher, on the team, Davis remarked in late August that "Plank is the best left-hander in the business."[21] W.A. Phelon concurred. Writing in *Sporting Life*, he observed, "The Gettysburg southpaw is as good a left-hander as any man could ask for, and is due to improve still further in future. He hasn't as much speed as Waddell, but somehow they don't bunch hits on him, and he doesn't grow fainthearted anywhere along the road."[22]

Philadelphians saw Plank the gentleman on display in mid–June. B.F. Keith's Bijou Theater—noted in 1895 for having the first public showing of a movie—advertised a "baseball night" with players from the Athletics and St. Louis Browns in attendance. The event occurred after Philadelphia swept St. Louis, which happened to propel the Athletics into first place by themselves. All the Browns players were corralled into attendance, however only two Athletics showed up (even more embarrassing because the theater had hung white elephant banners where the Athletics players were to sit, making the lack of participation even more noticeable)—Lave Cross, the team's captain, and Plank. Years later, writer Ernest Lanigan said Plank told him he felt obligated to attend because, as Lanigan conveyed, "it had been advertised that the ball players would be present."[23] It would not be the last instance of Plank being a do-gooder or being lauded for altruistic behavior.

♦ 6 ♦

The Workhorse

After the 1903 season, which included another city series against the National League's Phillies ("a dismal failure both from an artistic and a financial standpoint,"[1] according to local writer William Weart), Lave Cross and his wife visited Eddie Plank in Gettysburg, with the trio going hunting and bagging several partridges and rabbits (Mrs. Cross reportedly "shot 8 birds and 3 rabbits"[2]). Hunting would always be a big part of Plank's life, and over the years he went on trips with several teammates.

As he continued to do over the years, Plank worked with Gettysburg College's pitchers in the off-season, but he picked up a couple of new hobbies as well—bowling and holding out (or, at least, signing late), both of which he would continue being proficient at throughout his career. While many Athletics also got into bowling—Monte Cross owned his own alley, while Harry Davis was co-owner of another—most players signed their contracts for the upcoming season in relatively quick fashion.

By mid–February all but six players, including Plank, had signed, and one, Lave Cross, had agreed to terms but as was his custom delayed actually putting pen to paper. By the end of the month, all but Cross and Plank had signed. Finally, on March 1, 2½ weeks before the team left for spring training in Spartanburg, South Carolina, Plank signed on the dotted line.

As is the case in spring, positivity abounded. Mack looked at his team and saw a potential pennant-winner, which wasn't a far-fetched idea seeing as how the Athletics won the American League pennant in 1902 and were in the hunt for much of 1903. "I do not see anything wrong with my team," Mack said prior to heading south. "I can not see a weak spot in it. We certainly expect to win the pennant again this year. Barring accidents like last year when [Harry] Davis and [Topsy] Hartsel were out of the game so long on account of injuries and [Rube] Waddell did not do as well as we had counted on, I feel confident that we will win out…. With Waddell at his best this year, our pitching department will be the strongest of any club in the country and all we need to win the pennant is good pitching."[3]

6. The Workhorse

But as often happens, the promises of spring turned into the failures of fall. First baseman Harry Davis suffered an injury two-thirds of the way into the season and was lost for the year. He would lead the team in batting average (.309) and home runs (10). Outfielder Danny Hoffman suffered a horrific beaning and played in just 53 games (.299/.329/.426). His replacement, Ollie Pickering, hit just .226 with a .299 on-base percentage and 17 stolen bases in 124 games after batting .281 with a .353 OBP and 40 steals a year earlier. Both catchers were anemic at the plate as Ossie Schrecongost had a slash line of .186/.199/.232 and Doc Powers .190/.220/.207. Shortstop Monte Cross batted .189. Outfielder Socks Seybold hit .292, just seven points lower than in 1903, but saw his slugging percentage dip from .462 to .396. The team's hitting was so poor, Mack at times batted the pitcher eighth in the lineup.

While Mack claimed to have eight promising pitchers, he relied mainly on three—Plank, Rube Waddell, and Weldon Henley. Those three accounted for 123 of the Athletics' 155 starts. Chief Bender started 20 games and pitched 203⅔ innings but went 10–11, and his 2.87 ERA was worse than the league average (2.60). Henley wasn't much better. He pitched 295⅔ innings and was 15–17 with a 2.53 ERA.

That left, again, Waddell and Plank. Before the season, the Rube proclaimed, "We'll win the pennant in a walk this year.... If we don't win it will not be my fault. I'll pitch my arm off to win for Connie Mack."[4] He backed up his words by having his best season to date. Pitching a career-high 383 innings (almost 50 more than any other in his 13 seasons), he boasted a 1.62 ERA while striking out 349 batters, a major league record that wouldn't be topped for over 60 years. However, speaking to the quality of Philadelphia's offense and perhaps some bad luck, Waddell's record was just 25–19 (.568).

Plank also set a career high in innings (357⅓) while pitching in 44 games, with 43 starts, but he posted a .607 winning percentage (26–17) to go with a 2.17 ERA, seven shutouts and 201 strikeouts. Unlike Waddell, though, Plank made no preseason predictions or boasts. He just went about his business. "He is today the same quiet, modest, unassuming young man that he was as pitcher on the Good Intent team, or as the bleachers put it—'Plank isn't one but "chesty."'"[5]

That's not to say Plank didn't have his moments when he showed emotion. One of those times occurred September 10 at home against Boston, again challenging for the AL pennant it would eventually claim. The Athletics were technically in the race, at eight games back, but in fourth place with just a month left in the season. The matchup, though, was one for the ages—Plank against the venerable Cy Young, who at age 37 was in the midst of one of his final great years (26–16—he would never win more than 21 again—with a 1.97 ERA). For 12 innings the game was scoreless, with both pitchers getting out of jams and receiving ovations from the crowd. Finally, in the bottom of the 13th, it was Plank who won it when his two-out hit flew down the first-base line and into right field to score Danny Murphy from third with the only run of the game. Plank ran out to right field to retrieve the ball to keep as a souvenir, and as he worked his way back to the clubhouse, he found many of the over 14,000 fans surrounding him. At first he was pressed into shaking the hands of the hometown faithful as he tried to work his way through the crowd, but eventually members of the throng lifted him up and "carried him in triumph to the dressing room and gave him three cheers more as a final parting."[6] Those who remained in their seats celebrated by throwing whatever object they could find, including seat cushions, into the air. Wrote a visiting correspondent from Boston, "It was a demonstration following a game that will forever be remembered by those fortunate to have seen it."[7]

A baseball from a game-winning hit wasn't the only thing Plank earned in 1904. In July, with his club barely playing above .500 ball and falling further behind in the standings (as much as 10½ games out after splitting a doubleheader on July 9) as an incentive for his pitchers, Mack said he would buy anyone a new suit if he won three straight games. Plank quickly took advantage. After losing three straight decisions and seven of his last 10, Plank won four in a row, capturing his suit with a 5–1 win over Chicago and Doc White on July 15.

The streak started with one of the best-pitched games of his career. On July 8, he topped Washington at home 2–1, allowing a lone hit—a bunt single by Jake Stahl which the Senator "beat by a narrow margin"[8] in the fifth inning. Plank was so dominant against the mostly right-handed lineup (seven of the nine batters hit from the right side) that none could even get a fly ball to left field. Plank allowed three fly balls in the first two innings, and then nothing was hit out of the infield in the final seven frames. Of course, whereas over 14,000 saw Plank's epic showdown with Young months later, a scant 1,700 or so witnessed his command performance, mainly due to the threat of rain, which never came on this day.

Plank filled his closet more that summer. He won three straight games from July 29–August 8 and reeled off eight in a row from August 22–September 19, his final victory in that latter streak a 6–1 win at Boston in which he allowed three hits and fanned eight. At one point, Plank retired 18 batters in a row and 23 of 24, with no Boston runner even reaching second base from the second through seventh innings. In his last 40 innings against Boston, Plank allowed but three runs. No wonder the performance caused the *Boston Sunday Post* to gush, "Plank was almost invincible."[9]

But Plank tired a bit as the season wound down. He was yanked after one inning at Chicago on September 24, allowing four runs on three hits.

6. The Workhorse

Two days later, he started again in the Windy City and won, 2–1, but allowed 11 hits, his most since giving up 12 against Detroit three months earlier. The Tigers returned the favor on September 30, again getting 12 base knocks off Plank, although the Athletics hurler emerged with a 9–4 win. Philadelphia finished the season in Washington and in front of a sparse crowd (estimated at 1,500), Plank was batted around for seven runs and seven hits in three innings.

That finished off Plank's season, and two days later the Athletics' was done as well, ending with an 81–70 record, a disappointing fifth place in the American League, 12½ games behind Boston. But Plank wasn't done pitching just quite yet. There was an exhibition against the Trenton (NJ) YMCA, where he tossed five perfect innings, whiffing nine, and a charity game back in Gettysburg, where Plank and a band of professionals, including his brother Ira and Philadelphia teammate Lave Cross, beat a bunch of college players, 14–1, raising over $60 for the College Athletic Association and Women's Civic Club.

Plank had plenty of time to rest his arm, staying, as usual, in Gettysburg in the off-season. There was the rumored visit of New York Giants owner John T. Brush to the town, but after another lengthy delay in signing, on March 1 Plank was on board the train leaving Philadelphia for New Orleans, the team's destination before heading to Shreveport, Louisiana, their spring training site in 1905.

The newest edition of the Athletics was nearly identical to the previous season's. With Danny Hoffman back healthy, outfielder Ollie Pickering was sold to Columbus in January. Twenty-one-year-old Bris Lord filled in as the club's backup outfielder. Also, left-handed pitcher Andy Coakley, who went 4–3 with a 1.89 ERA after joining the team in late August, became a fixture of the staff and would make 31 starts. In fact, Mack used only 20 players *the entire season*. Philadelphia's five-man pitching core of Plank, Coakley, Chief Bender, Weldon Henley, and Rube Waddell accounted for 1,343 of the team's 1,383⅓ innings pitched. Mack also used only 13 position players, although 10 accumulated 250 or more plate appearances.

Despite the small roster (six of the other seven American League clubs used at least 25 players, topped by the New York Highlanders with 37), Mack was confident of this group early on. Early in camp he noted, "From present indications no team in the country will be stronger in the pitching department than the Athletics."[10] His belief in the team would only grow as the season progressed.

It didn't quite start that way. The Athletics did win their first five games to open the season but two weeks later were at .500. The team was inconsistent, standing at 19–15 and in third place at the end of May. Plank was inconsistent as well, going 4–5 in his first nine starts. He might have been still regaining strength in his arm. He also could have been trying out the spitball—a legal pitch throughout Plank's career and which became more popular after the New York Highlanders' Jack Chesbro went 41–12 with a 1.82 ERA using that pitch in 1904. Although future teammate Eddie Collins said he only saw Plank throw a spitter once, and in 1911 another eventual Athletic, Stuffy McInnis, claimed, "Ed Plank never threw a spitter in his life,"[11] *Sporting Life* said in mid–May that the Athletics pitcher had been throwing "a few damp ones."[12]

Things changed for Plank in June. On the opening day of the month, he had a no-hitter against Washington for 7⅔ innings before light-hitting Hunter Hill spoiled it. Plank weakened in the ninth and was taken out by captain Lave Cross for Bender with two out, but the Athletics held on for a 6–5 victory. Plank wouldn't lose a game in June, winning all seven of his starts, including a 1–0 six-hitter at Washington played in front of 21-year-old Alice Roosevelt, daughter of the president, in which he walked none and struck out 10.

The tide turned in July as Plank lost his first three starts, not able to

The Athletics' famed $100,000 infield: first baseman John "Stuffy" McInnis (left), third baseman Frank "Home Run" Baker (middle), shortstop Jack Barry (second from right) and second baseman Eddie Collins (far right). Also pictured is Danny Murphy (second from left), who might have helped lure Eddie Plank to the Federal League (George Grantham Bain Collection, Library of Congress).

make it out of the fourth inning in any of them. The Athletics' play was sporadic as well. From July 8–29, the team won back-to-back games just once, although they lost more than two straight games only once as well (a three-game skid from July 11–15). But there were signs things were getting better at the end of the month, especially from Plank, who won his last three decisions of July.

Plank's final three starts of the month were all against Chicago, a team in front of the Athletics (along with Cleveland, alternating first place). On July 23 in Chicago, in front of a capacity crowd of around 15,000 (with even more people watching from roofs), Plank outdueled Frank Owen, 1–0, fanning eight and allowing just two hits. Four days later, he was on the hill again in a game which ended in a 4–4 tie after 10 innings. The game was stopped at 5 p.m. because both teams had to catch a train to Philadelphia, where Plank would face the White Sox, now in first place, again on July 31. With Connie Mack in New England on a scouting trip, the Athletics won, 4–1, as Plank went the distance (as he usually did), allowing seven hits and a walk while striking out six.

Philadelphia was still in third place but only two games back. Just before the Chicago series, Mack was quoted as saying, "Barring accident, the Athletics should go right down the line from now on and by Saturday next they should be in the lead in the race for the American League pennant. No team in the league is playing smarter or better ball than our bunch."[13] A pretty strong statement by the manager of a team which went 4–5 to end the month.

But Mack knew what he had. Plank's win on July 31 started a five-game winning streak by the Athletics, and on Saturday, August 5, now winners of six of seven, Philadelphia was in first place, holding a two-game edge over Chicago and 2½ games in front of Cleveland. After his team lost three of four to the Athletics, including a nine-hit shutout by Plank in the first game of an August 4 doubleheader, Detroit pitcher George Mullin thought the Athletics were headed towards the pennant. "Unless their pitchers fall down, I can not see how the Athletics can be kept from winning," Mullin said. "They are certainly a great team and they play the game all the time."[14]

Others chimed in with similar thoughts later in the month as the Athletics maintained their lead by a slim 3½-game margin. "With a race as close as the present one, any upset that will change conditions is likely to come at short notice, of course. As it stands at present, however, I can not see how any club is going to beat Mack's men to the pennant," said Washington player/manager Jake Stahl.

St. Louis manager Jimmy McAleer was even stronger in his conviction regarding the Athletics. "I do not see how the Athletics can fail to capture the pennant, going as they are," he said. "In sporting parlance, they are a 10 to 1 shot. Mack has a splendid team. His pitching staff is first class. With the ash, his men bat well, hitting the ball hard whenever a long hit is necessary; at base running they have few equals and no superiors, while the outfield of the team is one of the strongest in the league. In my judgment, the Athletics will carry off the coveted honor—the pennant."[15] Mack was in no mood to argue. "Without making any immodest statements, Philadelphia has the best club in the league, and nothing but an epidemic of accidents or sickness can beat us out,"[16] he claimed.

Of course, those were the thoughts from managers of the two worst clubs in the American League plus Mack, presider of the team in question. The managers of those closer in the chase of the Athletics remained confident in their teams as well.

Things were going well for the Athletics. After a mid–August hiccup against the Browns where they lost three of four games and tied another, Philadelphia closed the month winning nine of 12. From August 28–September 4, which included two doubleheaders, the Athletics won seven straight. The only thing which was a cause for concern was Plank's arm at the end of August. After pitching 7⅓ innings against Detroit on August 28, Mack sent Plank out again on August 30 at Cleveland. Plank's arm was hurting enough that he needed help from catcher Ossie Schrecongost just to button his shirt collar … and then he went out and tossed a complete game, winning 6–2, allowing seven hits, and not issuing a walk. Plank wouldn't pitch again until September 6. The rest would do him well—and he would need it.

Plank won at Boston in that September 6 game, 2–1, and the Athletics took three of the four games. As the team boarded its train for home, it held a 4½-game lead with roughly 30 games to play. When the Athletics arrived back in Philadelphia, the tenor of the rest of the season had changed.

Rube Waddell had a fantastic season in 1904. He was possibly even better in 1905. Waddell led the league with 27 wins (against 10 losses) and a 1.48 ERA, both career bests, while pitching 328⅔ innings. But that innings total should have been higher if not for some shenanigans on the train ride from Boston to Philadelphia. Somewhere along the way, it was reported that Waddell and Andy Coakley got into a scuffle at a railway station over a straw hat, with Waddell injuring his shoulder in the process. Waddell later denied accusations that he had succumbed to the gambling element, who might not want the Athletics to win the pennant or World Series. Either way, his season was all but over.

That, of course, was not good news for the Athletics. Besides Plank and Waddell, the two stalwarts, the pitching staff was lacking. Coakley had a fine season in his first full year in the big leagues, with an 18–8 record and 1.84 ERA, but missed time down the stretch with a sore arm. Chief Bender again had an ERA higher than the league average, 2.83, although

6. The Workhorse

he sported an 18–11 record. Weldon Henley had a 2.60 ERA (AL ERA was 2.65) but finished 4–11. Mack brought in Jimmy Dygert, who pitched for the team during spring training, from New Orleans for some September pitching depth and ended up having to start him in three games. Dygert went 1–4 with a 4.33 ERA in his six appearances, and his only victory came in his major league debut on September 8, the final game at Boston before the fateful train ride, in relief of Waddell. That put a lot of onus on the left arm of Plank.

Starting on September 9, Plank made six starts over the next 18 days. It started with a doubleheader against New York, a 6–2 victory in the opener. He faced Boston at home on September 13 in a game that lasted just an hour and 15 minutes; Plank allowed just two hits, both singles, and walked none as the Athletics won, 1–0, thanks to a Danny Murphy home run over the right-field screen in the seventh inning. Plank retired the side in order in each of the final four innings. Two days later, he faced Boston again and even though the *Boston Globe* claimed Plank was in "poor form,"[17] he prevailed, 6–2, giving up six hits and one walk while fanning five.

In part because the Athletics had a couple of days off, Plank didn't pitch again until September 21, again at home, this time versus future Hall of Famer Addie Joss and Cleveland. Joss tossed a four-hitter while Plank allowed six hits, but the Athletics won again, 2–1. The Naps got the tying run on second base with two down in the ninth inning but Plank fanned pinch hitter Bob Rhoads. Two days later, Plank was at it again in front of an overflow crowd vs. Cleveland in the second game of a doubleheader. The Athletics scored two runs in the ninth to finish off a twin bill sweep with a 3–2 win with Plank allowing six hits and two walks while striking out eight in the victory.

But by the time Mack used Plank again—he saved him for Chicago, which came to town after a three-game series with Detroit—the Athletics were tied for first place with the White Sox. Philadelphia, which had been up four games as late as September 16, had lost two of three to the Tigers, with Waddell trying to pitch in the finale, an 8–7 loss. He barely could get anything on the ball, bouncing several pitches before leaving after facing just two batters.

Chicago was 11–4 on the road since September 19, coming off a series in Boston where it won five of six. There was no hotter team in baseball. The game was so pivotal that newspapers such as the *Philadelphia Record* put the game story on its front page—a rarity for a sports story—while the *Chicago Tribune* devoted nearly an entire page. Columbia Park in Philadelphia was filled, with many other fans, estimated in the thousands, turned away at the gate. The writers and fans had plenty to talk about, especially concerning Plank. He allowed only three hits—one of which normally would have been an out but fell into the overflow crowd—as the Athletics won, 3–2. Plank whiffed 12, striking out a batter in every inning but the sixth. "Plank ... had the Chicago players completely baffled, and was applauded time and again for his great work,"[18] reported the *Philadelphia Record*. In the ninth inning, Chicago loaded the bases with two out on an error, walk (one of just two by Plank), and a hit by pitch. Billy Sullivan then hit one off Plank's leg, the ball rolling towards first with the pitcher picking it up and throwing it to Harry Davis for the final out. After the game, Plank showed off bruises on both of his shins thanks to the play.

The Athletics smashed Chicago the next day, 11–1, and in the finale, Mack again turned to Plank on one day's rest, leading the *Philadelphia Record* to wonder "Can Plank stand the strain?"[19] In front of another packed crowd, estimated at over 25,000 (the three-game series drew 64,620), Plank allowed three hits and two runs in the first inning. He settled down but in the seventh inning, Chicago got to him for two more runs on three hits and the Athletics fell, 4–3, Plank allowing 11 hits. "Eddie had not strength enough left to get up half the customary speed and the wonder is that Chicago did not beat him worse than by a 4-to-3 score," observed *The Sporting News*. "If Mack would have had a pitcher in shape for the last game the Athletics could have taken the entire series without much trouble. But with Waddell out of it, Coakley handicapped with a lame arm and Bender pitching the day before, Mack had to stick with the overworked Plank again."[20]

Luckily for the Athletics, last-place St. Louis came to town next. Coakley blanked the Browns, 5–0, on October 2, and Henley and Bender combined to beat them 5–2 the next day. Plank made it a clean sweep with a 4–1 win. The rest helped, even against St. Louis, as he allowed five hits and struck out six. His "curves broke beautifully yesterday and he had the Browns standing on their heads."[21]

Philadelphia headed to Washington and took both games of a doubleheader against the Senators on October 5, putting the Athletics on the precipice of clinching—a win or Chicago loss would do the trick. Mack sent Coakley to the mound on October 6, but he lasted only two innings and was replaced by Waddell, who went six innings, allowing six runs on five hits and five walks plus two wild pitches. The Athletics lost, 10–4, but it didn't matter as St. Louis surprisingly beat Chicago, 6–2. The players didn't find out they won the pennant until they returned to their hotel, the Riggs House. They were greeted by a pennant which read "Athletics, champions 1905" and several small replica white elephants hanging from white and blue ribbons.

The Athletics finished out the season with an October 7 doubleheader, winning one and tying another (Waddell started the opener but lasted just one inning and allowed two runs). Plank, of course, did not pitch. He had made 10 starts from August 30–October 4 and won nine of those. He went the full nine innings each time. Five times he had followed an Athletics loss, and five times he emerged with a win. For the season he made 41 starts, completing 35, and finished with a 24–12 record and 2.26 ERA. But it was down the stretch where he really shined—when his team needed him, helping them reach their first World Series (just the second to be played between the American and National Leagues).

Coakley lost 15 pounds those final weeks, and he labored to a 5–3 record in September and October. Two years later, Mack looked back at that season and was stunned at what Plank gave the team. "In 1905 we went along for the final six weeks on virtually one pitcher," he recalled, "for Plank alone of our twirlers could be depended on for a victory, and we worked him so hard that I marvel he was able to stand the strain."[22]

There was still more baseball to be pitched, of course, as the World Series (or World's Series as it was then called) began just two days after the Athletics' final game. While Philadelphia captured the American League at the very end of the season, winning 92 games while leading the league with a .255 batting average, .310 on-base percentage and .338 slugging percentage, the New York Giants ran away with the National League, finishing with 105 wins, and had a much better slash line, .273/.351/.368, which also led their circuit. The Giants' pitching staff under John McGraw was formidable, with Christy Mathewson (31–9, 1.28 ERA) leading the way.

Still, Mack liked the Athletics' chances, of course, and intimated he would have his two frontline pitchers for the series even though Waddell barely pitched down the stretch and when he did was a shell of himself. "Waddell and Plank will mow down those National League fellow as sure as you live, and as for the rest of the team I am not a bit doubtful," he said the day before the series began. "We can bat as good as if not better than they can, while in the field there is nothing to it but the Athletics."[23]

Team captain Lave Cross also thought Waddell would pitch, although he wasn't too happy about the circumstances over the past month. "I'd like to clout him on the head with a bat," Cross said. "He worked out yesterday on the quiet and had both speed and curves. There is no reason why he should not pitch. He is jeopardizing our chances of getting the bulk of the money, and it is not fair to the team."[24] In addition to the series share, the Athletics had been promised $1,000 in gold by the *Philadelphia Inquirer* if they beat the Giants.

Waddell or no Waddell (and it turned out he did not pitch in the series), what Mack, Cross and the Athletics didn't have—although Mack once nearly did get him years earlier—was Mathewson, who pitched Games 1, 3 and 5 and tossed shutouts in each, defeating three different Athletics pitchers.

Before the first game of the 1905 World Series at Philadelphia's Columbia Park, the Athletics' Lave Cross presents Giants manager John McGraw with a white plaster elephant, much to the delight of the crowd (Michael T. "Nuf Ced" McGreevy Collection, Boston Public Library).

Plank got the assignment in Game 1, held at Columbia Park in Philadelphia. There was some levity before the game when Lave Cross presented McGraw with a plaster white elephant, the manager then stepping on the plate and putting the figure on his head, to the delight of the crowd. But there wasn't much to cheer for after that for the home fans. An overflow crowd of nearly 18,000, not to mention thousands more "watching" the game on a bulletin board at the *Philadelphia Record*'s office or listening to play-by-play being announced through a megaphone at the *Inquirer* building, saw (or heard) Mathewson shut down the Athletics on five hits, with only one runner reaching third base as the Giants won, 3–0. Plank was touched for 10 hits and expressed some displeasure about a number of called balls by home plate umpire Jack Sheridan, particularly in a two-run Giants second inning. "[The Giants] made the Athletics look like second raters,"[25] observed the *Philadelphia Record*.

The Athletics, behind Chief Bender, won Game 2 over Joe McGinnity, 3–0, but, after rain pushed Game 3 back a day, fell victims again to

6. The Workhorse

Mathewson, who beat Andy Coakley, 9–0. Plank went in Game 4 against McGinnity at the Polo Grounds and, despite all the innings his arm had gone through that season and it being a frigid day, he pitched a gem, allowing four hits and two walks with six strikeouts. "During the season you can go along easy and save yourself once in awhile. But in a world's series you put everything you have on each ball, and when you get through you've pitched as hard in one game as you would in a month during the stretch of 154 games,"[26] Plank explained in 1921, when he revisited the Polo Grounds as a retired pitcher witnessing another World Series.

Plank allowed just one run, in the fourth inning. An error by Monte Cross to open the inning put a runner on first, who moved to second on a bunt. With two down, light-hitting second baseman Billy Gilbert hit one that Lave Cross couldn't flag down, the single scoring the runner, Sam Mertes. It would be the only run of the game as the Athletics were once again shut out on five hits.

New York Giants manager John McGraw (right, in black uniform) and two Athletics players have a discussion with the umpires before a 1905 World Series game in Philadelphia. Eddie Plank, who started Game 1 at Columbia Park, appears to be the player to McGraw's left. The other player is likely Harry Davis, who was the Athletics' captain (Michael T. "Nuf Ced" McGreevy Collection, Boston Public Library).

The *Philadelphia Inquirer* described the scene at the team hotel later that night: "It was a rather dejected bunch around the Marlborough to-night. The boys felt confident of winning behind Plank, and they feel particularly sore on his account. Plank took his defeat philosophically as one of the chances of war."[27]

Mathewson finished off the Athletics in Game 5, 2–0, completing the best World Series performance by any pitcher—three shutouts. "I was greatly disappointed in the work of the Athletics," said American League president Ban Johnson, who would have liked nothing better than to beat McGraw, "aside from their pitchers, who did themselves proud, Plank and Bender particularly."[28] As victors, the Giants pocketed over $1,100 apiece. The Athletics received $380, although it was reported that several players agreed before the series to split their shares 50–50 no matter who won. Several Giants added to their take by winning bets placed before the series— it was reported that manager McGraw had bet $400 in Philadelphia while players Boileryard Clarke, Mike Donlin and Dan McGann (and likely others) had $50–$100 wagers, all at even money. Plank and the other Athletics also got a financial boon when team president John Shibe and Mack decided to give their 40 percent share of the gate receipts—over $8,100 or roughly $451 per man—to the players.

There was even more money to be made. The team went on a barnstorming trip around New Jersey and Pennsylvania that was said to have earned them a "neat sum"[29] (although many players apparently quickly spent their money on booze, with the exception of Plank and Doc Powers; in fact much of the team, again except for Plank and Powers, played drunk in a 7–1 loss to Pittston in Wilkes-Barre), plus a deal with the *Philadelphia North American* on a souvenir book—which reportedly sold all 10,000 copies which were produced—netted the players another $1,000 to be split among them.

♦ 7 ♦

Hitting 300 One Final Time

Despite losing the World Series, the city of Philadelphia held a parade for the Athletics, replete with floats (one, of course, featured a white elephant), fireworks and carloads of players—first the Athletics and then, surprisingly both asked and agreeing to attend, members of the New York Giants. "It was a magnificent and wonderful display, and I do not believe any other city in the country could duplicate it," said American League president Ban Johnson. "I knew Philadelphia was the corner stone of base ball in America, but no one could have made me believe that such a spectacle could exist unless I had seen it."[1]

A banquet was also held for the team at the Bingham House, with plenty of toasts and compliments—an apologetic Rube Waddell cried after being mentioned, sorry he couldn't pitch in the World Series. In addition to their winnings, each player received a gold watch fob from team president John Shibe, while the players in turn gave manager Connie Mack a piano. Eddie Plank, as well as Chief Bender and Andy Coakley, were singled out by Johnson for their pitching work down the stretch.

Plank returned to Gettysburg after the affair, a little richer and perhaps more well known nationally, but to his hometown he still came across as "the same Eddie."[2] Notoriety and fortune were not his goals in life. *Sporting Life* gave a glimpse into the man in an article shortly after all the ceremonies:

> Plank, by the way, is deserving of much credit for the aid he has given his parents. The son of a poor farmer near Gettysburg, Edward has saved his money and aided the old folks in accumulating one of the best farms in Adams County. Edward has told during his winter stays that he has no desire to secure fame like Waddell. "I realize that a pitcher's arm is not going to last many years. I mean to do my duty and perform in my share of games, but shall never try and earn [a] record for strike outs, etc.," said he.[3]

Plank's arm had certainly taken some wear and tear the past few seasons. He had thrown over 300 innings in the regular season four straight years—1,340 combined including 704 the past two seasons—and that doesn't include his 17 innings in the 1905 World Series or the times he took the mound in spring training games and exhibitions, before, during and after each season. It's no wonder then during spring training in 1906, this year in Montgomery, Alabama, newspapers on more than one occasion noted during games, both in scrimmages and against another opponent, that Plank was not "exerting himself."⁴

Eddie Plank in 1905. He led the American League that season with 41 starts and 35 complete games, posting his fourth consecutive 20-win season (Library of Congress).

As the team traveled north, Plank still was having issues. In a 3–0 win on April 3 over the crosstown Phillies in their annual preseason city series, "Eddie favored his arm all through the game and (threw) a medium slow cross-fire delivery practically all the time."⁵ Nevertheless he did pitch all nine innings, allowing just six hits and two walks with six strikeouts. It didn't affect his hitting, either, as Plank drove in all three runs in the game.

Much was expected of the Athletics in 1906. After all, they were the defending American League champions and largely returned the same team as in 1905. Lave Cross, who turned 40 in May, was gone, signing on to captain Washington. Finding a suitable replacement at third base would remain an issue for Connie Mack for a few years. The pitching staff was similar as well. Weldon Henley was dispatched to Rochester, with Jimmy Dygert and, eventually, rookie Jack Coombs both getting significant innings.

Dygert logged innings early in the season as Plank was sidelined with either a cold or the flu. Plank did pitch three innings in a scrimmage held in Atlantic City on April 13 but didn't make his first start of the season until April 19–16 days after his complete-game win vs. the Phillies. He lasted only five innings, giving up seven runs on nine hits. The *Philadelphia Inquirer*

7. Hitting 300 One Final Time

theorized that Plank had "not yet recovered from a severe attack of grip."[6] If that was the case, he recovered quickly.

In his next start, Plank blanked Boston on three hits. It was the first of seven straight wins as a starter (he pitched three innings of relief on May 4). He had a particularly good stretch from May 15–29, shutting out Chicago on May 15 on five hits, fanning eight Tigers on May 18 and doing the same, in 10 innings, against Cleveland on May 23, then allowing one run on five hits with seven Ks vs. Boston on May 29. The Athletics were in first place but dropped their next five games, with Plank losing two of those (on June 2 and June 4). He would lose only two more games the rest of the season.

Following those back-to-back defeats, Plank reeled off eight straight wins from June 9–July 12 as the Athletics worked their way back into a tie for first place. After suffering a loss to St. Louis in the first game of a doubleheader, Plank won his next four starts, although he was tagged for seven runs in his last one, a 10–7 victory over Cleveland on August 3. The Athletics were 2½ games out in front, but things turned suddenly.

Plank's next start was August 8 at Chicago. The Athletics had dropped the first three games of the series yet still held a one-game lead in the standings as second-place New York couldn't take advantage, and the White Sox had entered 7½ back. Plank, dubbed by the *Chicago Tribune*'s Hugh Fullerton as "the premier pitcher of the American League,"[7] was at his best.

Chicago player-manager Fielder Jones singled with one out in the first inning. It was the only hit Plank allowed in nine innings, and he walked just one as well. Unfortunately, the opposing hurler, Roy Patterson, was nearly as effective, allowing five singles to an Athletics lineup which featured a third baseman du jour in Ed Lennox, who was making his major-league debut (he would go 0-for-3 and commit an error). In the bottom of the 10th inning, Plank walked George Davis to lead off. After a bunt attempt was caught by Plank, Pat Dougherty ripped a triple on a 2–2 pitch to account for the only run of the game and send the Athletics to their fourth straight loss. Five years later, Plank considered that game his worst defeat. "I had two and two on him [Dougherty] and wanted to put the next one down around his knees, where Pat can't hit," Plank explained. "I put everything I had on the ball to get it low enough but miscalculated. I got the ball too high and Pat whacked a triple. That broke up the game, of course. That's the toughest game I ever lost."[8]

Mack displayed confidence in his team, declaring "Just wait till they get back to Philadelphia. We will show them a trick or two."[9] But the Athletics lost again in Chicago and then four of five in St. Louis, where Mack stated that Plank wouldn't pitch again until the team got back to Philadelphia. Once there, though, it was said it would be another week. Plank admitted his arm was sore but blamed it on a cold he contracted in Boston back in May. While he was tossing complete game after complete game and winning, his strikeouts were down. In his first seven starts, he fanned six or more batters six times, including in five straight. But once June hit, he whiffed six batters (and never more than six) twice, with the last occurring July 18.

There would be periodic announcements that Plank would be ready to pitch in a week—and he would be in full uniform sitting on the bench—but the weeks went by and he never took the field. When Plank last pitched on August 7, the Athletics were 59–38 and in first place, one game up. Exactly one month later, they had slipped to fourth place, 7½ games back. The team went 9–18 in the 27 games after Plank last pitched. "With Plank in shape they would likely have landed the pennant again, despite all the many obstacles in their path," wrote Horace Fogel, using the pen name Veteran, for *The Sporting News*. "When Eddie broke down it took the heart out of the rest of the team and at least some of them gave up the fight."[10]

Despite the Athletics all but being out of the pennant race—even Mack admitted so—Plank pitched one more time. On September 13 at home, he took on Boston and lasted five innings, giving up three runs on five hits. He wouldn't factor into the decision as the game went extra innings, with the Athletics losing, 4–3, in 10 innings. Philadelphia won just six of its final 16 games.

Even though he made only 25 starts, plus that one early relief appearance, Plank won 19 games (with six losses) and tossed five shutouts. His 2.25 ERA was topped on the Athletics only by Rube Waddell's 2.21, although his record was 15–17. Plank led the team in WHIP (1.058) but his 4.6 K/9 was his lowest since the advent of the foul-strike rule. The rest of the pitching staff was a little better than average. Chief Bender was starting to come around, going 15–10 with a 2.53 ERA and 6.0 K/9. Jack Coombs was brought in from Colby College in July and went 10–10 with a 2.50 ERA. Jimmy Dygert was 11–13 with a 2.70 ERA, while Andy Coakley couldn't follow up on his great 1905 season, finishing 7–8 with a 3.14 ERA, which ended his time in Philadelphia.

The Athletics had three good hitters in Harry Davis (.292, 42 doubles, 12 home runs), Danny Murphy (.301), and Socks Seybold (.316), but the rest of the lineup struggled. Veteran shortstop Monte Cross batted just .200 while 20-year-old third baseman Jack Knight, one of five to play that position, hit .194. Outfielder Topsy Hartsel (.255) and Bender (.253) were the only others to bat above .250. The Athletics finished with a record of 78–67. But even as Philadelphia finished out its season, Plank's time on the mound wasn't done.

As the Athletics' season wound down in September, Mack sent a group of notable players, including pitchers Plank, Bender, and Coakley, catcher

7. Hitting 300 One Final Time

Doc Powers (who served as team captain and de facto manager), Cross, Murphy, and Seybold, to face the Brooklyn Royal Giants, an African American team, in a series in Atlantic City, as he gave some younger players a tryout (including Eddie Collins, playing under the pseudonym Sullivan, for six games). Plank pitched in the September 19 meeting, a 5-1 loss, but otherwise played left field. He also tossed a complete game in a 7-6 win against Frankford on September 26. Plank's arm was feeling good enough to join some Athletics players on an October barnstorming trip, pitching in many of those games (five pitchers made the trip with Bender primarily playing second base and Coombs center field, although Plank did play in center one game while Coombs hurled), including a 5-4 win in Chester against the Philadelphia Giants, which won the World's Colored Championship each year from 1904 to 1906.

The tour began October 7, and Plank headed home to Gettysburg on October 23. How his shoulder and arm felt at that point is unknown, but he had the salve of roughly $100 extra in his pocket, his split of the profits earned from the trip. The extra cash couldn't hurt. While Plank had earned modest raises since joining Mack's squad in 1901—when he was paid $1,000—his contract for the 1907 season called for the same salary he had earned in 1906, $3,500. Plank probably felt he didn't have much of a leg to stand on to seek a raise (a problem he wouldn't have in later years). Despite leading the American

A baseball card of Mike "Doc" Powers made by the American Tobacco Company. Not much of a hitter, Powers was the catcher most often used with Eddie Plank, but he tragically died shortly after the opening game at Shibe Park in 1909 (Library of Congress).

League in winning percentage (.760), he made just 26 appearances and pitched 211⅔ innings, both easily season lows for him at that point in his career. Plank re-upped for $3,500, although he was among the last group of Athletics to sign for the 1907 season.

A group of 28 Athletics boarded a train in Philadelphia and headed to spring training on March 1. Plank wouldn't pitch in a game until March 13, partly due to saving him and having his arm get in shape, but he also took a line drive off the bat of Harry Davis while pitching batting practice on March 6, which could have slowed his progress.

Plank got work in scrimmages and tossed a few innings against Dallas on March 24, but the next day, according to the *Philadelphia Inquirer*, "Eddie complains of a little stiffness in his left shoulder."[11] Plank must have been feeling better because on March 28 he was called on to face the New York Giants in front of 2,000 fans in New Orleans. It turned out to be quite the exhibition.

In the top of the first inning, Plank retired the first two Giants hitters but then allowed singles to Art Devlin and Cy Seymour, with Devlin racing to third and Seymour advancing to second on the throw. Plank got ahead of the next batter, Frank Bowerman, 1–2. Then the madness began.

Plank turned and picked Devlin off third base to end the inning. Roger Bresnahan, who was coaching third base, was one of a few Giants to scream "balk" after the pickoff. Home plate umpire Charles Zimmer disagreed; he later said Plank was never on the rubber. Bresnahan and manager John McGraw, already incensed at some of the called strikes in the game, rushed at Zimmer to voice their displeasure with the ruling, and Bill Dahlen and Mike Donlin soon followed suit. The argument lasted 30 minutes before McGraw finally retreated to the Giants' bench, but as the dust cleared and Zimmer made his way back to his umpiring position, he happened to walk in front of McGraw, who yelled at the umpire, "You can't show any of us up here."[12] (Note: Also reported as "We are not here to be shown up by you."[13]) This started another argument as Zimmer was surrounded by McGraw and the Giants players. Police intervened to protect Zimmer and were able to fend off the Giants, but not off the field. Zimmer took out his watch and told the Giants they had five minutes to get back to their bench. When that didn't happen, Zimmer ruled the game a forfeit.

The teams returned to the park the next day, although McGraw was absent (the *New York Evening World* used the excuse that the manager was sick). Under instructions from McGraw, the Giants refused to take the field if Zimmer was the umpire. Zimmer walked to the New York bench and instructed the pitcher and catcher to be announced, but his words fell on deaf ears. Another 9–0 forfeit was declared in favor of the Athletics. But a second game would be played that day as Joe Rickert, a Southern

League umpire, agreed to officiate once Zimmer was gone. Plank pitched four innings as the Athletics won, 7–0. New Orleans officials, not happy with what took place, banned the Giants, who had two remaining games against the Athletics, from playing at the park. The New Orleans minor league team, playing exhibitions in nearby Alexandria, returned home to play Philadelphia on those dates.

The whole chaotic situation served notice as to how the Athletics' season would progress.

The Athletics returned home and lost four straight games to the Phillies in their annual preseason city series, although neither Plank nor Chief Bender pitched, electing to save them for the season. Pitching was a strength of the team, with the reliable Plank and Rube Waddell (well, reliable on the field), Bender, who was coming into his own, Jimmy Dygert, and Jack Coombs.

"The Athletics lost the pennant last year chiefly because our pitchers suddenly slumped and we had to experiment too much at third base. I believe these two problems have been solved," said Mack, who was counting on the now 21-year-old Knight at the hot corner. "We expect Waddell, Plank and Bender to show the form when [we] won the pennant in 1905. This is no idle prophecy. Whenever these men are in good condition they pitch winning ball. Their record in the past shows that, and we know that they are in proper shape this season. I do not say we will win the pennant, but we will be pretty close to the top at the finish."[14]

Early on, Mack looked prophetic. After Plank beat Washington, 3–2, on April 30, his third consecutive victory, in a tidy one hour and 35 minutes, the Athletics were 10–4 and in first place by a half-game. Philadelphia had allowed two or fewer runs in five of its last six games. But it went south quickly. The Athletics allowed four or more runs in each of its next six games, all defeats. Plank lost four of his next five starts, the only victory a shutout over Detroit on a blisteringly cold day on May 20—it was the first time the Tigers had been blanked; they had been the only major-league team not to have been held scoreless—and the Athletics dipped to three games under .500 on May 25, 7½ games out of first place.

The Athletics were up-and-down all summer, as was Plank. Third base remained a problem and Knight, who committed 21 errors in 40 games, was shipped to Boston for veteran Jimmy Collins, who at least by reputation was a better fielder, but even he, too, had 17 miscues in 41 contests. Also, young pitcher Jack Coombs, who did so well as a rookie in 1906, was injured in late June. He would not return until mid–August, pitching sparingly and, other than one start, was used in relief.

Coombs' injury left the Athletics' pitching staff down a key member. But they still had Plank. While he had an off game here and there, such as getting knocked around for 10 runs on 14 hits by Chicago on June 4, Plank went 8–3 from May 31–July 16. He shut out Detroit again, a five-hitter on June 20, hit the ball to the center-field fence in New York (likely on bounces or a roll, as it stood over 540 feet away from home at Hilltop Park), circling the bases for a home run in a 3–1 victory on July 3, and bested the White Sox's Ed Walsh, 2–1, on July 10.

But Plank fell to Detroit, 6–3, on July 22, the Tigers completing a three-game home sweep of the Athletics. It was a chance for Philadelphia to catch a contender, but now the Athletics stood six games in back of league-leading Chicago. Cleveland was in second, three games out, with Detroit one-half game in back of the Naps. But the Athletics had another opportunity, a five-game series with the White Sox in Philadelphia, and they took advantage, winning four of five, Plank winning the fourth affair, 4–3. Chicago won the finale, but four teams were now separated by just three games.

"If the Rube can keep to his present form—if he can—and Bender continues the magnificent work he showed yesterday [a two-hit shutout with one walk] and Plank, the old reliable, keep on his usual gait, the Athletics should make a great showing,"[15] Chicago player-manager Fielder Jones said after Plank's win.

Philadelphia kept on winning, taking all three games of a series at home against St. Louis. Plank won the final two games, pitching 2⅓ scoreless innings of relief in an 8–7, 11-inning win on July 31, then taking the ball the next day and tossing a four-hit shutout in a 2–0 victory. Cleveland was next in and Philadelphia took four of five, with Plank getting one of those wins. The Athletics were still in third place, but just one-half game behind Chicago and Detroit, who were tied for first. Six games with the Tigers were on deck, three in Philadelphia followed by three more in Detroit.

The Athletics opened with a 4–2 win in Philadelphia on August 7, Chief Bender topping Ed Killian, one of three Detroit pitchers who won 20 games in 1907. Plank faced another of those, George Mullin, the next day. The hot afternoon led to combustible tempers, setting the tone for games to come in the pennant race. Despite temperatures reaching 90 degrees, nearly 15,000 spectators—a large enough crowd to force a roped-off area in left field, not to mention benches placed on the field in front of a grandstand—jammed Columbia Park. The players battled the heat all game, often stepping out of the batter's box to wipe the sweat off the bat handle. It was no picnic for the pitchers either. Joe Jackson of the *Detroit Free Press* noted, "Mullin, by the time the game was half done, looked as though he had been swimming."[16]

Plank had problems of his own as well. Pitching on just two days' rest

7. Hitting 300 One Final Time

and for the third time in a week, he had nothing on the ball and was hit freely for six hits and four runs before mercifully being taken out of the game by captain Harry Davis. Detroit's Germany Schaefer, coaching on the sidelines and known to be very talkative when occupying that spot, took every chance he could to needle Plank.

That wasn't the only confrontation between the two teams or involving a player coaching the bases. After the Athletics batted in the bottom of the first, Monte Cross took some gum he had been chewing out of his mouth and pegged it at Mullin's face. Cross claimed Mullin had done the same to him and he was just retaliating. Umpire Tim Hurst had to separate the players. Later, in the Tigers' third, Ty Cobb, who earlier socked a two-run triple off Plank, tried to score from third on a grounder and, as he was wont to do, went in hard at Athletics catcher Doc Powers, unsuccessfully trying to jar the ball loose. Detroit won, 5–3, but the tenor of a heated summer pennant race had begun.

Plank got his revenge five days later. Working on a four days' rest this time, he blanked Detroit on three hits as the Athletics beat Mullin, 3–0, in front of over 6,000 fans, including American League president Ban Johnson. Over the last seven innings, Plank pitched to just 22 batters, and the

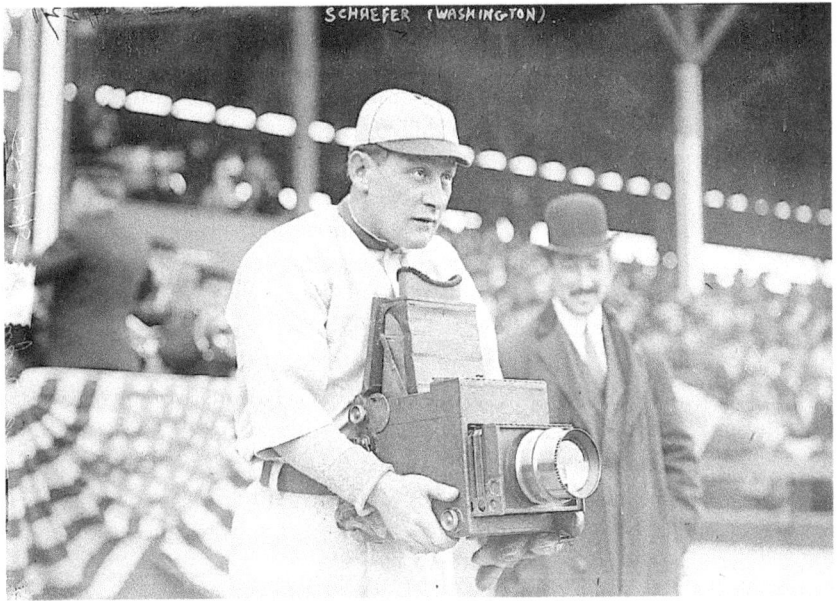

Germany Schaefer, pictured in 1912, tried to get in Eddie Plank's head by bantering with the pitcher. Schaefer opposed Plank when he played for Detroit from 1905–1909, Washington from 1909–1914, and Newark of the Federal League in 1915 (George Grantham Bain Collection, Library of Congress).

only one to reach base was Cobb (who went 0-for-4 with three strikeouts) in the sixth inning on a third strike which got past Powers. Of Plank's final seven innings, the *Philadelphia Inquirer* surmised, "That should most eloquently suggest the kind of flinging stunts performed by the pride of Gettysburg."17 The win was the third straight over the Tigers for the Athletics, who were now 1½ games atop the AL, with Detroit in second place. Chicago was third, 2½ games out, while Cleveland was in fourth place, just three games back.

However, Plank, being worked often, lost three of his next four starts to finish out August as Philadelphia slipped to second place. He opened September, though, by winning his next three starts, including his first matchup with Walter Johnson, who joined Washington just a month earlier. After taking three of four from Washington and beating New York on September 4, the Athletics were back in first place. Philadelphia built its lead up to 2½ games after a doubleheader sweep of Boston on September 14, but lost three straight, all at home, two to New York and one to St. Louis, and were back tied with Detroit after the games of September 20. After Plank shut out St. Louis the next day, scattering seven hits in a 6–0 win, the Athletics were alone on top by a half-game.

But the Athletics were hurting. First baseman Harry Davis was playing, but his legs were causing him so much trouble that he couldn't slide without difficulty. Hitting .277 on August 15, Davis saw it plummet as low as .258 on September 20. Third baseman Jimmy Collins and outfielder Rube Oldring were also playing through injuries. The pitching staff was in worse shape. Chief Bender's arm was hurting; he wouldn't pitch after September 14. Jack Coombs tried to come back in mid–August, but his elbow still wasn't right and he was shut down September 17 after allowing nine runs in his last 11 innings. Rube Waddell was being used more sparingly than usual. Pitching 13 innings of shutout ball against Boston on September 9 probably didn't help his arm. In his next three starts he allowed four runs in four innings (a 6–6 tie vs. Boston on September 13), four runs in six innings (4–1 loss to St. Louis on September 20), and eight in a complete game (8–3 loss to Chicago on September 24). Even Jimmy Dygert wasn't immune to overuse. Dygert pitched four innings on September 10 and nine on September 12 and was used in both ends of a September 14 doubleheader, going 2⅔ innings in the opener and a full nine in the second. He didn't pitch again until September 26.

That left Plank, who kept taking his regular turn—and irregular ones, too. Four days after blanking St. Louis, he did it again, this time vs. Chicago, allowing just two hits (no runner got past second base) while striking out 11. Dygert beat Chicago the next day as well, 3–1, and the Athletics were just a half-game behind Detroit, which was coming to town for a pivotal

7. Hitting 300 One Final Time

four-game series. It was important that Plank, fresh off two complete games over a four-day period, the latter just two days prior, was on the slab for the September 27 opener against the Tigers and Bill Donovan. In front of an overflow crowd, Plank was game for the task but ran out of gas in the seventh inning, allowing three runs as the Athletics fell behind, 5–1. Plank doubled into the overflow crowd to lead off the bottom of the seventh, one of his three hits, and Philadelphia scored three times in its half, but a double play helped kill the rally as Detroit won, 5–4, despite 13 hits for the Athletics, who twice had the bases loaded and didn't score, leaving 12 runners on base in the contest.

Rain wiped out the scheduled game the next day, and after an off-day (no baseball was played in Philadelphia on Sundays), the teams readied to square off in a Monday doubleheader on September 30. Dygert faced Donovan in the opener. It was a day many would never forget and still talked about, and complained over, years later. With only a week left in the season, every game was precious—and wins over Detroit were paramount, as this was the last time the clubs would meet in 1907.

Dygert lasted only two innings, but the Athletics staked a 7–1 lead after six. Waddell replaced Dygert and allowed four runs in the seventh inning, two errors helping Detroit's cause, and another in the eighth. Trailing 8–5 in the ninth inning with a man on base, Ty Cobb clubbed a 3–2 offering from Waddell over the right-field fence to tie the game. Waddell finished the ninth and Plank took over in the 10th, along with Doc Powers, who came in at catcher for Ossie Schrecongost. Detroit scored in the 11th inning, but so did the Athletics. In the 12th, the Tigers loaded the bases with one out and couldn't score. In the 14th, it appeared as though Philadelphia won the game.

Harry Davis led off the inning with a deep blast to center field off starting pitcher Donovan. Tigers outfielder Sam Crawford moved back further and further, towards the roped-off crowd. He reached for the ball ... and then the ball was in the crowd. The outfielder claimed he had been interfered with by patrons, that he caught the ball but dropped it after being jostled. Detroit quickly came to his defense and ordered that Davis be called out. The umpires, Silk O'Loughlin and Tommy Connolly, conferred. As they did so, players rushed out to argue their cases and fans spilled out onto the field as well. Monte Cross led the charge for the Athletics, followed by Waddell, who had already changed out of his uniform. Detroit's Claude Rossman entered the fracas (and eventually was arrested by the police, which also fended off the crowd). O'Loughlin ruled that Davis was out, much to the chagrin of the Athletics, their fans, and newspaper reporters. "That the Athletics did not win in the regulation nine innings was owing solely on their own fielding misplays; that they did not win out in the fourteenth was due to an outrageous and high-handed usurpation of umpirical authority on the part of 'Silk' O'Loughlin," the *Philadelphia Inquirer* claimed. "There was not the slightest evidence of interference. Crawford reached the ball while on a full run. It struck his mitt and dropped out again. The claim of interference was made and, to the surprise of everyone, it was allowed by O'Loughlin."[18]

Mack never forgave O'Loughlin, saying his team was "robbed"[19] and that the umpire made the decision to get back at the Athletics for previous indiscretions. Five years later, the manager and umpire were still bickering about it to reporters. In a 1912 article, O'Loughlin discussed his reasoning for the decision.

> Harry Davis started the fourteenth with a drive that looked good for a double. Sam Crawford backed up against the crowd, got the ball in his hands and muffed it. At the time I felt certain that he had been interfered with in making the catch. I was convinced of this fact as Crawford raced to make a protest. I conferred with my partner and decided to call Davis out because of the interference on the part of a spectator.... Very unfortunately for me, in the game of the day previous I called Schaefer safe on a very close play, and he scored the winning run of the game. [Note: Schaefer scored twice in Detroit's 5–4 win on September 28, but neither was a contested play at the plate.] The game was called on account of darkness in the seventeenth, and was never played off, there being no open date. Yet the Athletics always blamed me for losing the game and the pennant on that decision, which I would be compelled to render the same way if it came up again.[20]

Mack, of course, disagreed with O'Loughlin's characterization of Crawford's so-called catch. In an article for the *Saturday Evening Post* just over month after O'Loughlin's article appeared in 1912, Mack said of the lost hit:

> If he [Crawford] had mounted a stepladder he couldn't have touched it. Now—and note this fact in connection with what I shall say about the present-day fan—not a single person in the crowd tried to interfere with Crawford, though each and every man was "pulling" for the Athletics to win; but a policeman happened to pass in front of Crawford as he backed up against the ropes and the Detroit player claimed interference. The best that could have been said was for the protest was that advantage was taken of a slim technicality to defeat the merits of play.... That decision cost us the championship.[21]

Without O'Loughlin's decision, Davis would have had a double, as per the ground rules of the day. The next batter, Danny Murphy, singled, thus further enflaming the rage of Mack, Athletics players, and boosters. Philadelphia wouldn't score in the 14th, and the game remained tied after 17, when it was finally called for darkness. After three hours and 50 minutes, neither team emerged with a victory that day, as the second game of the doubleheader had to be canceled. But Detroit really won, as games lost weren't made up, so the Tigers didn't lose any ground in the standings and were done playing their nearest competitor.

Plank pitched eight innings in relief and allowed just the one run, throwing 71 of his 100 pitches for strikes. A few years later, in 1911, he called it his "best effort"[22] in his career to that point, although better ones were to come.

Two days later, Plank pitched again, losing to Cleveland, 4–2. And then again two days after that, he fell, 2–1, to Walter Johnson and Washington in the first game of a doubleheader, in a contest which lasted 10 innings. Not that it much mattered. Detroit had won four straight entering Philadelphia, then peeled off five more consecutive victories, including four at Washington, to clinch the pennant. With suspicion that Washington laid down in its four games and murmurs among fans that the contests were thrown, Powers confronted Senators manager Joe Cantillon before the start of the series, sarcastically proclaiming, "You guys must have made a beautiful showing against Detroit."[23] Cantillon retorted, "Well, we didn't get six runs ahead of them and let them catch us in two innings."[24]

Dygert and Plank had started all 11 games for the Athletics since September 21. Plank pitched 74 innings in September—easily his most of any month of the season—plus another 18 in two October starts. Overall, he tossed 343⅔ innings, the fifth and final time in his career he topped 300. Plank finished the year with a 24–16 record and a 2.20 ERA with an American League-best eight shutouts (two National League pitchers, New York's Christy Mathewson and Chicago's Orval Overall, also had eight). His 183 strikeouts and 4.8 K/9 were both third in the AL. Dygert also toiled the most in September, with 54 innings, in addition to 27 innings in three October starts. He finished 21–8, led the league in fewest hits per nine innings (6.9), and had career bests with a 2.34 ERA and 261⅔ innings.

Finally, with the Athletics eliminated, Mack used Waddell and Rube Vickers in a season-ending doubleheader. "We lost the pennant last season because we fell short of good pitchers right in the crisis," Mack said a short few weeks later. "I thought I had enough but the injuries to Bender and Coombs, and Waddell's tough luck, left me with only Plank and Dygert, and great as was their work they could not carry us through. Therefore my first thought for next season has been to look after the box material.... Dygert and Plank will as usual form the backbone of my staff."[25]

Mack didn't name Waddell in his plans for 1908. The pitcher had finally worn out his welcome. He had accused his teammates of not playing hard for him, and during a postseason barnstorming trip around the area he claimed that those in charge of the trip and the finances—Monte

Cross, Harry Davis, Topsy Hartsel, and Socks Seybold—were holding back money from him. The players kicked Waddell out of the traveling group, which only had a couple more games to play, but upon completion Davis headed to Mack's office and told him of the team's desire to rid themselves of Waddell.

8

The Gettysburg Guide

Privately Connie Mack might have promised his players that Rube Waddell would be off the Athletics for the 1908 season, but publicly the manager maintained a different stance. "I will not part with Rube Waddell," Mack said at the beginning of the year, "and am counting on him being as valuable in 1908 to my team as he ever was."[1]

Eventually, however, Mack succumbed to what he knew he had to do, for his team's sake and probably for his own sanity. On February 7, 1908, the St. Louis Browns acquired Waddell—one of the greatest pitchers of his era and a future Hall of Famer who won 131 games in six years with the Athletics, posting a 1.97 ERA and an unheard-of, for the time period, 7.6 K/9—for, well, money. Mack had hoped to get a package of players for Waddell, but had to settle for cash, reportedly $6,000, which made St. Louis the high bidder.

Detroit owner Frank Navin said he could have had Waddell for $2,000. Despite his pitching acumen, there didn't appear to be a big market for Waddell, who could have been considered more trouble off the field than his worth on it, especially since the pitcher's quarrel with his teammates appeared to be common knowledge inside the game. That didn't help Mack's bargaining power. "I did all I could to make him behave, and no one can blame me for letting him go," Mack said weeks later as the team traveled to New Orleans for spring training. "I hope he makes good with the Browns."[2]

Mack could have traded his other star left-hander as well. The *Pittsburgh Press* reported that the Chicago White Sox "will give Connie Mack a dozen players for Pitcher Plank if Connie will listen to him."[3] But with Waddell gone, Mack needed the anchor to his pitching staff even more. Plank thought the same. After the season he just had, he wanted more money.

Plank earned $3,500 in 1906 and 1907. He didn't think that was a fair salary, but coming off a 1906 season when he had arm trouble and pitched only 211⅔ innings, Plank accepted the same amount for 1907, especially since he wasn't exactly sure if his arm would hold up. But after being used for 343⅔ innings, and called upon by Mack often down the stretch, he had no more concerns.

What would Plank do instead of play baseball? Some might have you believe he would be a guide at the Gettysburg battlefield. This was first mentioned in *The Sporting News* in 1903, in an article which claimed, "In the off-season Plank picks up considerable coin as a guide for parties of visitors to the historic battlefield."[4] It resurfaced again in 1907. In an August 21 game recap, the *Chicago Tribune*'s Charles Dryden repeated the assertion. A few weeks earlier, the *Washington Star* told a story which seems apocryphal and against the common public perception of Plank. Of course, the tale might have been true, or just a way to set up a groaner of a joke:

> Eddie Plank of the Athletics, and one of the most reliable pitchers, is from up in the neighborhood of Gettysburg, Pa., where in the off season the gentle Eddie acts as a guide, and, it is alleged, sells the gullible tourists bullets supposed to have been shot away during the war of the rebellion, but which his ball-playing friends claim are buried by Eddie several days before he makes the sale. But, as Plank says with a grin, what's the difference, as long as the tourists are happy? Eddie says that, at any rate, selling bullets supposed to have been fired away during the time the blue and gray armies were playing rings around the rosies is not as bad as copping the coin for pieces of chips said to have come from the ark sailed by Noah. They are separating Americans in Europe today from their coin on this game, and, as Plank once told Lave Cross, if an American wants to get "stung," let it be done by some good fellow-countryman, if only from a patriotic standpoint. As a Gettysburg guide and from constant talk about the dead who lie there in the cemetery, Eddie Plank has developed a hankering after the occult, and the other night in Philadelphia, he purchased a couple of tickets for a lecture to be given at the Academy of Music on Buddhism. He was going to take Dr. Mike Powers, the catcher, with him, as Mike is a deep student on such things, but at the last moment Mike failed to appear, and the only player around the hotel was Rube Waddell, who had just that day shown up after his prolonged absence, so Eddie, turning to Waddell, asked him did he want to go up to the Academy of Music to hear a lecture on Buddhism. "Sure thing," said the big pitcher, as he jumped up with alacrity. "I'm a great lover of flowers."[5]

This is the only claimed occurrence of Plank discussing his supposed job as a guide at the battlefield. Plank was never a registered guide (his cousin, E.P. Plank, was), however the caveat is that guides weren't registered until 1915. However, Plank being a battlefield guide is never mentioned in the local Gettysburg papers, including in the articles and obituaries following his death. Yet it remains a part of the pitcher's historical background lore, oft repeated by credible sources, including sportswriter Red Smith, a Spink Award honoree and winner of the Pulitzer Prize, who in 1974 wrote, in part,

"Eddie made an independent income between seasons as a guide on the Gettysburg battlefield."[6] Regardless of the veracity, a nickname was born—"the Gettysburg Guide."

But Plank did have work in Gettysburg. He helped the Gettysburg baseball team and, just days away from the Athletics leaving Philadelphia to make their way south, made arrangements to stay as pitching coach. He also made claims that he would go help his brother Luther, who recently purchased the Table Rock flour mill (which Luther would own and run until his death in 1972 at the age of 99), which, like Gettysburg, was located in Adams County. At least that's what he was telling Mack. "Plank is not a man who would make a bluff of quitting for the purpose of boosting his salary. He knows me too well for that," Mack said. "Well, if Plank lost his arm or if he died, the Athletic Club would have to get along without him and if he really means to quit, which I think he does, we will have to find someone to take his place."[7]

Plank's talk, though, was just that, talk. It was a bluff and it worked. "Although confident in his own mind all the while that Mack would meet his terms, Plank launched the coaching scheme to hurry up his manager, so that he could go along the Southern trip,"[8] reported the *Philadelphia Inquirer*. Plank's raise was either a $500 increase in his yearly stipend, as reported by the *Gettysburg Compiler*, or $750 more, as reported by the *Gettysburg Star and Sentinel*.

Mack might have been buoyed by Plank's return but had concerns. "I will have practically the same line-up as last year, but I am not so sure about our pitching staff," he said in late February. "That may be the Athletics' weak point in 1908, yet I should not say this. Bender, Plank, Vickers, Dygert and Coombs are still with us, and I feel that they will be as good as ever, but it is hard to tell about twirlers. They are the uncertainties of a ball team."[9]

Mack should have been worried about his hitters as well. The 1908 season was not a good one for the Athletics, and the less said about it probably the better. The hitting, even for the Deadball Era, was abysmal. Philadelphia finished last in the American League in batting average (.223) and on-base percentage (.281) and had a slugging percentage of .292, which amazingly was only third-worst in the circuit. Injuries forced Jack Coombs to start 43 games in the outfield, which actually might not have been the worst thing to occur since the pitcher finished with a slash line of .255/.287/.355 in 235 plate appearances. Catcher Ossie Schrecongost, Waddell's drinking partner, slumped to a .222 average in 71 games before he was shipped off to Chicago in September. Shortstop Monte Cross left to manage in the minors, and his replacement Simon Nicholls batted .216. Veteran third baseman Jimmy Collins struggled to stay healthy and hit only .217 in 115 games. Even slugger Harry Davis, who led the lead in home runs in each of the past four years (with 10, 8, 12 and 8) dipped to a .248 average with five homers.

The Athletics' pitching was barely better than their hitting, posting a 2.56 ERA, which was the second-highest in the AL. Coombs, thanks to his place in the lineup, only pitched 153 innings, while Chief Bender was limited to 138⅔ innings due to injuries. Jimmy Dygert (2.87 ERA in 238⅔ innings) took a big step back as well. Rube Vickers helped save the staff by pitching 317 innings in 53 games, with 34 starts, posting a 2.21 ERA but likely ruining his arm in the process. The team finished with a 68–85 record.

Not that there weren't some highlights. Eddie Collins, who played in a handful of games in 1906 using the pseudonym Sullivan so he could retain his college eligibility (it didn't work) and joined the team for good after finishing up at Columbia in 1907, earned a full-time role in the summer, hitting a team-high .273. Collins moved from shortstop to second base late in the year to make room for another former collegian, shortstop Jack Barry of Holy Cross. Barry hit just .222, but Mack had his middle infield set for nearly a decade.

Then there was Plank, who as usual was steady. He pitched fewer

A cartoon captures the images from an Athletics doubleheader sweep at home over Washington on May 27, 1913. Chief Bender won the opener, 7–1, with Eddie Plank tossing a shutout in an 8–0 win in the second game (Library of Congress).

8. The Gettysburg Guide

innings, 244⅔, as Mack sat him and Bender out often early in the season during the colder months. He made only five starts combined in April and May. Plank finished with a 2.17 ERA, tossing four shutouts in his 28 starts (he also was used in relief six times) and struck out five batters per nine innings, good enough for eighth in the league. However, for the first time in his career he had a losing record, 14–16. That wouldn't happen again until Plank's final season.

The most exciting thing to happen to the team occurred in the off-season. Following a few barnstorming games, including an exhibition with the Red Sox in New Britain, Connecticut, to raise money for tuberculosis (unfortunately, because only 185 people attended, none of the proceeds went to the fund, partly because the players didn't play for free, but even they got less money than promised), Coombs, Plank, Daniel Murphy, and team secretary John Shibe (son of Athletics president Ben Shibe) went on a hunting trip to Maine, Coombs' home state. The purpose was to hunt deer and moose, which they did.

After canoeing up the Allagash River, the group camped. While Coombs and Plank went off in one direction, Murphy and Shibe walked in another. Versions vary on what exactly happened next—either Shibe was tracking bear paw prints in the snow and was surprised by the animal or he discovered a bear cub, shot at it and missed, and the angered mother heard and attacked. Either way, Shibe was pounced on by a black bear. Murphy, who was either with Shibe or discovered the incident as it occurred, managed to get near the occupied bear and put a bullet in its skull, killing it and saving Shibe, who had cuts on his head, arm and hand as he tried to fend off the larger animal. Coombs and Plank arrived to help bring the bear back to camp. It was eventually stuffed, and Shibe gave it as a present to Murphy along with a gold watch. Plank didn't leave empty-handed either; he sent home the hide of one of the two deer he shot.

The rest of Plank's off-season was much tamer. As usual, he worked on his farm, which took up most of his hours. But there was time for some of his other hobbies, such as trap shooting and duck pin bowling, both of which he became quite good at. In February he held an oyster bake at his premises, which became an annual affair. There was no holdout leading up to the 1909 season, although the same couldn't be said for one his rotation mates, Chief Bender.

While Bender had a 1.75 ERA in 1908, he made the mistake of asking for more money after pitching just 138⅔ innings and sporting an 8–9 record. Plank at least knew when it was appropriate to ask for a raise. But that also trended with the two personalities of the pitchers, who while not total opposites, did provide contrast. Plank was introspective, quiet and humble, and a teetotaler. Bender wore his emotions on his sleeve and also was known to be one of the heavy drinkers on the team (perhaps the biggest now that Schrecongost and Waddell were gone). "Plank is of the serene, nonchalant type, but he warmed up as a raconteur when he told about Bender, his colorful pitching mate," wrote Cullen Cain of the *Philadelphia Daily Ledger* in 1923. "The big Chief offered a striking contrast to the mild and placid Plank."[10]

Mack had an affection for Bender, whom he always called Albert (Bender's full name was Charles Albert Bender). But while Mack bemoaned the potential loss of a possibly retiring Plank a year earlier, he had no such sympathy for Bender, who also was threatening to quit and instead take up trap shooting, in which the pitcher claimed there was "lots of money in this game, and I find that it has greatly improved my health."[11] Bender probably was underpaid by Mack, relatively speaking. His obituary claimed Bender never made more than $2,500 in a season, which is false as he would be paid $4,000 in 1914. But 1914 was six years away, and no doubt Bender's salary was more likely in the $2,500 range—which was at least $1,500 less than Plank was making.[12]

None of that mattered to Mack, who was clearly angry with Bender.

> The contract which I will send to Bender will call for a salary so small that he will no doubt scoff at it. To be frank, I have not been counting upon Bender in planning the makeup of my team for next season. The reason must be obvious to everybody. To make it plainer, Bender has been receiving the best of treatment from the Athletic Club, but in turn has not given the services he should have rendered. Last year, for instance, he got what he wanted—everything was made satisfactory to him—and what did he give us in return? The records show that he pitched in 17 games, of which he won eight and lost nine. During the last two months of the season he didn't work at all for us. I want to make this clear. If Bender signs at any figure, no matter how small, and then turns around and takes his regular turn next season, pitching as well as he is capable of doing, and renders first-class services, I am willing to pay him the same salary next fall as I paid him last year. In other words, I will give him the extra money as a present.[13]

Much like Plank, despite his threat to quit, Bender eventually signed with the Athletics in early March, helping solidify the pitching staff on a team which, despite its bad 1908, had Mack and team captain Harry Davis feeling optimistic. "There seems to be a disposition to count the 1908 second-division teams of the American League out of the running in the race for the championship this year," Davis said during spring training. "I think we can stop Detroit [the Tigers again won the American League in 1908]."[14] While Davis, who turned 36 in July, was a mainstay at first base, he was now surrounded by a youthful infield: second baseman Eddie Collins, shortstop Jack Barry, and third baseman Frank Baker, who played in nine games in 1908 after being acquired in September from Reading of the Tri-State League, were all 23 years or younger—and all had upside both offensively and defensively. Mack also had acquired an 18-year-old shortstop, John "Stuffy" McInnis, who debuted in 1909 and eventually was part of the core infield at first base. Also, the rotation appeared to be strong with Plank and a healthy Bender and Coombs (who wouldn't be needed as an outfielder), plus a young left-hander in 20-year-old Harry Krause, who showed Mack something in four appearances in 1908. "We will be a contender for that pennant and if we don't win it, we'll come mighty close to doing so,"[15] Mack predicted right before the start of the season.

Perhaps Mack was also buoyed by what awaited him in Philadelphia—a new ballpark for his team. With the Athletics perennial contenders and drawing good, often overflow crowds, it had been announced prior to the 1908 season (probably a good thing as momentum might not have been there for a new park after a lackluster effort that year) that a stadium for the Athletics would be built a short distance northeast of Columbia Park at 22nd and Lehigh, to be readied for the 1909 season. The ballpark—eventually named Shibe Park after the team's owner and president—was made

Shibe Park, with its Beaux Arts tower greeting fans at the main entrance, had architecture unlike any other baseball park when it opened in 1909 (George Grantham Bain Collection, Library of Congress).

entirely of concrete and steel, with walls of brick. The cost of the stadium reportedly was around $500,000. "Nothing is too good for Philadelphians, for Philadelphians have certainly been good to us,"[16] John Shibe said upon the announcement.

It wasn't just the steel and concrete which differentiated Shibe Park. It didn't look like a baseball stadium from the outside. The architecture was French Renaissance, and it was enclosed by buildings which housed the team's offices. The front of the structure, the home plate entrance, stood out with its Beaux Arts tower. But that was not the only entrance, as 17 gates

One of the grandstand entrances to the Athletics' Shibe Park, which opened in 1909. The statue head above the entrance is that of team owner and president Ben Shibe (George Grantham Bain Collection, Library of Congress).

were spaced all around the façade, more than double the number at Columbia Park, including eight for the grandstands.

The Athletics waited until the start of the regular season to debut their new park. The entirety of the preseason interleague series against the crosstown Phillies was played at the National League team's Baker Bowl. Despite the Athletics' poor 1908 season, fans were drawn to Shibe Park for the April 12 opener. The gates were to open at noon—with no tickets sold before then—which caused a line of fans waiting to enter. One, George McFadden, arrived at 7 a.m., ensuring he would be the first to buy a ticket.

The game had all the hoopla of a World Series game. Bunting lined the walls, a 48-page booklet on the history of the Athletics and the new park was made available, free scorecards were handed out, a pregame concert was held, Shibe and mayor John E. Reyburn raised the flag, the players paraded about the field, "The Star Spangled Banner" was played, and special guests—including American League president Ban Johnson, members of the 1883 Athletics, and George Wright, one of the first professional players with the 1869 Cincinnati Red Stockings—were among the throng of 35,000, a record crowd ("by far the largest gathering ever assembled in any major league park in the history of the game,"[17] declared the *Boston Post*), to fill the park, which only seated 25,000, so areas had to be roped off. All were impressed. "It is the most remarkable sight I have ever witnessed,"[18] Wright said. Proclaimed the mayor: "The park is a masterpiece. It is unparalleled anywhere."[19] Johnson stated, "Shibe Park is the greatest place of its character in the world."[20]

For the Athletics' opening game at Shibe Park, the first regular-season game of the 1909 season, Connie Mack gave the honor of starting the game against that day's opponent, Boston, to his most veteran pitcher, Eddie Plank. It was the first time Plank had started on Opening Day since 1904, but that game was in Washington. This one was at home, in a new park, and in front of a huge crowd. It would end up being a memorable day for all involved. But not because of the result of the game.

◆ 9 ◆

A Death in the Family

Philadelphians were in a festive mood. The previous day was Easter, and many from the city headed to Atlantic City for what the *Philadelphia Inquirer* proclaimed was "the greatest seen in years."[1] Of the estimated 100,000 people who went down to the famous boardwalk, the paper estimated half were from Philadelphia. Another 800,000 attended music-filled services in the city. Spirits were high (well, except for those who were robbed by burglars who took advantage of those who made the sojourn to New Jersey), and now the Athletics were opening their spanking new ballpark.

The day had a slight chill to it, with temperatures around 60 degrees. That didn't stop the fans coming out, many of whom climbed buildings to witness the opener. They saw a slightly puzzling lineup put out by Connie Mack—with 20-year-old Amos Strunk in center field, as Rube Oldring wasn't fit to play yet, and 18-year-old John McInnis at shortstop. Simon Nicholls, the regular shortstop, was stationed at third base because Frank Baker, who injured his leg in an exhibition against the Phillies, was still hobbled.

But there were still several recognizable faces. Topsy Hartsel played left field and led off, Eddie Collins, who forced his way into the lineup in 1908, was at second base and batting third, cleanup hitter Danny Murphy was pushed out to right field due to Collins being in the infield and Harry Davis batted behind Murphy and as usual was at first base. Then, of course, there was the battery of Eddie Plank and Doc Powers.

By this point in their careers, the pitcher and catcher were a fine-tuned machine. Powers was in essence Plank's personal catcher. The opening game of the 1909 season was Plank's 282nd career start. Powers was his catcher for 206 of those, or nearly three-quarters (73.0 percent). Also, when Mack brought in a new pitcher he also changed catchers, with Powers usually the backstop called upon when Plank entered. Whether it was true or not, it was thought that Powers was the only catcher on the club who could consistently deal with Plank's crossfire delivery.

9. A Death in the Family

"'Doc' handled everything Plank could use without any apparent extra effort or trouble. Plank is not the easiest pitcher in the business to handle, as many a catcher who has tried it will testify, but Powers apparently reveled in Plank's stubborn delivery," wrote Stephen O. Grauler in 1910. "Crossfire 'Doc' seemed to fairly eat up, and no matter how hard or low did some of Plank's shoots go, Powers invariably mitted them, which other catchers would have let slip away to the grandstand."[2]

Powers certainly wasn't around for his offense. While he hit .251 and .264 in his first two seasons with the Athletics, he was a career .216 hitter with a .268 slugging percentage. He hadn't hit over .200 since 1903, when he batted .227. When Powers re-signed in 1907 after hitting .157 with one extra-base hit in 185 at-bats the previous season, *Sporting Life* noted, "Mike Powers is the only catcher who can handle Eddie Plank right. That's Connie Mack's reason for holding him."[3]

Another reason Mack kept Powers is that the catcher and Plank got along well on the field. Unlike other teams, when the pitcher and catcher had a disagreement on which pitch to throw, Mack let the hurler cast the deciding vote. "'Take the pitcher's judgment,' was an early season order from manager Mack, and he never changed it," said Paddy Livingston, who caught for the Athletics from 1909 to 1911 and also played for Cleveland, Cincinnati, and the St. Louis Cardinals. "There was never a call-down for the pitcher or catcher when Connie believed a fastball should have been used instead of a curve, or vice versa. We were expected to know what to do. Advice came before or after the game. And then it was up to both pitcher and catcher. Mack does a lot of things different from other managers I have played for. Every man on the team has his ear when a suggestion is offered. We were all called upon to dig up something at daily meetings."[4]

Not that everything was perfect between Plank and Powers. They often squabbled during the game over how to handle situations, but like most old married couples it was quickly forgotten. Powers shouted encouragement to his longtime throwing partner and was known for uttering, "Work hard, old boy, work hard."[5]

The pair were in tune, mostly, once again, on April 12 against Boston in Shibe Park's christening. Plank allowed just six hits and got out of a no-out, bases-loaded jam in the fourth inning by inducing two pop outs—Tris Speaker to Powers and Heinie Wagner to Collins—before Jack Thoney hit into a fielder's choice to end the inning. The Athletics led, 3–0, at that point and went on to win, 8–1, Boston getting its only run in the sixth inning. Murphy had four hits, including a pair of doubles, Nicholls had three hits and four runs, and Collins was on base four times with two singles and two walks. Philadelphia banged out 13 hits with only Strunk and Plank taking an 0-fer.

In the seventh inning, Powers started feeling pain in his abdominal area; the *Philadelphia Inquirer* reported it (incorrectly as it turned out) as a "seizure of acute gastritis."[6] Nevertheless, Powers kept on playing, but by the time the game ended he was in so much pain he asked the team trainer, M.P. Lawlor, to give him a rubdown. But even that proved too painful. He was in so much agony he couldn't be taken to Northwest General Hospital for at least 30 minutes because he didn't want to be moved. Powers' given name was Michael, but he wasn't called Doc by accident—he had a medical degree from Louisville and spent his off-season nearby Philadelphia as a practicing physician. It was reported that Powers should be able to return to the team in a few days.

The Athletics continued their homestand against Boston and then New York before heading on a road trip. Powers was still hospitalized as the Athletics took two of three from the Red Sox, with Plank starting twice in the series, losing 6–2 in the opener and winning, 4–1, in the finale. "Manager Mack wanted the game bad enough to put in his star performer, Eddie Plank. He had Dygert and Krause warming up before the game, as well as Eddie, but the latter looked good enough to him to put in the box,"[7] reported the *Inquirer*. Plank pitched to Jack Lapp and Ira Thomas, not Powers, who was still laid up and getting worse.

Philadelphia next traveled to Washington, D.C., where it was to open a series on April 26. Early that morning, at 9:14 a.m., the end came for Powers. He died five months shy of his 39th birthday. Powers didn't have gastritis, but rather intussusception of the bowel, which is extremely rare in adults and perhaps why Powers didn't—or couldn't—make a self-diagnosis. There has been much speculation on what caused Powers to be afflicted, from eating too many pregame sandwiches to wearing a heavy belt. However, there is no known cause for intussusception. The doctors in Philadelphia discovered the issue—where one intestine telescopes into the other—during surgery. Other problems arose—gangrene, for one, which developed after his first of four operations—helping contribute to his early demise. Reportedly, Powers' last words were "I've got no pulse; no pulse."[8]

Somehow, after learning about the news, the Athletics went out and played a game. Wearing black ribbons on their uniforms, and playing under flags which flew at half-mast, the Athletics beat Washington, 3–1, Chief Bender pitching a three-hitter with eight strikeouts. But the mood around the team was understandably glum. There was little chatter in the dugout, in the coaching box, or on the field, and what words were spoken were in hushed tones.

As the players milled about the Arlington Hotel later that night, the despondent mood of all was evident. The *Washington Herald* observed, "there was a gloom thick enough to cut with a knife."[9] The Athletics might have been in Washington, D.C., but their hearts were in Philadelphia. Powers' funeral was to be held there three days later, and there was no question the Athletics would abandon their road trip to be in attendance.

"Powers was the most popular man of the Athletics, and his loss is felt keenly by his teammates individually and collectively," remarked Mack upon his arrival back in Philadelphia, where he had traveled to as soon as learning of Powers' death. "To me his death comes as a great personal shock. He was the only player left of the team which opened the first American League championship season at Columbia Park, and there existed between us a bond of friendship that makes the separation doubly hard to bear."[10]

Mack wasn't the only one with a deep history with Powers. Of all the players on the team, Plank had been his closest confidant. The players not only got along, but also Powers helped nurture the young, raw pitcher who arrived from Gettysburg in 1901. He even helped teach him how to throw his signature delivery, the crossfire, which served Plank so well throughout his career. "I could not feel the loss of a brother's death more than I do Mike's," Plank told the *Washington Herald*'s William Peet. "He was more than a brother to me, and I owe my success in the baseball world to his untiring efforts. When I first broke into the big league I was raw and apt to go up into the air, but he would always steady me down and talk to me in such a manner as to give me encouragement, and many games that I won and was praised for really belonged to Powers."[11] Weeks later in talking about the catcher, Plank offered this sentiment: "my dear friend, Doc Powers, to whom I owe more than ever could have been repaid."[12]

With Powers behind the dish, Plank had some of the best years of his career, winning 20+ games five times in his first seven seasons. "What do I think of Eddie Plank?" Jack Coombs pondered in 1914. "Well, just this: He's one of the greatest pitchers that ever lived, and when he paired off with poor Doc Powers, they formed the greatest battery of modern times."[13]

While Powers' passing surely hit the Athletics, and particularly Plank, hard, this was not exactly the age of enlightenment for men. There were no outward displays of emotion, and the games went on. Both the Athletics and Senators, however, did agree not to play Thursday, the day after Powers' death. Powers was on all their minds—and their uniforms, as players adorned their jersey top with a black ribbon, which they would wear for a month—as the Athletics, perhaps not surprisingly, lost to Washington, 3–2, in 10 innings on Friday. Both teams left D.C. for Philadelphia following the contest so they could attend Powers' funeral the next day—Athletic players had vowed they would attend the service and not play on that day.

Upon the request of Powers' widow, Eddie Plank and Jack Coombs were two of the pallbearers. They were joined in that duty by teammates

Harry Davis, Danny Murphy, Simon Nicholls, and Ira Thomas. The service was well attended—besides members of the Athletics and Senators, players from the crosstown Phillies showed up as did Athletics team officials and the city's sportswriters. It was estimated that 10,000 people gathered outside the church to see the procession of the casket.

The Athletics didn't have to play another game until May 3 because of rainouts, but the time away from ballparks didn't help as they lost two straight in New York by scores of 9–6 and 11–3. With the flags at Shibe Park lowered to half-mast, Plank made his first appearance since April 24, starting against Washington on May 5 with Ira Thomas as his catcher. The Athletics lost, 4–3, and Plank was particularly testy during the game, often barking at home plate umpire Rip Egan, then turning his attention to base umpire Tom Connolly when his complaints went unheeded.

Connie Mack observed to *The Sporting News* a week earlier that his team hadn't been playing its best baseball early on because they were worried about Powers' condition. The weekly opined that the Athletics would find their footing a week after their teammate's funeral. Indeed, after Plank's loss, Philadelphia won the next three games against Washington, then took two of three in St. Louis, with Plank besting Rube Waddell, 5–1, on May 10.

A hot streak ensued. The Athletics went into Chicago and swept a four-game series from the White Sox, with three straight shutouts (including back-to-back, 1–0, extra-inning affairs, the first 13 innings and the next going 12). Next up: A trip to Detroit to face the first-place—as well as two-time defending American League champion—Tigers.

Games between the Athletics and Tigers were often heated, especially so during Detroit's reign atop the league. Incidents from 1907, especially how the Athletics felt they were robbed of the pennant, lingered.

Plank wasn't immune to stirring things up. Besides his tête-à-tête with Germany Schaefer, he and Ty Cobb often exchanged words during games throughout their careers—Cobb trying anything to get Plank off his game. It didn't usually work. While Cobb hit .340 in his career off Plank, that's below his lifetime average of .366. In the 11 years they played against each other (Plank didn't face Cobb in the latter's rookie season in 1905), Plank held Cobb below his season average in eight of those seasons. In 1908, Cobb led the AL with a .324 average but was just 5-for-21 (.238) vs. Plank. In 1909, he hit a major-league best .377, however had only nine hits in 31 at-bats against Plank (.290).

It wasn't just Cobb who had trouble with Plank on the Tigers. They had three other left-handed-hitting regulars—fellow outfielders Sam Crawford and Marty McIntyre and first baseman Claude Rossman. Switch-hitting shortstop Donie Bush also proclaimed a dislike of facing Plank, telling teammates, "I'd rather hit against Walter Johnson any day."[14]

9. A Death in the Family

Detroit star Ty Cobb in 1910. Cobb and Plank faced each other often and had many wars of words on the field. In the end, though, Cobb respected Plank and continually named him as one of the best pitchers of all time (George Grantham Bain Collection, Library of Congress).

Nearly two decades later, Eddie Collins claimed, "Plank liked to pitch against Detroit. He didn't bother Crawford and McIntyre much, but he made it tough for Cobb, Bush and Rossman and with those three out of the picture, we usually won."[15]

While the memories of players sometimes aren't the most reliable, Collins wasn't too far off. From 1906–1914—years in which Plank pitched for the Athletics and also faced Cobb—the pitcher had a 36–20 record against Detroit. Over that span, that is the most wins he had against any American League club.

May 22, 1909, was one of the easier of those 36 victories. Plank and the Athletics beat Detroit, 7–1, to put the two teams in a tie for first place. Plank went the distance, allowing six hits and two walks while striking out four, and even bettered Cobb at the plate. While he held the Georgia Peach to an 0-for-4 day, Plank had a pair of hits and scored a run.

The Athletics served notice to Detroit. They scored 38 runs and had 54 hits in taking three of four games. Philadelphia had put the 1908 season behind them, and despite—or perhaps even fueled by—the death of Powers, appeared to be headed for another pennant run.

The race wouldn't heat up until the summer, however. The Athletics stumbled a bit in June and fell seven games behind Detroit after a loss at home to New York on June 28. No one was struggling more than Plank, who opened the month going 0-4 in his first five starts, failing to go the distance in four of the five (with the one complete game an eight-inning outing on the road in which he gave up 11 hits and six runs), plus a relief appearance in which he allowed two runs in one inning. Plank remained confident, as relayed in "The Old Sport's Musings" column in the *Philadelphia Inquirer*: "Plank has not been at his best for some time, but he believes that his setback is but temporary, and declares that he will be pitching as well as ever he did before the season gets much older."[16]

Things did take a turn for the better—for both Plank and the Athletics. The team took four of five games at Boston and swept a five-game series in New York. That left the Athletics three games back of the Tigers, with a four-game series in Detroit upcoming from July 8-11. Plank had won his last two starts but wasn't sharp in either. He allowed four runs—including a home run to Jake Stahl—in beating Boston in the first game of a doubleheader on June 30 and recovered from a slow start, allowing three hits in the opening inning, in a 7-2 victory at New York during a July 5 doubleheader.

But the Tigers brought something else out in him. The Athletics took the opener in the series, 3-1, behind rookie wunderkind Harry Krause, a left-hander who finished the year 18-8 with a league-best 1.39 ERA and who gave a lot of credit to Plank for his advice during the season. That put the Athletics 1½ games behind Detroit. Cobb jawed at Plank, claiming he would "get him"[17] if he tried to field a throw at first base if and when he laid down a bunt. It turned out Cobb's bark was worse than his bite as there was no incident when he did bunt, but perhaps Cobb did get into Plank's head a little as he went 2-for-4 with a double in the July 9 game.

Plank, though, once again outhit Cobb. He had three hits in four trips to the plate and even knocked in a run. It's the only run he needed as he tossed a seven-hit shutout, fanning seven. There was a bit of nervousness in the ninth inning, however. Plank had two on with one out when George Moriarty tried to steal third base—the problem was that Plank hadn't pitched yet and easily threw out the runner. Germany Schaefer was at the plate and, according to umpire Billy Evans, the pitcher and batter were yelling at each other, as always. Evans penned a story in 1926 telling of such an at-bat with Schaefer in a close game and Ira Thomas catching—this would be the only such instance. Although not every detail in Evans' account matches what happened in the game, as such in journalism in early 20th century there was little if no fact-checking (as we will come to see later).

With just one out to go to end the game, Plank, according to Evans, leveled this volley at Schaefer: "Pack up the bats, boys; it is all over; this

9. A Death in the Family

fellow never made a hit off me in his life."[18] To which the batter replied, "If they were all as soft as you, Eddie, I would be leading the league."[19] Plank yelled to his catcher, asking whether he should end the game on a strikeout or popup. "Better not strike him out, Eddie," Thomas answered. "I understand Jennings is looking for a new second baseman, and I'd hate to see good old Schaefer go back to the minors."[20] Schaefer gave it back to both catcher and pitcher before stepping into the batter's box, telling Plank, "you're so old someone ought to give you chloroform and put you out of [your] misery."[21]

Plank got the last laugh, both figuratively and literally. After retiring Schaefer for the final out, Plank, according to Evans, while on the mound "laughed harder than he would have at the funniest joke ever pulled."[22] Schaefer, of course, objected and followed Plank as he headed off the field, yelling more barbs at the pitcher. It didn't escalate, and Schaefer indeed was gone from the Tigers soon enough—traded to Washington in mid-August—but the fire between these two teams was burning.

For a while, it didn't look like it would matter. After taking three of four games from Detroit, the Athletics dropped three of four in Cleveland, three of five at St. Louis, and four straight at Chicago—the latter two teams both sub-.500 clubs—putting Philadelphia a season-high 7½ games behind Detroit. But just as quickly the Athletics rebounded, finishing a long road trip with a four-game sweep of Washington before returning home and taking four of five from both Cleveland and Chicago, with the Tigers coming into town for a four-game set leading Philadelphia now by only three games.

Krause lost the opener to Ed Summers, 3–1. Plank got the ball the next game, Saturday, August 7. Fans filled Shibe Park's outfield, and ground rules were established for a double hit into the roped-off overflow crowd. Plank allowed a run in the top of the first inning, but in the bottom half the Athletics-Tigers fire burned bright once again.

One run was already plated when Harry Davis stepped to the plate with runners on the corners—Collins was on third and Frank Baker on first. Davis either hit a slow grounder or bunted, depending on the report, towards third, where Detroit's Moriarty had no chance to make a play. Collins raced home in what looked to be an easy run until he was greeted with a shoulder from 26-year-old rookie catcher Oscar Stanage. Collins was leveled to the ground and remained there for what the *Philadelphia Inquirer* deemed "several minutes."[23] Umpire Bull Perrine ruled Collins should have scored and gave the Athletics the run, much to the dismay of the Tigers, who argued with Perrine and Billy Evans over the call vociferously—to no avail, of course. Detroit finally left the field after being threatened with a forfeit. Collins returned to the game and collected another hit. Stanage was booed loudly in his two plate appearances. He eventually had to leave the game—and missed two weeks—after taking a foul ball off his thumb. Some in-game karma, perhaps.

The Athletics led 5–3 in the eighth when Plank put two on to open the inning. He then struck out both Bush and Crawford before getting Cobb, who went 1-for-4 with a strikeout, to hit a weak fly. The hoots and hollers from the crowd of nearly 26,000 (or 24,000, depending on the newspaper) grew exponentially with every out. "There wasn't one of the crazed ones present who is likely to forget the spine-chilling eighth, when Eddie gave one of the most remarkable exhibitions of an iced think tank ever seen on any ball tossing field,"[24] observed the *Philadelphia Inquirer*.

With no baseball allowed in Philadelphia on Sunday, that gave the teams an extra day of rest. That allowed Connie Mack to go back to his lefties on two days' rest each. Krause beat Ed Willett, 7–1 on Monday, Baker homering, meaning the Athletics were just one game in back of Detroit. A win Tuesday and the teams would once again be tied.

It was a hot summer weekday, but over 19,000 fans turned out to watch Plank face off against Summers in a pivotal matchup. Pitching on short rest, Plank wasn't at his best. He allowed 10 hits and the Tigers loaded the bases three times—but just one run crossed the plate, on a sacrifice fly in the eighth inning.

Despite it being over 90 degrees, Plank came to bat in the third inning of the scoreless game wearing his Athletics sweater—a blue knit jacket adorned by a white elephant. Whether it was superstition, luck, or trying to keep his arm loose, it didn't hinder him as Plank hit a ball which bounced over the head of center fielder Red Killefer and kept on rolling to the flagpole at the deepest part of the park. Plank easily rounded the bases for the third—and final—home run of his career.

Slumping right fielder Danny Murphy—he was hitless in his previous seven games—tripled in a run in the seventh inning, then stole home to give Plank a couple of insurance runs. Plank allowed the one run in the eighth after filling the bases and loaded them again in the ninth with one out, walking McIntyre and Bush back-to-back to bring up Detroit's two heaviest hitters—Crawford and Cobb.

Plank retired Crawford for the fifth time in the game, on a pop to Collins. He ran the count full to Cobb before inducing a grounder to Collins. Bush stopped running towards second and instead made a beeline for Collins and jumped up and down in front of the Athletics' second baseman. Collins booted the ball and complained to umpire Evans, who called Bush out for interference. The distraction was so obvious—and illegal—that nary a Detroit player (save Bush) argued the game-ending call. The Athletics and Tigers were tied for first once again.

9. A Death in the Family

Philadelphia won nine of its next 11 games, but the Tigers played just as well, and the Athletics held just a one-game lead when they headed to Detroit for a three-game set beginning August 24. Plank only pitched once during that span due to a stomach ailment, allowing a run in the ninth inning before getting George McBride to take a called strike three with two out and runners on second and third to beat Washington, 2–1.

It was Plank's fifth straight win, all complete games. His record was now 14–8, but *The Sporting News* thought it should be better: "Plank lost at least a half a dozen games early in the season which he would have won if Powers had been behind the plate to coach and steady him."[25]

Plank had another idea of how the Athletics could have done better. He pointed a finger at Murphy. In *The Sporting News*, Horace Fogel quoted Plank as saying:

> Even with some of the others in a batting slump we would have won nearly all, if not all of our games, if Murphy had been hitting up to his old-time form. We lost at least a dozen games by one run in each of which Danny had several chances with men on bases to drive in runs, and would have driven them in if he hadn't been in such an awful slump. Yes, if Murphy had been in his batting stride we would have won at least a dozen games which went to the other fellows. Now, add a dozen games to our won column and take them off the lost column, and we would have that pennant clinched a month before the finish of the season.[26]

This is some kind of accusation from Plank, who was rarely quoted in print, and when he was, it was nothing inflammatory like this. Are we to believe he said this? Well, Plank and Murphy were good friends (and remained as such), so perhaps they had a good enough relationship. Or perhaps this quote was said tongue-in-cheek. The truth is that Murphy did slump, especially in July (when he slashed .238/.316/.333 in 126 plate appearances) and August (.202/.248/.303 in 112 PA). Murphy rebounded in September, batting .348/.381/.554 with 24 RBI in 32 games.

There was pointing of fingers at the Tigers once again as well. In the opener of the key series in Detroit, Cobb spiked Baker on the arm while sliding into third on an attempted steal, on which he was thrown out rather easily. Mack said Cobb spiked Baker intentionally; Cobb always insisted it was unintentional and he later pointed to a photograph as proof (Mack never gave ground). Baker remained in the game and the Tigers beat Krause and the Athletics, 7–6. Another first-place tie.

Plank took the hill on August 25, nearly four months to the day after Powers' death, for the biggest game of the season to date. It was another hot day—Plank again wore his Athletics sweater when batting—although a rain cooled off the teams all day. Philadelphia led, 2–1, after seven innings but had the bases full in the first inning and couldn't score. A rain shower hit, and some thought the game could be called—and thus the Athletics would win—but it tapered off and the game went on.

In the eighth inning, Plank had two strikes on Cobb but lost the battle as the Detroit star singled in Bush to tie the game. Cobb smartly hustled to second on the throw to the plate, which allowed him to score the go-ahead run on a Crawford single. The Athletics, though, tied it back up in the ninth on Davis' two-out RBI single. The tie was only momentary. Stanage, back in the lineup, singled to center to plate Moriarty with the game-winner. Plank, in his first start in a week, allowed 10 hits and didn't walk or strike out a batter.

The Tigers won the next day as well. From August 26–September 2, Detroit won 14 consecutive games, all at home in Bennett Park. The excitement for the Tigers and Athletics wasn't over yet, though.

The teams wouldn't meet again until mid-September. The season was winding down with roughly 20 games remaining and the Tigers holding a four-game advantage. September 16 would also be Cobb's first game at Shibe Park since he spiked Baker. The third baseman missed no playing time (although he did play with a bandage on his arm for a while), but Philadelphia fans were still livid—and they let Cobb know.

Precautions were taken, especially since Cobb had received his share of hate mail and threats. It was reported that 100 police officers were on duty at the park to preserve the peace. One potential hurling object was banned—soft drink bottles—but fans still threw seat cushions at the Tigers outfielder (he didn't get hit, but some surrounding fans found their noggins worse for wear). Cobb tried to defuse the situation with some humor, tipping his cap to the crowd of 25,000 before his first plate appearance. That of course just increased the jeering. When Plank fanned Cobb, those jeers turned into thundering cheers.

Plank struck out Cobb again in the third inning, this time with the bases full, and after getting out of the inning unscathed by inducing Crawford to bounce out to Davis, the cheers by the Philadelphia faithful were directed to the pitcher. Although Plank held Cobb hitless in four at-bats, he was a bit unsteady in the early innings, causing Mack to warm up Chief Bender, but after Plank's performance in the third inning he was allowed to stay in and ended up with a 2–1 win, allowing six hits, four walks, and hitting a batter while striking out five. The *Philadelphia Inquirer* deemed it "brilliant yet erratic work."[27]

The Athletics and Tigers split the next two games—Krause lost, 5–3, and Bender tossed a three-hitter in a 2–0 shutout—before the usual off day Sunday. Three games behind Detroit and with time running out, there was no doubt who Mack was going to turn to in the final game of the series—and final meeting between the two teams—on Monday.

9. A Death in the Family

"I feel confident we have just a bit better ball team than Detroit," Mack said.

> I think our loss Friday was due to Krause's wildness [he walked four and hit a batter; the Tigers also stole seven bases—teams found out that Krause had trouble holding on runners]. But you can't blame the boy very much. It's enough to make a seasoned veteran weaken to face the Tigers in such an important game. However, I feel certain that Plank can win another game. To tell the truth, I felt from the first that we could be satisfied if we won three from the Tigers. For you know, if we stick strictly to business, the advantage of playing at home, which will be ours, should easily overcome the two-game lead which they will have. I cannot predict what will be the outcome, but I feel mighty good about our chances for the pennant.[28]

Plank, the Tiger-killer, was feeling confident, perhaps because the Athletics had won his last five starts, and his two recent appearances were a 1–0 shutout over Boston and his 2–1 win over Detroit. After coming to Shibe Park in the morning, Plank made his way up to Mack's second-story office. From there he and his manager watched a throng of people make their way to the stadium. The *Philadelphia Inquirer* and *Detroit Free-Press* reported there were over 29,000 people in attendance. The *Philadelphia Evening Telegram* put the number at 32,000. "Gee, I guess I am the only man in Philadelphia that is going to work today," Plank said, perhaps to himself, as Mack stood nearby. "Well, I am feeling fit for the job and I hope to send them all home happy."[29]

This being an Athletics-Tigers game, the fans might have gone home happy, but there was also potential vitriol. In the fourth inning, Cobb slid into second base and spiked shortstop Jack Barry, who, as it turned out, would be lost for the rest of the season as a result. After the game Cobb (once again) said the spiking was not intentional, but this time the Athletics backed him up, although not all were pleased. Catcher Ira Thomas, who played for Detroit in 1908, said, "That fellow Cobb wears the sharpest spikes of any player in the country and something should be done to prevent him crippling men like he has this season."[30] The proclamations of the other Athletics came later, but with all that had gone on with Cobb and Baker, after Cobb ended the eighth with a strikeout (which the crowd, of course, loved), the Tiger exited via the Athletics bench, changed his clothes, and went to the team hotel before the game was even over.

As for the game, the Athletics took an early 4–1 lead. In the sixth, Plank allowed a two-out, bases-loaded single to Moriarty which plated two runs before getting Stanage to pop to Collins. Detroit couldn't get to Plank again. Crawford singled in the ninth but was erased on an inning-ending double play. The large throng did indeed go home happy as the Athletics crept to within two games of the Tigers.

But that's as close as Philadelphia would get. Even though the Athletics won four of their next five contests, they lost a half-game in the standings. Losing four of their next six, coupled with Detroit putting together a three-game winning streak, sealed the Tigers' third straight pennant. Plank got one last start in the first game of a September 29 doubleheader at home against Chicago, which he lost, 2–1, in 10 innings.

The loss cost Plank a chance at a 20-win season. His 19 wins (against 10 losses) were still fourth-most in the American League, while his 1.76 ERA ranked seventh—but fourth on his own team behind Krause, Cy Morgan (16–11, 1.65) and Bender (18–8, 1.66). The Athletics' team ERA was an AL-best 1.93.

Collins, just 22 and playing his second full season in the big leagues, emerged as a superstar, batting .347 with 104 runs and 63 steals. Baker, a 23-year-old rookie, burst on the scene with a .305 average, 19 triples, 73 runs, and a team-high 85 RBI. Murphy rebounded from his prolonged slump and finished at .281 with 14 triples, 61 runs, and 69 RBI. The young shortstop, Barry, still only 22, didn't hit well but played solid defense. Davis was 35 but still managed to hit .268, score 73 times, and drive in 75 runs. The Athletics might not have won the pennant, but the pieces were falling in place.

✦ 10 ✦

California, Cuba and Everywhere in Between

The 1909 season certainly wasn't the best in Eddie Plank's first nine years in the major leagues, but his notoriety continued to grow.

In August, Plank was one of a handful of players who started appearing in advertisements for Coca-Cola. Among the others were his manager, Connie Mack, teammates Harry Davis and Eddie Collins, and future Hall of Famers Ty Cobb and Pittsburgh's Hans Wagner (better known now as Honus, but more commonly referred to as Hans in that era).

The advertisement which appeared throughout September as well in *The Sporting News*—which claimed to have the "largest circulation of any Sporting Paper"[1]—featured Plank's mug shot in a circle and right below that his signature (E.S. Plank) as well as a quote from the pitcher: "Am very fond of Coca-Cola. Have been drinking it for some time."[2] The advertisement also featured these selling points: "A Professional ball player, ranking high in this profession, watches his health like a hawk—he must. That's why he Drinks Coca-Cola the beverage that best quenches the thirst without the ill effects of alcoholic stimulants and sweet soft drinks. Delicious-Refreshing-Cooling 5¢ Everywhere."[3]

If being one of a few ballplayers in such a national ad campaign wasn't enough to raise Plank's reputation, he also was one of five pitchers included on an "all-American team" as selected by 19th century star Adrian "Cap" Anson. Two of the other hurlers were also American League pitchers— Detroit's George Mullin, who led the league with a 29–8 record and .784 winning percentage, and Chicago's Ed Walsh, who had a 1.41 ERA in 1909. *Baseball Magazine* also tabbed Plank for its postseason all-star teams, placing him both on the publication's All-American League and All-American (players from both leagues) teams.

That fall, Plank's fame expanded as he traveled to places where fans previously only could have read about him. For the first time, people west of the Mississippi River and St. Louis could see Plank pitch. After the Athletics' usual postseason barnstorming trip around Pennsylvania and New Jersey, most of the team—with the exclusion of shortstop Jack Barry and catcher Paddy Livingston, both injured, and outfielder Daniel Murphy—headed west to play a string of exhibition games against local teams as well as a traveling National League all-star club, which featured players from every team in that circuit.

Mack's crew began in Chicago with a game against the Cubs and didn't stop to play again until Montana, where it faced the National Leaguers in Billings and Helena, Plank pitching in the latter. Stops were also made in Seattle, Portland, Los Angeles, and Bakersfield before an extended stay in San Francisco. Other cities visited included San Jose, Stockton, Ventura, and Pasadena. The final game was played in Los Angeles on December 12. Well, that wasn't *supposed* to be the final game. There were exhibitions scheduled in New Orleans, but poor weather waylaid any opportunities from the West Coast to the Bayou.

The overall trip was an unmitigated disaster. The games were fine, but not much to write about. A contest against the National Leaguers in Bakersfield in which Plank pitched was played in only 52 minutes. The Athletics won, 4–0, as Plank allowed five hits while walking one and striking out none. Swinging early and often in the count likely was the standard of the day. Perhaps as a result of the snappy play—most games were played in under an hour and a half—crowds weren't as large as expected. Each player earned all of 30 cents in gate receipts at one venue—and those who participated barely escaped without losing money. A $200 deposit had to be forked over before the beginning of the trip, which all were fortunate enough to get back—but nothing more.

The worst of it, though, was suffered by Jack Bliss, a backup catcher for the St. Louis Cardinals. In a game November 29, he broke his ankle so badly that the bones ripped through his skin. He would appear in only 16 games in the 1910 season and wouldn't make his season debut until June 22.

Plank, as usual, kept himself in shape during the off-season by working on his farm. He also picked up a new hobby—golf (he quickly earned a reputation as one of the best golfers on the Athletics). There was no holdout for Plank as his contract for the 1910 season was received by Connie Mack in early February. He did, though, in a short while discuss retirement. Nothing impending, mind you, but for Plank his baseball life expectancy clearly was on his mind. He would turn 35 in August; the clock was ticking on his professional days in baseball.

"Last year, I felt as good if not better in fact than the first year I entered the Athletic fold. If I continue in this way I'll stick, but just the minutes that I know I'm going back I'll quit the game while the going's good," he said in the Gettysburg area newspapers. "I figured that in about three years it ought to be time for me to say 'Farewell,' but of course if my condition is good I'll stay till the bell rings down the curtain. You never can tell in baseball anyway. I may go out this year and in the very first game break my arm, or get injured in such a manner that I'll be useless and never come back."[4]

Plank planned on never playing for another team other than the Athletics and said he would never pitch in the minor leagues. "When I quit the big show it will be for good as far as twirling is concerned,"[5] he said. Of course, life doesn't always go the way we plan.

Three years was just an estimation, he said, based on the way he was feeling. And he was feeling good at the start of the 1910 season. Besides, he noted, there was no reason to complain or worry too much about the future. "We all get old and I guess that farm down at Gettysburg will be all right for me."[6]

The opinions others had of Plank weren't as confident as the pitcher's feelings about himself. Detroit manager Hughie Jennings, who took his team to the World Series three straight years (and lost all three) figured a fourth consecutive appearance was in line, and he wasn't overly worried about the Athletics, even though they won 95 games a year before, finishing 3½ games behind the Tigers.

> Any club that beats Detroit will have to be 20 per cent stronger than last year.... As for the Athletics, I cannot see where they will be as strong as last year. I don't think there is a chance in the world for [Harry] Krause to repeat the record he hung up. As for [Chief] Bender and Plank, they are getting old, and they may not be as good as last season. There are many veterans on the Philadelphia team—too many, in fact, to make the team as strong as last season.[7]

Former teammate Simon Nicholls, who appeared in 307 games for the Athletics between 1906 and 1909, including 21 in 1909, told a Cleveland newspaper that his frontrunners for the American League pennant were Boston and Detroit. *Sporting Life* paraphrased some of Nicholls' thoughts, including that he "can't see the Athletics in the pennant race this season"[8] and "Nicholls does not expect Plank to do much this season, as his pitching days are about over. He said that last season Plank was in misery every game he pitched, being bothered with a sore arm the whole season."[9]

Saying Plank had a sore arm after a season in which he tossed 24 complete games and set a personal best with a 1.76 ERA might seem like an unfounded claim. However, over his career Plank often claimed his arm was sore. And that usually was a good thing. "Plank usually had a muscular soreness in his left arm. But if Eddie complained of a sore arm he usually went out and pitched a swell game," longtime Athletics trainer Doc Ebling explained in 1937. "When he didn't complain, he was likely to wind up being knocked out of the box in a few innings."[10]

Plank was in fine form during spring training and the yearly spring series against the National League's Phillies. In his final three appearances, he allowed just one run on eight hits over 19 innings. With the season nearing its start, Mack summoned Plank, Chief Bender, and Jack Coombs to his office. Near the end of his life, Coombs recalled the incident. "He said: 'Boys (he always called us boys) I've got this figured out. If we can win 95 games, we'll win the pennant. If you boys can win 75 for me, I think I can get the other twenty from the rest of the pitching staff.'"[11] The trio wouldn't quite meet Mack's goal. But the Athletics would win more than 95 games.

The Athletics' quest for the 1910 pennant began in Washington. Plank was given the nod to start Opening Day, and it turned out to be a momentous occasion—but not because of the Philadelphia pitcher. About 30 minutes before the start of the game, a band struck up "The Star-Spangled Banner" as President William H. Taft—along with his wife and several dignitaries—made his way to a box seat near Washington's bench along the first-base line. This marked the first time a sitting U.S. president had attended a major league game. Taft shook the hands of several players as well as managers Mack and Jimmy McAleer before throwing out the first pitch while standing in his box seat (now adorned with a comfortable armchair, which was quickly ushered there upon his arrival). Instead of throwing to catcher Gabby Street, as was expected, Taft tossed the ball to Washington's starting pitcher—Walter Johnson. Johnson wisely did not use that ball in the game. Taft autographed it the following day (Johnson brought it to the ballpark to show players from both teams). The Hall of Fame is now in possession of that baseball.

Before the game began, the captains of both clubs—Harry Davis of the Athletics and Germany Schaefer of the Nationals—brought umpire Billy Evans pieces of paper with the lineups of both teams written upon them. This was a new rule put in place in 1910—the pregame lineup card.

Plank was just a footnote in this game, however. He went the distance but allowed 13 hits and three runs while walking none, hitting a batter, and striking out six. Johnson, just 22 years old and beginning his third full season, gave a hint of what was to come in the years ahead. The Athletics could barely touch the fireballer and were fortunate not to be no-hit. With two outs in the seventh inning, Frank Baker lofted a fly to right field. Doc Gessler raced for the ball but due to an overflow crowd (attendance was around 14,000), he ran into a fan and fell over, doing a flip while reaching for the ball, which fell out of his reach. One account said the fan was reading a newspaper; another said he was a "cripple and simply could not get out of the way."[12] Johnson walked three but that was the only hit he allowed in a 3–0 Washington victory.

10. California, Cuba and Everywhere in Between

"I wanted this game mighty bad," Mack told reporters that night at the team hotel. "It always encourages a team to win the opener. Eddie Plank seemed to be in such grand shape that I felt sure he could stop the Washington hitters. I did not figure on Walter Johnson. He surprised me by his work. The Athletics simply could not connect, and you know a team looks awfully bad when it isn't hitting. I believe Johnson is in better form than he ever was in his life before."[13]

Plank wouldn't lose again until June. He injured his thumb in the fourth inning of the opener on a liner back to the box by Street and didn't pitch again until April 23, when he went all 11 innings in a 5–3 win at Boston. He made five starts in May, winning four (the Athletics won the other as well). At the end the month, Philadelphia was 26–9 and had been in first place every day but one.

June opened with a thud. In the midst of a long road trip, the Athletics lost four straight, getting swept in a three-game series at Detroit. Plank pitched the finale, a 2–0 loss to Ralph Stroud, a middling 25 year old in his first year in the majors. "You will see a different looking ball club when we come back here," Mack proclaimed. "We don't mind losing a game like that one today, but it hurts to throw them away. We played bad ball and deserved to get beaten in the first two games."[14]

Plank was inconsistent the next two months. He won four in a row from June 21–July 9 and then lost his next three starts. His record was 10–7, a winning record, but hardly the production he had given in years past. The Athletics, however, were playing well overall. On July 30, they led Walter Johnson, 7–0, heading into the ninth inning, but Bender started faltering, allowing three runs and loading the bases with nobody out. Plank was brought in to clean up the mess. He struck out Bob Unglaub, walked Schaefer to force in a run, got Red Killefer to hit into a force, which also scored a run, and fanned pinch hitter Doc Reisling to give Philadelphia the win and a six-game lead in the standings.

Around this time, Detroit manager Hughie Jennings and outfielder Ty Cobb labeled the Athletics as "quitters."[15] The Athletics had gone through a bit of a rough patch, losing six of nine games and tying another, but lost only 1½ games off their lead over that stretch. Less than two weeks later, on August 12, Plank beat Ed Summers and the Tigers, 7–4, not allowing a hit after the fourth inning, giving Philadelphia three of four games in the road series. The win also put the Athletics 10½ games in front of second-place Boston, the first time their lead reached double digits. The pennant was all but theirs and everyone knew it.

When Plank beat Chicago, 6–1, a week later in front of around 7,000 fans, the *Philadelphia Inquirer*'s Edgar Wolfe, writing under the pseudonym Jim Nasium, took offense to what he considered a poor turnout.

Honest, fellows, we ought to be ashamed of ourselves. Many a town that is only a dump flag station compared with this city of ours would be buying up all the pasteboards and getting up on its hind legs and yelling itself into an epidemic of vocal paralysis over this ball team of ours if they had it in their midst. Let us cut loose a little enthusiasm, fellows, and show the boys we appreciate their grand work. Who the dickens wants to win a pennant in the midst of funeral silence and apparent indifference?[16]

The lead was so large—now 12 games—that questions started to be asked about the World's Series. Team owner John Shibe was queried by Chicago reporters—the Cubs were in the midst of running away with the National League pennant as well—about which team would host Game 1. "Oh, I'm not all sure we are going to win out. There is always the danger of a train wreck that might kill all our players," Shibe joked.[17]

By September, it was all but official. Philadelphia and Chicago would meet up for the championship. Cubs manager Frank Chance took a dig at the Athletics in early September—there was still a month to go in the season—saying, "I do not consider the Athletics are a much stronger combination than the Tigers were when we faced them."[18] The Cubs played Detroit in the 1907 and 1908 World Series and lost just one game.

Philadelphia kept rolling along, and Plank was again up and down. He won four consecutive decisions to start August, then lasted three innings in back-to-back starts, both losses (part of a string of three consecutive defeats). He won at Detroit on September 15, 7–1, allowing only four hits and no walks with six strikeouts for win No. 15. Five days later, Plank upped his record to 16–10 with a 6–3 win at Cleveland. Coupled with a loss by New York to Chicago, the Athletics clinched the American League pennant. There were still 15 games remaining (only 14 were played).

Plank pitched only two more times—eight innings on September 25 and five innings on October 5—getting a no-decision in both. The Athletics went "only" 8–5 (with a tie) in those final 14 games, giving them an American League-record 102 victories with just 48 losses. New York finished in second, 15½ games out, at 86–63.

Bender, Coombs and Plank didn't quite combine for the 75 victories Mack had asked of them. The trio finished with 70, Coombs leading the way with an incredible 31–9 year along with a 1.30 ERA over 353 innings. Bender finished at 23–5 and a 1.58 ERA, with Plank at 16–10 and a 2.01 ERA. Cy Morgan chipped in with an 18–12 record and 1.55 ERA. The Athletics as a staff had a 1.73 ERA, the lowest in American League history. No team has had an ERA under 2.00 since (only two other teams in AL history have done so—the 1905 White Sox, 1.99, and the 1909 Athletics, 1.93).

The offense was nearly as proficient, leading the league in batting average (.266) and slugging percentage (.355) and finishing second in runs (671)

10. California, Cuba and Everywhere in Between

and on-base percentage (.326). Eddie Collins led the way once again, batting .324 with 81 runs, 81 RBI and, yes, 81 steals. Outfielders Danny Murphy (.300, 18 triples) and Rube Oldring (.308) were the only other regulars who hit .300 or better. Third baseman Frank Baker (.283) and shortstop Jack Barry (.259) were solid at the plate and in the field.

The Athletics won a lot of games and had a good time doing it. The team was a tight-knit bunch—Plank was especially friendly with Bender, Collins, Coombs, Davis, and Murphy—and nicknames abounded, even with little-used players or newcomers. Not all were that creative. Catcher Jack Lapp was, for example, called "Jackalapp," shortstop Jack Barry "Holy Cross," after the college he attended, and Jack Coombs "Kennebunk," after a town in Maine, his home state. Eddie Collins' nickname was "Cocky," which seemed an apt description of the player. Younger players could get tagged with interesting nicknames. Outfielder Amos Strunk was called "Cupid," and pitcher Tommy Atkins was stuck with "Nickel in the Slot." Nineteen-year-old first baseman John McInnis was tabbed "Stuffy"—a nickname which stuck with him for his lifetime. Plank had a nickname as well—"Kingnutt"—but no explanation was given. Earlier in his career, Lave Cross had started calling Plank "Bunny,"

Popular Reuben "Rube" Oldring, "the idol of the left-field fans," was a teammate of Eddie Plank's from 1906–1914 (George Grantham Bain Collection, Library of Congress).

because, Plank surmised, "Lave thought I was so mild-looking, like a rabbit, you know."[19]

Mack's choice for Game 1 of the World Series was a pitcher he referred to by his middle name—Albert—but everyone else called "Chief."

The Athletics prepared for the World Series by playing a team made up of some of the best American League players in the game, such as Washington pitcher Walter Johnson and outfielder Clyde Milan, Boston first baseman Jake Stahl, second baseman Larry Gardner, and outfielder Tris Speaker, and Detroit outfielder Ty Cobb, who arrived a few days late due to a car accident.

The teams played five times and Plank pitched in three of them (Mack mostly had pitchers last just three innings in these exhibitions). The *Pittsburgh Press*, among others, projected Plank to pitch the opener in Philadelphia. As it turned out, Mack only used two pitchers the entire series—Bender and Coombs. That surprised many, but Mack tipped his hand back in early September. This tidbit appeared in *The Sporting News*: "When Connie Mack, in discussing the world's pennant prospects while he was here [Washington] last week, got to the matter of pitching, he said directly at one time and let it be understood by inference at others that he expected to rely on Coombs and Bender against the Sox [Cubs], and that unless something occurred during the progress of the series to change his mind, he might let that pair go the entire route."[20]

Mack theorized that Chicago hit left-handers well. The Cubs only had two left-handed hitters in their lineup—outfielders Frank Schulte and Jimmy Sheckard (a third, second baseman Johnny Evers, did not play in the Series due to a broken leg). The manager confirmed his strategy with Plank, right-hander Cy Morgan, and catcher Paddy Livingston, who would sit because Ira Thomas and Jack Lapp were the personal catchers for Bender and Coombs, respectively (Thomas played well enough in Game 1 that he was the catcher in four of the eventual five games, with Lapp playing in the other).

"Connie told us before the first game, that is, Plank, Morgan and myself, that we would be the battery in case anything happened to Coombs and Bender," relayed Livingston a week after the series ended. "So we had to be the men-in-waiting every day, as 'nothing happened' that affected our chances. It was tough in a way, but we knew were next in line, and we thought we would be called upon."[21]

Bender won Game 1, 4–1. and Coombs took Game 2, 9–3. David L. Plank, Eddie's father, showed up at Shibe Park thinking his son might pitch. It nearly happened. Coombs loaded the bases in the first inning, and Mack had Plank start warming up. Coombs allowed only one run, and Plank sat down. "You'll get in some day, Ed," the elder Plank told his son, "and you'll lick 'em, too."[22]

10. California, Cuba and Everywhere in Between

"The boss told us after Coombs had won the second game that Plank or Morgan might do better than either Coombs or Bender in the games to come, but he was going to use Coombs and Bender because he believed they would have more luck,"[23] Livingston recalled. Mack was so true to his word that he used Coombs on one day's rest in Game 3 in Chicago, a 12–5 Athletics win. Bender started Game 4 and got in trouble in the fourth inning, allowing three straight singles as the Cubs narrowed Philadelphia's lead to 3–2. Both Plank and Coombs were sent to warm up, but a double play and fly out finished Chicago in the inning without any more runs. The Cubs ended up winning, 4–3, in 11 innings.

The Athletics still led the Series, three games to one, but Mack was having second thoughts. Coombs, who allowed just 1.88 runs per game (including unearned runs) during the season, had let up eight in 18 innings and walked 13 batters, including nine in Game 2. Following the Game 4 loss, Mack told the team to decide who should pitch in Game 5—Coombs or Plank.

Eddie Collins ran into Tigers second baseman George Moriarty at the team hotel and asked him, "As a player who has batted for years against Coombs and Plank, whom do you favor for tomorrow's game?"[24] Moriarty said if it were left up to him, he would pitch Coombs in Game 5 and save Plank for Game 6 back at Shibe Park if the Athletics couldn't close the series in Chicago. "That's what our whole bunch has decided," Collins responded. "Leave the big game for Plank, he'll beat them for sure."[25] However, there would be no Game 6.

In his pregame talk with the team, Mack turned to Coombs. Livingston recalled the conversation: "He said: 'John, you've pitched two poor games. Now, you've got to go in there today and win. Everything depends on this game, and I expect you to pitch the finest ball of the series.' John did."[26] The Athletics won, 7–2, as Coombs tossed this third complete game, allowing nine hits but only walking one. Every player on Philadelphia—even Plank, who didn't throw one pitch—received $2,062.74.

Plank still got a chance to pitch in 1910, however, but first came a celebration of the World Series victory, which took place November 5 in Philadelphia, and also ... a wedding? Plank was one of several Athletics rumored to be married soon, including Mack, Barry, Collins, and Coombs. Plank was reportedly going to "wed an old schoolmate"[27] but that was the last such talk was heard of again. In February, Mack left one to assume the report was entirely fictitious when, discussing his own nuptials as well as those of Collins and Coombs, he commented, "This leaves only Oldring, Strunk and Plank unmarried and there is no telling when they will join the majority and take unto themselves a wife."[28]

Twelve Athletics agreed to head to Cuba to play some exhibition games. The group was originally guaranteed a $7,000 split, but after Collins and Frank Baker decided not to go (Mack also did not attend; he was in Rome on his honeymoon and met Pope Pius X), it was reduced to $5,000. Instead of $500 per man, now it was $387. One player who likely didn't mind was Claud Derrick, who took Collins' spot and now had himself this stipend and a World Series share despite striking out in his only appearance of the 1910 season.

The Athletics opened with a game against Detroit, which was finishing up its own exhibition tour on the island, in Havana. Plank was on the mound in front of a crowd of 12,000, which included Cuban president Jose Miguel Gomez, as well as others who "perched themselves on the fence and points of vantage in the near vicinity of the park."[29] The Athletics lost—either 6–2 or 5–2 depending on the report—and that set the tone for their play.

The Athletics played 10 games during their trip and won just four. Plank pitched three more times and lost all three. On December 10, the Athletics led Habana, 3–0, but Plank allowed five runs in the eighth inning in a 5–3 defeat. He faced Jose Mendez—considered one of the best pitchers to never play in the majors (due to the color of his skin, he was relegated to playing in Cuba and, later, the Negro Leagues)—and Almendares in his other two games and lost, 5–2 and 7–5. Plank allowed 25 hits and four walks with 10 strikeouts in his three outings, covering 24 innings.

Reports were that the Athletics didn't take the games seriously—but that could also have been emanating because players who weren't allowed to play in the major leagues put a thumping on the world champs. Umpire Billy Evans went on the trip but never got to officiate, Cuban umps being used instead. "Umpiring of the rankest sort in the first game may have had something to do with the Athletics' horseplay," Evans claimed. "The two Cuban teams played steady ball throughout. They were after the games in earnest, and they made good—with the able assistance of the umpires in the first game [the contest against Habana in which Plank pitched]. They did have their batting eyes with them, though, and their fielding was sharp and clean."[30]

The *Washington Post* reprinted a critique from the *Havana Post* after the final games, a December 18 doubleheader in which the Athletics lost 7–5 (Plank's game) and 6–2:

> Burlesque baseball by the Athletics, the kind that would shame any schoolboy club in the United States was passed out to the 8,000 people who paid their good money at Almendares park to see the real article. Spectators were disgusted with the showing of the Athletics. Hundreds quit the grounds before the second game was half over. Their opinion was that the work of the big leaguers was rotten in the superlative degree.

10. California, Cuba and Everywhere in Between

Cuban fans say they have never received such a raw deal from a big league team that was paid a small fortune to come here. There is no denying that baseball enthusiasm in this city has receive a severe blow because of the Athletics' conduct.

However, the exhibition by the Athletics yesterday was only on a par with their past performances on this trip. It didn't matter to them that they had received a princely guarantee to come here and that they were facing one of the biggest crowds that ever turned out on this island, they simply put up a bluff at playing.[31]

A few years later, while training in Cuba, Plank looked back on his first experience in the country. His only reference to the Athletics' play, or lack of it, came in an indirect reference to the team possibly not being in good condition. Otherwise, he had fond memories.

> They treated us like a parcel of kings. We had all our expenses paid and enjoyed ourselves to our hearts' content without laying out a nickel. These people were making barrels of dough at the gate, too. We played twelve games [sic] and the park was packed to over-flowing on each occasion. And, believe me, it was an occasion, for these Cubans to watch a real big-league club in action. We were the one big attraction of the city. The men who were in back of the trip could well afford to lay out the guarantee they did, for they were holding a full house at every game with the prices sky high. The way they taxed these natives to get a look at us was a shame.[32]

An illustrated picture of Eddie Plank on a baseball card from the Nadja Caramel Company after the 1910 season (Library of Congress).

◆ 11 ◆

Catching Ire

Eddie Plank entered the 1911 season as a 35 year old. That already made him the 10th-oldest player in the major leagues—but just the third-oldest on his own team, behind Harry Davis and Topsy Hartsel. However, neither Davis nor Hartsel, as well as many of those born before him still playing, were being counted on for (or would play) as a big a role as Plank.

Plank pitched 250⅓ innings in 1910. He was expected to carry the same, or greater, load again in 1911. The Athletics' pitching staff which did so well the previous year was largely intact, with Plank, Chief Bender, Jack Coombs, Harry Krause, and Cy Morgan expected to lead the way to another Philadelphia pennant.

The critics were out again, calling for Plank to start falling off his game. Said the *Washington Herald*: "In Coombs and Bender, the Athletics have the best pair of boxmen, possibly in the league. But those two men are the only real class pictures Mack has on his roster. Morgan, Plank and Krause are fair, but not about the ordinary by any means."[1]

Not many pitchers his age were even still on the mound, and even fewer were putting up major innings like Plank. In 1909, three pitchers who were 35 or older—or turned 35 during the season—toiled at least 200 innings. Forty-two-year-old Cy Young of Cleveland led the way with 294⅓ innings. In 1910, he would pitch just 163⅓ innings with a 2.53 ERA, barely better than the league average. The St. Louis Browns' Jack Powell, who turned 35 in July, pitched 239 innings but just 129⅓ the next year. Cincinnati's Bob Ewing went over 200 innings in 1909 at age 36 with 218⅓ and followed that up with 255⅓ innings for the Phillies in 1910, but with a 3.00 ERA (he would last just 24 innings in 1911 with a 7.88 ERA). Brooklyn's George Bell was 35 in 1910 when he went 310 innings (with a 10–27 record). He would last just 101 innings with a 4.28 ERA in 1911 and be out of the majors for good. Since the start of the American League in 1901, only 15 times had a 35 year old pitched 200+ innings in a season—and seven of

11. Catching Ire

those instances were by Young. In other words, there was reason for pessimism when it came to Plank's career trajectory.

Plank himself reiterated what he said a year earlier: His plan was to pitch through the 1912 season and then call it quits. While walking to the park during spring training at Savannah, Georgia, Plank and Coombs, who turned 29 in April but had pitched over 600 innings (including postseason and exhibitions) the past two seasons, discussed the wear and tear pitching has on a body and mind. "Two more years and back to the farm to stay there the rest of my life," Plank relayed to his fellow starter.

> I shall quit the game in 1912 and all that I ask is that I have two more good years. I have earned a long rest. In 1912 I will have been a dozen years in the game as a pitcher. I started with Connie Mack, and I want to quit with him. Most of these fellows who sit in the bleachers and roar at you when you have a bad day think that all you have to do is travel around the country and work a couple of hours a day. I want to tell them that there is more actual work in pitching one game of baseball than there is in two days' work on the farm. I get up at sunrise and work until sundown in the country and then sleep like a baby. But let me pitch a game of ball and my arm aches. I'm sore all over and cannot sleep for pain. Two more years for me and then I'm through. If I haven't enough to live on then I

Manager Connie Mack in his familiar bowler and suit, taken in 1911. A former catcher, in his early days with the Athletics, Mack often got into his old position to take warmups from pitchers he was trying out (George Grantham Bain Collection, Library of Congress).

never will have if I stick in baseball twice as long. Goodby baseball for Eddie in 1912.[2]

Spring training in the early 20th century consisted mainly of teams playing minor-league clubs to get into game shape. The caliber of opponents varied and often weren't much competition for a veteran major league hurler like Plank, who often wouldn't give it his all in exhibitions (which could cause some concern to his manager). March 24 against Charleston wasn't one of those times. Plank allowed only the leadoff hitter to reach base in pitching four shutout innings with a pair of strikeouts. "Any talk of Plank's being all in would have been shamed today if the 'knockers' could have observed the hoop on his fast one, and snap to his benders," observed second baseman Eddie Collins after the game. "Watch this old war horse this coming season. The forebodings are bright for the 'Gettysburg farmer.'"[3]

Questions about Plank aside, the Athletics were highly thought of entering the season. After all, this was a team coming off 102 wins and a World Series title. The *Cincinnati Enquirer* asked members of the Baseball Writers' Association of America who they thought would meet in the 1911 World Series. The consensus: the Athletics and New York Giants. That prediction didn't look so good early.

Due in part possibly to bad weather in Philadelphia which limited their ability to practice once they returned from spring training, the Athletics lost six of their first seven games, Plank earning the only victory, a 1–0 win over Boston in which he got out of a two-on, nobody-out jam in the top of the ninth. Plank also won the team's second game, at Boston on April 24, 5–1.

Plank won his first five starts and pitched the ninth inning in a two-run win in another. In games in which he hadn't appeared, the team was 7–9. Following his fifth win—a 7–0 shutout of St. Louis (Plank already had three shutouts; he had just one in 1910 and three in 1909)—the Athletics went on a six-game losing streak, falling to fifth place at 13–15 and already 12 games behind American League-leading Detroit, which was 27–5 after beating Philadelphia (including Plank in the opener) in the first two games of a four-game series.

The Athletics broke the skid in their next game, May 20, but needed Plank to relieve Coombs in the eighth inning. Philadelphia led 13–8 entering the inning when Coombs allowed a single, triple and walk. Plank replaced Coombs (and Ira Thomas also came in for catcher Jack Lapp). He got Donie Bush on a short fly, but then allowed back-to-back singles to Ty Cobb and Sam Crawford (the *Detroit Times* said Crawford reached after shortstop Stuffy McInnis fumbled the ball). Jim Delahanty singled in a pair of runners to cut the lead to 13–12 but fortune started shining on the Athletics. Crawford was thrown out going to third base by right fielder Danny Murphy, and Delahanty was gunned down by Thomas trying to steal second. Only one batter was retired—and four runs had crossed—but the Athletics still had the lead and held on, 14–12.

The victory catapulted the Athletics on a seven-game win streak, a loss in the second game of a May 27 doubleheader ending the run. Plank won both his starts, 9–1 at Cleveland on May 23 and 8–1 vs. New York in the opener of the twin bill. Philadelphia promptly reeled off another seven-game winning streak. Plank saved another for Coombs, coming in with the bases full and one out in an 8–5 win over the Yankees and beat Cleveland, 5–1, in a seven-inning, rain-shortened game on June 2. Before the start of the latter contest, the team took down its American League pennant, which it had put up a month earlier, and raised a World Series pennant up the flagpole—upside-down on the first attempt, as it turned out. The blue and gold flag read, "Philadelphia Americans, 1910, Champions of the World."[4]

With the win, Plank was now 8–1 on the season, allowing just 10 runs in his eight victories (six of those came in one game) and striking out 5.3 batters per nine innings. "Eddie Plank appears to be the only sure-fire pitcher on Connie's staff"[5] was an observation printed in The Old Sports Musing's column in the *Philadelphia Inquirer*.

June, however, wasn't as kind to Plank. The Athletics' latest seven-game streak was stopped when Plank lost to, of all teams, Detroit on June 8. Another six-game win streak ensued—including Plank blanking St. Louis for his fourth shutout—but he would be the next one to lose again, 8–6 to Chicago on June 17. No one else was losing, though, and after a four-game sweep of Washington from June 19–22, the Athletics were just 1½ games behind the Tigers. A doubleheader loss to Boston on June 23 (Plank suffering one of the defeats) was such good news to Detroit that Tigers manager Hughie Jennings wired Red Sox manager Patsy Donovan a message: "I thank you. The Tigers thank you. Detroit thanks you. Keep it up."[6]

Boston did not comply. The Athletics won the next three games from the Red Sox before heading to Washington. Plank's slump continued. He lost his third straight game, 4–3, in the first game of a doubleheader on June 28, then allowed two runs in two innings of relief the following day. "Plank and Coombs, who for weeks have done all the work for the champions, appear to have overworked themselves,"[7] noted the *Washington Evening Star*. The *Philadelphia Inquirer* was more succinct in summing up Plank's performance: "He did not look good."[8]

July started off a little better—Plank won on July 3, pitching four innings of relief, allowing one run in an 8–7, 12-inning win at New York.

But two days later, that same team pounded him for four runs on nine hits in 4⅓ innings. Plank didn't pitch again until July 11, when he relieved Coombs in the eighth inning against Detroit and allowed two runs charged to Coombs and five of his own. The Athletics had gone into a slump as well, dropping five straight. (Plank was not involved in a decision in either of his appearances, including getting swept in a four-game series at Detroit.)

Suddenly, just as quickly as he went into a pitching slump, Plank snapped out of it. He wouldn't lose a game until September. It started with a six-hit shutout at St. Louis on July 15. He followed that up with a 10–2 win at Chicago on July 21, seven innings of two-run relief in a 6–5 win vs. Cleveland on July 26. and finally, in front of a packed Shibe Park, an easy 11–3 win over Detroit—striking out nine—on July 29. That last win put the Athletics just one-half game behind Detroit, but the Tigers beat Philadelphia in the next two games.

The good news for the Athletics was that St. Louis was coming to town next. The Browns had lost all 12 matchups against Philadelphia thus far. Plank pitched the opener in an August 4 doubleheader and won a quick contest, 5–1—it was the first time he allowed a run to the Browns all season—and Cy Morgan won the second, 5–2. Coupled with the Tigers losing in Boston, 7–3, the Athletics were now in first place by one game.

The Athletics did finally suffer a defeat to St. Louis—Jack Coombs taking the loss—but kept winning (or at least kept winning enough) to grow their lead to four games by mid–August. Plank should have been in a good mood. His team was in first place, he had won five straight decisions, and he had allowed two runs in his last 24⅓ innings.

Plank was not the typical ballplayer. In an era when many players used tobacco and imbibed alcohol, some to excess, off the field and a few played dirty on it, Plank was promoted as a paragon of righteousness by the press. "Many scribes have thought Plank a grouch and he may become one in his olden days. As a youngster, though, there was no one more keenly alive to doing the right thing,"[9] baseball scribe Ernest J. Lanigan wrote in 1917.

According to reports throughout his life, Plank didn't smoke or drink. Willis Johnson, a traveling secretary on some of Plank's later teams, said as much in an article in *Sporting Life* in 1916. It's hard to say whether that was the truth or just a characterization, but in 1915 Plank did attend a temperance sermon in Philadelphia given by former baseball player-turned-evangelist Billy Sunday.

Plank was also modest. There are scant few articles of the pitcher talking personally, and even then, it is not to compliment himself but rather to explain his thinking, pitching style, and so on. "It is almost impossible to get Plank to talk about himself," said Cullen Cain of the *Philadelphia Ledger*, "but he talks most interesting of the men who made up that wonderful

Mack machine of which he was a part for so many years."[10] Said Joe Bush, his teammate on the Athletics from 1912 to 1914. "I've never had the pleasure of meeting a more wonderful fellow."[11]

Not that Plank was purely an angel. He loved a good prank, for example. When a photographer tried to take his picture, Plank threw pebbles at the camera or made a funny face. He threw pebbles at other players who were getting their picture taken, in order to get them to react with some kind of twisted face. "This was just fun for Plank, however and nobody ever found fault with him for it,"[12] said *Chicago Evening Post* photographer Malcolm MacLean. "He just loved to have fun, is the best way I can express it, in that anything he could do to pull a trick on you, to just to really get a laugh, for you or for somebody else,"[13] recalled Charles C. "Junie" Bream, who was a child living in Gettysburg when Plank resided there after his baseball days.

There were ways to truly draw Plank's ire, though. "I'll never forget the day I called Plank a tight-wad, he wanted to lick me on the spot,"[14] said Joe Engel, who pitched for Washington from 1912 to 1915. Plank wasn't afraid to get into a shouting of words on the field, either, as evidenced by his battles with Germany Schaefer and Ty Cobb. And umpires. He wasn't shy to complain to umpires.

On August 20, he had his fill with Dr. Harley Parker, who was in his first—and only—year working as an American League umpire. The Athletics and White Sox were scoreless when with one out Pat Dougherty stepped to the plate. After calling a strike on Dougherty which upset fans, Parker declared Plank's next pitch a ball—ball four. There's no indication that Plank had been previously upset with Parker—he had walked just two in the game previously—but something about this decision set off the pitcher, who threw his glove to the ground quickly and angrily. Accompanying that action were, as one Harry Daniel of *Chicago's Inter Ocean* relayed it to his readers, "sassy remarks."[15] Plank's words were stronger than sassy. "Plank made his kick so strong when Parker called four balls on Dougherty that folks seated in the boxes were greiviously [sic] shocked,"[16] reported the *Philadelphia Inquirer*.

Parker ejected Plank, who rushed the umpire to offer a few more choice words before leaving the field. It didn't take long for Plank's anger to turn to embarrassment. When he reached his bench, there was manager Connie Mack waiting for him. Plank recalled the incident to teammates a few years later.

> As I walked over to put on my sweater, Connie said in a slow, deliberate way, with a piercing note of sarcasm in his voice: "Nice work, Eddie, you showed excellent judgment." That was all, just seven words, but believe me boys, I'll remember those seven words as long as I live. They hurt me worse than if he

had lit in and cursed me until he was blue in the face. I don't retain their memory with any hard feeling toward Mack—far from it. I simply remember them as forming the most cutting rebuke I have ever received. It taught me a lesson I never forgot—I never lost my head to such an extent as to get myself chased for it. And so, fellows, my little word of advice to you is that you try to keep the temperature in the neighborhood of your cranium in the vicinity of 70 degrees Fahrenheit or lower, if possible. This especially applies to the pitchers and catchers who often are wont to kick up the dust and create a row over pitched balls. When a man forces the ump to send him to the clubhouse he is hurting his teammates, not himself, and therefore it is his teammates he must consider, rather than himself. To kick and pout at a bad decision is only a mark of weakness on the part of the player, and the possible results do not justify it. The umpire can not change his decision, and to fight him means to jeopardize your chances of fair play. My policy has been "Never kick on a decision," and I have found it a very good rule to follow.[17]

This game in Chicago turned out to be the first—and only—time Plank was ejected from a game in his career.

Mack didn't stay peeved at Plank long; he allowed him to pitch the next day at St. Louis, and Plank won, 6–1, allowing just two hits and fanning nine (including all three batters in the eighth inning). The only run the Browns scored was as a result of a dropped fly ball. By this point in the season, young Stuffy McInnis was ensconced at first base. He had filled in at shortstop with Jack Barry sidelined but had played so well he took over for veteran Harry Davis at first. Barry and McInnis pulled off a 5–4–3 double play in the game, started by third baseman Frank Baker. Eddie Collins was implanted at second base. All four were having good seasons, and each was 25 years old or younger. It was a great infield—so valuable that the *Philadelphia North American* for the first time, in the recap of the above game, referred to them as the "$100,000 infield" (not for their contracts but for what they'd be worth on the open market).

Plank won his next two starts as well, 10–2 at Chicago and 6–5 vs. Cleveland. Next up for the Athletics was Detroit, the only team which could give Philadelphia a run for the pennant. Entering the series, the Athletics led the Tigers by 4½ games. Third-place Boston was 15½ games behind. Tensions were usually high when Philadelphia and Detroit met—but not always. In a game in August 1909, outfielder Rube Oldring ripped his pants and had to have them repaired. While Oldring was getting a quick sewing job, Cobb put on a catcher's mask and took warm-up pitches from, of all pitchers, Plank, and then tossed the ball to Athletics fielders. Earlier in the 1911 season, on May 18 (another game which Plank started), Cobb threw batting practice to Athletics hitters as they had no one available themselves to hurl.

However, despite these moments of levity, the games were often

11. Catching Ire

First baseman Harry Davis was one of the sluggers of the Deadball Era, leading the American League in home runs four consecutive years from 1904–1907, with a high of 12 in 1906. He and Eddie Plank were not just longtime friends, but later in his career Plank lived with Davis and his family during the season (George Grantham Bain Collection, Library of Congress).

contentious, and usually surrounded Cobb. Back on June 8, in yet another game in which Plank pitched, Cobb was caught stealing third base and spiked Baker's hand. The pair already had a history of spiking, which might be why Baker "grabbed the foot and gave it a nice ladylike twist."[18] Two innings later, Cobb again spiked Baker, this time on the foot, after a pick-off attempt. An upset Baker kicked Cobb, and soon the two combatants had their fists held up and were ready for a fight. Detroit manager Hughie Jennings, who was coaching third base, and players from both sides intervened before any punches were thrown, but Plank had a few words for Cobb and those two nearly came to blows.

Fast forward a couple of months later, and the Tigers won the first game of the three-game series in Detroit. Plank pitched Game 2. A loss and the lead would be down to 3½ games. Detroit scored three times off Plank in the second inning to take a 3–1 lead, but Philadelphia tallied six times in the third inning and five in the fifth. This would be the Athletics' day—and Plank knew it. And he wanted to gloat about it, especially to Cobb.

Detroit didn't score again off Plank. The Tigers collected nine hits in the game—Cobb had none, going 0-for-4. Cobb was 1-for-4 in their previous matchup. In the seventh inning, Cobb grounded out to Barry—which he did three times on the day. As the Georgia Peach headed out to his position in center field, Plank made sure to stick around the mound and said something to Cobb which triggered the Detroit star (albeit that might not have taken much to do so), who made a rush at Plank, looking for a fight. Infield umpire Bull Perrine quickly intervened before any fisticuffs ensued. The Athletics won, and Plank had his 19th win.

Detroit won the next game and technically was still in the race, but it didn't last long. After going 12–16 in August, the Tigers meandered to a 13–12 mark in September. Meanwhile, the Athletics went 21–6 during the month and at one stretch won 10 in a row (with a tie). Plank went 4–3 in the month, although one loss was a farcical 2–0, rain-shortened loss to Washington in the season's final week. One of the victories was a 2–0 blanking of New York, his league-leading sixth shutout. Plank also pitched the final inning of a 1–0 victory over Boston on September 1, his fourth save (as determined by modern rules), which tied for most in the AL.

The Athletics won 101 games, one fewer than the previous season, and took the pennant by 13 games. Making 40 appearances with 30 starts, Plank went 23–8, finished second on the team with 256⅔ innings, and led the Athletics with a 2.10 ERA. His 5.2 strikeouts per nine innings ranked seventh in the American League. Jack Coombs once again pitched over 300 innings (336⅔), but his ERA skyrocketed to 3.53, although he did have a 28–12 record. Chief Bender had another strong season at 17–5 with a 2.16 ERA. Cy Morgan was 15–7 with a 2.70 ERA, while Harry Krause struggled to 11–8 with a 3.04 ERA.

While the pitching was mostly good (third in the AL in ERA but seventh out of eight teams in walks), the Athletics' offense flourished, leading the league in runs (861), batting average (.296), on-base percentage (.357), slugging percentage (.398) and home runs (35). In his first full season, McInnis batted .321 with 76 runs and 77 RBI in 126 games, Collins batted .365 with a .451 on-base percentage, stole 38 bases, and scored 92 runs, and Baker hit .334 with a .508 slugging percentage, socking 42 doubles, 14 triples, and 11 homers while scoring 96 runs and driving in 115. In addition, outfielders Bris Lord (.310, 92 runs) and Danny Murphy (.329, 104 runs) both topped .300, while Rube Oldring (.297) fell just short. Even shortstop Barry batted .265, the second-highest average of his career.

The Athletics' opponent in the World Series, as predicted by members of the BBWAA before the season, would be the New York Giants. In early September, even before the pennant was assuredly wrapped up, Athletics manager Connie Mack discussed a potential opponent, with the National League race coming down to New York and Chicago. "The Athletics don't fear the Giants any more than they do the Cubs," Mack proclaimed. "They expect to win the series again, no matter which National League club they have to face. If New York wins, they fully expect to atone for their defeat at the hands of the Giants in the series of 1905."[19]

Five players remained on that Athletics team which lost in five games to the Giants in the 1905 World Series: right fielder Danny Murphy, who played second base in 1905; Harry Davis, the veteran first baseman who had been relegated to a backup role but was back in the lineup after McInnis got hurt at the tail end of the season; outfielder Topsy Hartsel, who had only 47 plate appearances during the season and wouldn't play in the World Series; Chief Bender, who won the only Series game for the 1905 Athletics; and Plank, who lost his two starts and had yet to win a game in the World Series. If anyone was looking to atone for anything against the Giants, it was Plank. And unlike in the 1910 World Series, this time he would get his chance.

◆ 12 ◆

36 and Stronger Than Ever

Connie Mack took a similar route for his team before the 1911 World Series to the previous year's. Mack had the Athletics face off against a team of other American League players in a series of games to get his team in shape leading up to the series against the New York Giants.

There wasn't much to be gleaned from the games—Mack used Jack Coombs, Eddie Plank, and Chief Bender in the first couple of exhibitions before allowing others to hurl in later games. But he had done the same in 1910 and Plank never pitched. One thing was for sure—young first baseman Stuffy McInnis hadn't healed from his wrist injury and would miss the Series (even though Mack had insisted McInnis would play), leaving the job in the hands of 38-year-old Harry Davis, who had all of 15 plate appearances from July 21 until the end of the season, and all but two of those coming in the final week (the others occurred September 25).

If Mack or the Athletics had any idea of who would pitch in Game 1—to be played in New York after the Giants won a coin toss; the remaining games alternated between the two cities—no one was letting on. At the Hotel Somerset on the night before the opener, Mack declared he wouldn't name his starting pitcher. The three contenders—Bender, Coombs and Plank—all pleaded ignorance to the writers' queries. "It may be any of us,"[1] said Bender, who did confirm that McInnis was out.

The general consensus, though, was that this year Plank would play a role, and potentially a big one. Venerable pitcher Cy Young, who just completed his final season, picked the Giants to win but also predicted, "Plank will prove the best pitcher, as he is doing better work than Coombs or Bender."[2] In its lead-up to the series, the *Philadelphia Inquirer* reasoned: "Owing to the Giants' well-known weakness against southpaws [note: according to the splits on baseball-reference.com, the Giants hit very well against left-handers during the regular season, with Al Bridwell, Josh Devore, Chief Meyers, Fred Snodgrass, Red Murray, and Art Wilson all batting better than .300 and Larry Doyle, who batted left-handed, .284] and the form in which Plank is now pitching, Plank will likely figure in the series, and there is a chance of Eddie jumping into the limelight as a big factor."[3]

Mack wasn't tipping his hand even on the day of the game. He had Bender, Coombs, and Plank all head out on the Polo Grounds field to warm up (Giants manager John McGraw had Christy Mathewson and Rube Marquard do the same). The choice was Bender, who matched up against 1905 Series hero Mathewson. Bender pitched well, but Mathewson was better. The Athletics at least scored off Mathewson, on an RBI single by Davis, no less, but lost, 2–1.

Game 2 was at Shibe Park on Monday, October 16 (no games in Philadelphia on Sunday). It was expected that Coombs would get the call from Mack. Out onto the field emerged Lawrence Phillips. For years Phillips had been, with the use of a megaphone, announcing the batteries (the pitcher and catcher) and changes in the lineup during a contest for both teams at games in Washington. American League president Ban Johnson had seen Phillips and liked the idea of more people at a park knowing

Eddie Plank, who didn't like having his picture taken, stares out from the dugout during the 1911 season. He led the American League in both shutouts and saves that year (Library of Congress).

what was going on. In other places—which didn't have Phillips—the home plate umpire turned to the crowd and made the announcements. It's hard to imagine anyone beyond the first couple of rows near the umpire hearing those words. Add in a crowd of over 26,000, as there was in Game 2, and who knows if anyone would know what was said. Johnson sold the idea to the National Commission—a three-person board, of which he was a member, which governed the game—to use Phillips at the upcoming World Series. It was agreed upon, and the 1911 Series became the first to have such announcements bellowed to the crowd, a fair many of whom now knew what was going on.

On this day, Phillips made the announcement that Plank was starting for the Athletics (Rube Marquard toiled for New York), and the crowd reacted with "a yell of surprise."[4] Plank himself might have been astonished by the choice. According to an account in the *New York Tribune*, while he was warming up (as he had in Game 1), an acquaintance of Plank's asked how he was feeling and whether he was going to pitch. "Dunno. Connie's keepin' quiet," said Plank, before adding, "If he puts me in, I'll lick 'em."[5]

Facing a Giants team wearing all-black uniforms (a nod to their 1905 champions), Plank opened the game by striking out Josh Devore—it would not be Devore's day. Plank's only blemish in the opening inning was hitting right-handed batter Fred Snodgrass, who liked to lean over the plate, on the shin. The Athletics quickly got a run for Plank when Bris Lord led off with a single, moved to second on an error by right fielder Red Murray, was sacrificed to third by Rube Oldring, and scampered home on a Marquard wild pitch.

Plank made his only mistake of the game in the top of the second. With two outs and Buck Herzog, who had doubled, on second, Plank intended to pitch around the No. 8 hitter, catcher Chief Meyers, and instead pitch to light-hitting pitcher Marquard. An intentional walk in 1911 meant just not giving the batter anything to hit. Plank attempted to do that, but one of his pitches didn't get outside and Meyers stroked a single to center, Herzog easily scoring. In a politically incorrect quote attributed to him, Plank after the game said of that at-bat, "I intended to walk the Indian on purpose as two were gone and Marquard is a weak hitter. Instead of a waste ball it cut the heart of the plate and the redskin pickled it."[6] Plank struck out Marquard to end the inning and further cement the soundness of his strategy, albeit not his execution of it.

The game remained tied at 1 until the seventh inning. With two down, Eddie Collins doubled, and Frank Baker followed with a home run—this clutch shot and another in Game 3 earned him a lifetime nickname, "Home Run" Baker—and that's all the support Plank needed. The left-hander was masterful throughout. Herzog was the only Giant to reach second base all game, and Plank allowed only three more hits after Meyers' single. Snodgrass singled twice: In the third inning, he was stranded, and in the sixth he was thrown out trying for an extra base. In the bottom of the seventh, Fred Merkle singled to open the inning. Two batters later, he was still there. He faked a steal and Plank, never known for a great pickoff move despite being left-handed, caught the runner flatfooted for the final out. While the fans cheered Plank, some also shouted "Bonehead" at the Giants infielder, a reminder of his errant play in 1908—dubbed "Merkle's Boner"—which helped cause New York to lose the pennant.

Plank ended the eighth inning by striking out Josh Devore for the fourth time—three times the Giants outfielder was caught looking. The Athletics were nearly as loud in their cheers after that strikeout as they were after Baker's home run. Devore complained that he had trouble picking up the ball from Plank's delivery, which he deemed illegal. "They shouldn't allow that Plank to pitch from first base. He's tough enough when he stays on the mound,"[7] he said in 1913 while playing with the crosstown Phillies. Plank, though, claimed it was something else. He figured out that Devore had difficulty with a curveball. He was completely fooled by it, as evidenced by umpire Tom Connolly ringing him up three times. After Devore's fourth time going down on strikes, again on a called strike, he turned to Connolly and spewed, "It is easy to see how you hold your job in the American League."[8] To which Connolly fired back, "It's hard to see how you hold yours with the Giants."[9]

Plank finished off the game with a 1-2-3 ninth inning, including a strikeout of Snodgrass, his eighth, to become just the fourth left-hander to win a World Series game (Nick Altrock and Doc White of the White Sox in 1906 and Jack Pfiester of the Cubs in 1907). Plank didn't walk a batter and threw more than 13 pitches in an inning just twice—16 in the first and 19 in the second. Overall, he threw 108 pitches, 71 for strikes, and the Giants hit only three fly balls. He faced the minimum 18 batters over the final six innings. "The inability of the Giants to time Plank's delivery made the chances rather easy,"[10] observed the *Philadelphia Inquirer*. The praise was, as expected, effusive.

In a syndicated and ghost-written article, Ty Cobb noted, "Plank's work was brilliant and too much cannot be said of the way he subdued the Giant batters."[11] Two Giants—Mathewson and Meyers—were providing first-hand (and ghostwritten) accounts in syndicated columns. Mathewson complained about the field, saying the Athletics watered down the baselines (which Mack denied) and lit into his teammate Marquard for the fastball he threw Baker which resulted in the homer, but also did compliment Plank, saying "Plank pitched a beautiful game and had a lot of things on the sphere,"[12] before going into about the "mistake" he threw Meyers.

The Giants catcher was impressed by a couple of things: The Athletics pitcher and the crowd. "Eddie Plank pitched a corking good game," Meyers wrote in his column. "Any man who can fan little Josh Devore four times in a row I'll take my cap off to. That portside crossfire of Plank's is a mighty hard thing for a lefthander to get to."[13] Meyers also spoke directly to Giants fans, asking them to take a lesson from how loud the Athletics faithful were during the game. "I never heard such a racket in my life as the Philadelphia fans made to-day. They had horns, strings of bells, rattles, tin pans, and all sorts of noise-making things. And they kept yelling to their boys, cheering even the easy plays, and hurrahing every time Eddie Plank put over a strike on us. That sort of thing helps win ball games."[14]

Some Giants were damning in their praise. "Our players simply could not see the ball. I don't believe Plank ever pitched or ever will pitch such a game again,"[15] Art Devlin, who didn't even play in the series, would later say. Said manager McGraw: "I'll admit that Plank pitched better ball than I expected, but he can't do it every day."[16]

Cincinnati manager Clark Griffith, who pitched against Plank with Chicago and New York from 1901 to 1907, had no dog in the fight, so perhaps his thoughts might have the most meaning of all. And to say he was impressed would be an understatement.

> Eddie Plank pitched the greatest game in the recent world's series between the Giants and Athletics that the game of baseball has ever known. Plank worked to perfection. He had terrific speed and his curves broke to a nicety. His sidearm delivery was very baffling ... I have seen games in which pitchers struck out more men and did more sensational pitching stunts, but for some wonderful pitching which took advantage of the opposition at every turn of the road, Plank carried off the honors. Plank had the Giants bewildered at all times. They did not seem to know where the ball was coming, and their efforts with the stick were woefully weak. I have seen the Giants in action, too, and know that when a pitcher gets them in that condition he was doing some little twirling.[17]

In attendance at Shibe Park for Game 2, as he was in 1910, was David L. Plank, Eddie's father. This time he got to not only watch his son pitch but also win a World Series game. "Great day for Eddie. He pitched a nice game of ball. I've wanted to see such a thing as this for eleven years," he said. "Now I'm happy and there isn't anything that I want except ... except to see Eddie win another one and take the series."[18]

Coombs beat Mathewson in Game 3 back at the Polo Grounds in New York—3–2 in 11 innings; Baker's homer in the ninth tied the score and cemented his legacy. Then the rains came in Philadelphia. It had rained before Game 2, part of the reason for the wet field and Mathewson's complaint, but this time it didn't stop for days—reporters began to refer to the

12. 36 and Stronger Than Ever

Athletics' home as Shibe Lake. It took a week before Game 4 was played with Bender beating Mathewson, 4–2.

Up 3–1 in the Series, Mack sent Coombs back to the mound for Game 5 at the Polo Grounds. McGraw went with Marquard. Rube Oldring's three-run homer in the third inning staked the Athletics to the lead, but the Giants got one back in the seventh and Coombs just couldn't get the final out in the ninth. With two down and a runner on second, Doc Crandall, who entered the game as a pinch hitter and stayed in to pitch (Crandall swung a pretty good bat and even started six games at shortstop in 1911), doubled and scored on a Devore single. In the 10th, Coombs, a fairly good hitter himself, hit a chopper in front of the plate and beat the throw to first base. However, he aggravated a groin injury he suffered earlier in the game when his spikes got caught in the dirt.

The Athletics failed to score, and Plank, who had warmed up in the sixth inning when Coombs injured himself, was summoned by Mack. It made sense with the left-handed-hitting Doyle leading off—although the bigger mystery might be why Plank wasn't brought in with Devore up in the ninth—but it backfired when, with two strikes on him, the Giants' second baseman chopped the ball down the third-base line for a double. Snodgrass bunted, which Plank fielded and threw to third base but too late. After Red Murray's fly ball to right field was too shallow to score Doyle, Merkle lifted one deep enough and just fair to score the tagging-up Doyle with the winning run. Well, kind of. When Doyle slid home with the apparent winning run, one leg was to the side of home plate and the other was raised above it. Home plate umpire Bill Klem would have called Doyle out if the Athletics tagged him or protested, but none was forthcoming. Mack and Davis both said they saw Doyle miss the plate but decided the Giants deserved the run, and they also didn't want to cause any unrest. This game being at the Polo Grounds and there being some history of umpire's decisions on apparent winning runs not going their way (see Merkle's Boner), the latter is more likely the case. "If any of my players had raised the point about Doyle's run," Mack said, "I would have felt so sore that I believe I would have tried to take him by the scruff of the neck and thrown him over the grandstand."[19]

For Game 6 at Shibe Park, despite pitching to a few batters the previous day, Plank was thought to be the choice to finish off the Giants. The *New York Tribune* reported it as such, and McGraw used left-handed pitchers for the majority of New York's batting practice. "We all figured that Plank would work and McGraw had my name in the lineup to hold down left field. I was dying to play, too. In fact, I kidded Plank before the game—said I was going to get him,"[20] said the Giants' Art Devlin, a third baseman who had never played outfield in his career to that point and didn't play at all in the 1911 Series. Much to the Giants' surprise, and Devlin's dismay, Mack decided on Bender.

There are a couple of theories as to why Mack went with Bender. One was that he saw McGraw using the lefties in batting practice and thus thought it the best strategy. Another, oft-quoted over the years, is that Mack liked using Bender in a big game, and a possible clinching Game 6 certainly qualified. Months later, that's the explanation the manager himself gave. "If I had to bet my life on a ball game and wanted to pick a man to pitch that game for me," he explained, "I would take Chief Bender for that one game."[21] There's one other explanation, though, and it's the one Mack offered immediately after the game. "I warmed up both him and Plank, and Bender showed me more. I simply picked the fitter of the two."[22]

The pitching choice probably didn't matter. The Athletics pounded Red Ames and Hooks Wiltse over the first seven innings. Bender allowed just four hits as Philadelphia won the series in a blowout, 13–2. Bender, Coombs, and Plank held a Giants team which led the National League in batting average (.279) and runs (4.9/game) to 13 runs in six games and 33 hits in 55⅔ innings, a .175 batting average. The Athletics were back-to-back champions, joining the 1907–1908 Chicago Cubs as the only repeat champions in the short history of the World Series. Over a decade later, McGraw said, "I have no hesitation in expressing the opinion that the Athletics of this period were one of the greatest clubs of all times."[23]

Although Plank had mentioned the past couple of years that 1912 was his likely last season in the majors, since the Athletics won the World Series and Plank got his elusive postseason victory, rumors began to spread that he would retire a year early. Mack, for one, was having none of the talk. "Plank has had one of the best years of his career this season, and I don't see why he should want to quit," the Athletics manager said the day after the Series win. "There is no sign of Eddie going back, and I don't see why he should want to give up a good salary unless there was some cause. Plank, I believe, will have another good season next year, and he may be a star for a number of seasons more to come. No, I don't believe Plank has any intention of quitting the game."[24]

Indeed, winning the series might have given Plank pause, if indeed he was interested in earning more money. The Athletics had just won back-to-back World Series, and that meant more cash in his pocket. There seemed to be no slowing down this team in the near future. "In short, the Athletics are a well-rounded baseball machine, and I believe that they are in line for another world's championship and possibly two,"[25] predicted Chicago Cubs player-manager Frank Chance. For beating the Giants, each Athletics player received $3,654.58—the previous high for a winner's share was $2,142.85 in 1907 (the loser's share in 1911 even beat that, at $2,436.39).

Plank, as well as some of his teammates, used the newfound money to purchase an automobile, which was a luxury item at the time. According to the Federal Highway Administration, there were only 618,727 automobiles registered in 1911.[26] Five years later there were over 3.3 million registered, and in 1922 it topped 10 million. Each Athletic also received a gold watch fob which included a diamond baseball within and the inscription "World's Champion, 1911" as well at the player's name and "Philadelphia Athletics" on the back side. The fob was presented in a leather box engraved with the player's name and encased in white satin.

After another banquet in Philadelphia in which the Athletics were honored—roughly 300 people attended the event at the Hotel Majestic on November 2—Plank headed back to Gettysburg and to his farm. Eddie Collins visited Plank a week later, and the pair went off hunting and driving around in Plank's new car. Plank also held his annual oyster bake—he had a new brick building constructed, presumably to be used for doing laundry, but the local paper noted it also had a stove which could roast shelled oysters. When he wasn't hunting, driving, roasting oysters, or farming, Plank took up another sport—duckpin bowling. It wasn't quite as exciting an off-season as a couple of his teammates had—Chief Bender, Jack Coombs, and Cy Morgan were hired to perform in vaudeville—but then again, that was true to Plank's character.

Plank said he was going to pitch in 1912, and indeed his signed contract was received by Mack in late January. There had been rumors that the New York Yankees had tried to acquire Plank—with Ban Johnson as an intermediary—but there's no evidence of terms ever even being discussed. A couple of players were gone, however. Harry Davis signed on to manage Cleveland, and longtime outfielder Topsy Hartsel was sold to Toledo. That left Plank as the only member of the 1901 Athletics, his initial season and the first year of the American League. Outfielder Danny Murphy, who was named captain in place of Davis, arrived in 1902.

Critics kept anticipating the bottom falling out on Plank, who turned 37 in August. The *Washington Times* mused that Plank "is expected by many American League fans to crack this coming year and rapidly fade away before the sluggers of the circuit. Plank has been with Connie Mack ten years, taking his turn with great regularity, never refusing to work when able to get anything on the ball. Last year he lost much of his effectiveness and all signs point to his disappearance in 1912."[27] In predicting that the Athletics' pitching staff would be weakened in 1912, Boston Red Sox right-hander Eddie Cicotte offered the opinion that "Plank didn't show a great deal at the end of the season."[28]

Plank proved not to be a problem for the Athletics in 1912. Early on, it was injuries, inexperience, and ineffectiveness. Chief Bender had tendonitis in his throwing shoulder and wouldn't make his first start until two weeks into the season, on April 25. He made another start May 1 but was sidelined again, this time for three weeks. Jack Coombs was injured in his second start, on April 20, and didn't pitch again until May 14. Cy Morgan pitched a one-hitter with 11 strikeouts in his first start, April 12, then three scoreless innings of relief on April 20. It slowly went downhill after that. On May 2, he gave up five runs in four innings, and in his next start allowed 11 runs on 10 hits and eight walks. He would mix in an occasional good start but there were more bad than good and by mid–July, sporting a 3–8 record and 3.75 ERA, he was sold to Kansas City of the American Association. Morgan made one more start in the majors for Cincinnati in 1913. He allowed four runs in 2⅓ innings. Harry Krause didn't last as long in Philadelphia as Morgan. The phenom of 1909 could never replicate that success. In his first two starts—both against Boston on April 16 and April 30—he didn't make it past the first inning in either, allowing seven runs in 1⅔ innings combined. He was sold to Toledo in late May.

Mack had to resort to unproven youngsters to fill out his staff. Carroll "Boardwalk" Brown got four starts in late April and early May—he allowed five or more runs in three of them and went 1–3. To give the team innings,

Left-handed pitcher Harry Krause in 1911. Krause stormed upon the scene in 1909, posting a league-best 1.39 ERA. Krause in part credited the tutelage of Plank for his success (George Grantham Bain Collection, Library of Congress).

Mack used a lot of unproven rookies in relief situations—a rare role in the Deadball Era. Twenty-year-old Byron Houck and 18-year-old Herb Pennock had mixed results, although Houck eventually landed in the rotation. On May 3, enjoying an 18–5 lead, Mack put in Roger Salmon, a left-hander who had twirled at Princeton, for his major-league debut. He walked four and allowed two hits, retiring just one batter before being pulled. Lefty Russell, a major acquisition by Mack in 1910 from Baltimore of the International League (the first of many lefties thought to be Plank's eventual replacement) faced five batters and got none out. Ten runs had scored and there was a runner—Hack Simmons—on first base. Mack had seen enough and called in Plank, who fanned Birdie Cree. On the third strike, catcher Ben Egan threw out Simmons trying to steal.

Egan was only playing because Jack Lapp was injured and Ira Thomas had caught 10 straight games. The hitting for the Athletics had been a problem as well. In early May, only Eddie Collins and Stuffy McInnis were batting over .300. Danny Murphy hit that mark with a hot streak at the end of May, but on June 3 he hurt his knee while trying to steal and was lost for the season. He was slashing .323/.401/.446 at the time. The inconsistency all over the lineup led to a poor start to the season. At the end of May, the Athletics were 17–16, in third place, and 7½ games behind the leaders, Chicago.

Despite it all, Plank was the constant, taking his regular turn in the rotation and being used in relief in close games when needed. The 36 year old opened the season with a 4–1 win over Boston, which had won its first three games. He tossed a four-hit shutout in New York on April 24 in a tidy one hour and 29 minutes, allowing only one runner for New York (known as either the Highlanders, as referred to by the *New York Sun*, or Yankees, as called by the *New York Tribune*) then on a wet day at brand-new Fenway Park held down Boston once again, 7–1. "Other southpaws, and righthanders as well, usually lose control of everything else in the face of a steady rain, but Plank never seemed in difficulty but once,"[29] noted the *Boston Post*.

Not that there weren't speed bumps along the way. The day after his two-out performance in the Athletics' 18–15 win over New York, Plank started and allowed five runs on 15 hits, three walks and a hit batter (but still won, 10–5). A week later, he allowed just one run on three hits in seven innings against Chicago, but then gave up a run on three hits in the eighth and was hammered around for seven runs in the ninth as the White Sox, winners of six straight, handed Plank his first loss, 9–5. He was also knocked out early in his next two starts, lasting just 3⅓ innings against St. Louis on May 21 and four innings at Boston on May 27.

June, however, was a different story. Plank made seven starts and one relief appearance and went 7–0. He beat Detroit twice (and had words with Cobb, of course) and Washington twice, including a 6–0 shutout on June 20. After Plank and Jack Coombs, who pitched the final two innings, topped the Senators and Walter Johnson 2–1 on June 29, the Athletics were in second place and six games behind Boston. The Athletics and Red Sox played six games—with two doubleheaders—between July 3–6. Plank beat Joe Wood, just one of five losses the Boston ace suffered in 1912, but Philadelphia lost four of six. By mid-July the Athletics trailed Boston by double digits. A third straight American League pennant was not in the offing. That didn't mean there weren't some interesting moments.

Plank faced Detroit five times in July—in fact, it was the only team he pitched against from July 17 until the end of the month. He started the first game of a doubleheader on July 17 but was pulled after two innings in which he gave up five hits. But these weren't normal at-bats by Tigers players. As Plank finished his crossfire delivery, Detroit hitters ran up—and out of—the batter's box to hit Plank's offering before it completed its sharp curve. Team captain Murphy, still with the club despite his season-ending injury, argued vociferously with the home plate umpire, who happened to be, of course, Silk O'Loughlin, he of the 1907 Athletics-Tigers controversy which didn't go Philadelphia's way. He was hearing none of Murphy's arguments and ordered him to "Get out of the grounds."[30] Seeing this take place, Tigers hitters became even more obvious in their new batting strategy. Pitcher Jean Dubuc and shortstop Donie Bush both tripled. Plank was hit for in the bottom of the second and replaced by 21-year-old Hardin Barry, who made this third and final appearance in the majors, allowing nine runs on 14 hits in seven innings.

Between games of the doubleheader, Athletics president Ben Shibe sent a telegram to American League president Ban Johnson relaying his disgust at the situation and specifically at O'Loughlin. There is no mention in reports about what, if anything, was done or said between Johnson and O'Loughlin. Interestingly, Plank relieved Chief Bender in the second game and retired seven of the eight batters he faced in a 5–4 victory. Three days later, Plank beat the Tigers again, 4–3. Plank's next start came in Detroit on July 27, and it might have featured the only time he threw a spitball in a game. That is, if Eddie Collins is to be believed.

Plank was touched for five runs in the first inning by Detroit but buckled down after that and didn't allow the Tigers to score. The Athletics managed to tie the game and send it to extra innings, where they tallied four times in the 10th inning. In a syndicated article, Collins told this story concerning Plank and the Tigers:

> I recall a game he saved by pitching a spitter, the first and last he ever threw. There were two out and runners on second and third when Cobb came up, and we were one run to the good. Plank and Catcher Jack Lapp held a conference. It

wasn't much of a conference, but it deceived Tyrus. Cobb thought he was to be passed, but there was Crawford waiting, and Sam like to hit against Eddie. This was the dialogue: "If I get two strikes on Ty I am going to throw a spitter," Plank calmly announced. Lapp nearly laughed out loud. Being assured that Eddie was in earnest, Jack whispered: "I will be looking for it," and went back to his position. The first two pitches were balls, with Ty tense and anxious. Then, after stalling around extra long, Plank shot over a strike, catching Cobb off guard. Cobb was vexed. Next, a nice tantalizing curve, and the ball was slammed down the right field line, foul by inches. The next pitch was a ball, making the count three and two. As Lapp returned the ball on that pitch Plank moistened his fingers and no one saw him. He fiddled around, changed his pose, then changed back, but at last he pitched. That spitter sure broke. It would have been a credit to [noted spitballer Ed] Walsh and it went over the pan for a perfect strike. Though Lapp had given the sign, he had not anticipated the terrific break, and the ball knocked him over as he blocked it. Cobb, however, was paralyzed, and Jack pounced on the ball and touched him out. The game was over. It was Plank's first and last spitter.[31]

The inherent problem with Collins' tale—besides it being told in 1927, 15 years after the fact—is that this was not a one-run game. However, there were only two games in Plank's career in which Lapp was his catcher, the Athletics beat Detroit, and Cobb struck out. The other was a 5–2 win on May 20, 1910. In this instance, though, Cobb did make the final out. Crawford, as usual, batted behind Cobb in both games. True story or fiction? Backing up the point that Plank never used the pitch was an incident in 1911. White Sox outfielder Ping Bodie singled off Plank in a game in Chicago on August 19 of that year. When he reached first base, Stuffy McInnis asked what was the pitch Plank threw? Bodie responded that it was a spitball, to which McInnis answered, "Ed Plank never threw a spitter in his life."[32]

Two days after the supposed thrown spitball, Plank pitched the final 2⅔ innings of a 7–6 win over the Tigers. The *Detroit Free Press* made sure to mention, "There were no complaints yesterday of batsmen stepping out of the box in hitting the ball. So far as cold be seen from the grandstand all the players kept within the lines of their position."[33] That made four straight appearances with a win for Plank, who then won his next three starts, including a 2–0 shutout over Cleveland for his 20th victory of the season—the second time since 1907 he reached 20 wins.

Plank lost two of his next three starts but in September he went 5–0 and saved a game, heading into a start against Washington on September 27. However, the Athletics—nor any other team—could keep up with Boston, which ran away with the American League. Mack pointed to the disappointing season of Cy Morgan, the young pitchers' inconsistency, several players being out of condition—code for drinking too much—including

Chief Bender and Rube Oldring (Mack suspended both), Danny Murphy's injury, and more. However, he admitted, "Even if my team had been in the pink of condition and playing the class of ball that won them the world's championships in 1910 and 1911, it is doubtful to my mind whether they could have beaten out Boston's great team this year. We all have to take off our hats to Jake Stahl."[34] He saved his praise for Plank and Jack Coombs, who did "everything that has been expected of them in the pitching line."[35]

Plank proved Mack's last statement in his final start of the 1912 season. A doubleheader was on tap but with a light drizzle descending from the clouds, Shibe Park was desolate. It was estimated fewer than 200 people were in their seats by the time the game started, and although the official attendance was 2,500, the *Washington Herald* estimated one-fifth the size. The paper remarked that the few in attendance, however, "were rewarded with the best ball game played on the Shibe Park enclosure."[36]

It didn't start that way. Plank allowed four runs in the first two innings, including three in the second. As he walked back to the bench, Washington manager Clark Griffith bellowed across the field to Mack, "Put the blanket on him, Connie, and send him to the barn. He was a good old wagon, but he done broke down."[37] Mack did have a pitcher warming in the second inning, but he stuck with Plank. And the veteran buckled down.

While Plank held Washington off the scoreboard, the Athletics got one run in the seventh inning and three more in the ninth off Bob Groom—an RBI single by Oldring, back from his suspension, tied it. Walter Johnson replaced Groom in the 10th, and the zeroes kept piling up. Both teams had a scoring chance here and there, but the game kept going and going ... through the 14th, when Plank got Eddie Foster to fly out with two down and the bases loaded ... through the 16th, with both Plank and Johnson getting out of jams, the latter striking out Oldring and Jack Barry with the winning run on third ... and through the 18th, when George McBride was pegged out at the plate by Oldring trying to score on an overthrow after he stole second. In the top of the 19th, Foster hit what looked like an inning-ending double play, but Barry's throw was low and caused Collins to misfire on his relay throw. The ball bounded away from McInnis, and Johnson, who was on second, was able to race around to score before the first baseman could retrieve it. Johnson set down the Athletics in order in the home half.

Plank pitched all 19 innings, tossing 16 consecutive shutout frames. He allowed just seven hits in the final 17 innings and at one point gave up just two hits over 11 innings. Bob Thayer of the *Washington Times* called it "one of the greatest pitching exhibitions ever seen," adding, "Plank is a hero."[38] The game lasted, depending on the source, either three hours, 57 minutes or four hours, two minutes. Either way, it was long, and the planned second

12. 36 and Stronger Than Ever

game of the doubleheader was called off. The game ran so late, Washington missed its train out of town and had to catch a later one.

The Athletics had a handful of games left and finished with 90 wins, one back of Washington (this caused McInnis to lose a bet with Griffith) and 15 behind the eventual World Series champion Red Sox. Plank had given it his all for the Athletics and Mack in that 19-inning affair, and the manager, wisely, kept him out of the final seven games. The question now was: had Plank thrown his final pitch in the major leagues?

◆ 13 ◆

Slowing Down

Eddie Plank was one of two pitchers on the Athletics who began the 1912 season in their 30s. Cy Morgan, 33, was jettisoned to the minor leagues in the summer. Plank, who turned 37 on August 31, was the unquestioned ace of the staff.

He led the team in ERA (2.22), just one of three Philadelphia hurlers under 3.00 (Chief Bender, 2.74; Byron Houck, 2.94), and also topped the team in wins (26) and shutouts (5) while tying Jack Coombs for the most complete games (23) even though he had two fewer starts. Plank's season gained notice, even from American League umpires, who included him as their first-team choice for pitcher on their 1912 all-star squad. "He was as good last year as he ever was in his major-league career,"[1] Washington manager Clark Griffith said early in 1913.

Plank's 1912 season was one for the ages—or maybe make that aged. Since the advent of professional baseball leagues in 1871 with the National Association, never had a pitcher who began the year at age 36 or older won 20 or more games with an .800 or better winning percentage. At 26–6 (.813), Plank became the first. No one did it again until the next century, when 38-year-old Roger Clemens went 20–3 (.870) in 2001 (38-year-old Randy Johnson accomplished the feat the next season with a 24–5 record [.828]; it hasn't been done since).

Plank wasn't done pitching in 1912 yet, however. There were the usual barnstorming games—he pitched a few innings in a game at Shenandoah in front of a reported crowd of nearly 10,000 and later blanked New Brunswick on four hits—as well as the renewal of a city series between the Athletics and Phillies. Plank pitched the first game at the Phillies' Philadelphia Park and won 6-1 (he actually committed an error in the game, something he didn't do during the regular season) and was in midseason form, striking out seven. The Athletics won four straight games in front of small crowds, with each team member pocketing all of $82 (the losing Phillies got $54 per man). Each team did make a profit, but "less than $500 each."

13. Slowing Down

Connie Mack, who in November increased his stake in the club and Shibe Park from 25 percent to 50 percent, declared that there would be no more postseason series between the Athletics and Phillies.

There was one more opportunity for the Athletics to play ball. Harry Davis had signed a contract for his Cleveland team in Cuba for some games, much as he did with the Athletics in 1910 when he was playing first base. However, Davis was ousted as manager before season's end, and the new boss, Joe Birmingham, called off the arrangement. Mack took over the contract and sent the Athletics to Cuba.

Things went much better for Plank and the Athletics on this trip compared to their 1910 sojourn as they won 10 of the 12 games played. Plank, Bender, and Coombs were the only pitchers to make the trip, and when they weren't pitching they were playing in the field (the team brought only two outfielders, Frank Baker would miss a couple of games due to injury, and Jack Barry left the island early after his sister-in-law was in a car accident). "We haven't seen any pitching yet that we can't solve, and, say, the way Bender, Coombs and Plank are fooling those sluggers, it's really a shame,"[2] second baseman Eddie Collins said towards the end of the trip. Bender and Coombs appeared in all 12 games. Plank made only two starts and won them both (Bender suffered both losses).

On November 3, the second game on the trip, Plank tossed a three-hit shutout against the Habana Reds. "When a twirler is in the shape Eddie was in this game, I guess nothing else shall be told to explain the rest of the contest,"[3] relayed Victor Munoz, sportswriter for the Cuban newspaper *El Mundo*. Plank won his other start as well, a 7–4 victory over Almendares on November 11. Overall, he struck out 14 but was surprisingly wild, walking 10.

Unlike Bender and Coombs, Plank appeared in only two games in the field, perhaps due to not feeling well much of the trip. Many players came down with what was reported as colds, but Plank had something more severe, left Cuba and headed back early to Jacksonville, from where the team made its way home to Philadelphia. "The climate did not seem to agree with us. You can gamble that there is not one member of the party who is not glad to get back home,"[4] said Collins, who nevertheless hit .417 (15-for-36) with 14 runs in the 12 games.

One person who had a decidedly worse time than the Athletics in Cuba was umpire Joe O'Brien, who was brought along to help officiate. After O'Brien ruled in favor of Philadelphia on a couple of close calls in an 8–7 win over Almendares on November 7, one Cuban newspaper brought up the idea of hanging the umpire. "I don't mind being hit with pop bottles and bawled out by rival captains, and even beaned with a bat, but when it comes to the point where you are lynched if you give a close decision, I think it is time to resign and get a safe job such as working in a dynamite factory or soldiering in the Turkish army," O'Brien said. "I am sorry that I ever came to Cuba."[5]

Plank headed back to Gettysburg with another $500 in his pocket, the guaranteed payout for the trip to Cuba. Money was never an issue for Plank. He was making a good salary playing baseball—in 1912 it was over four times the average U.S. income of $1,033[6]—and also had whatever he earned from his farm, where he lived and worked in the off-season. Plank also had the reputation of being a bit miserly. "I hear that Plank does his own washing while on the road,"[7] one unnamed Washington player was quoted as saying.

Baseball wasn't a necessity. He had been saying for years that 1912 would be his final season and had lamented to Coombs that every year he pitched seemed to take two years off the life of his body and mind. His major-league career started late, at age 25 in 1901, but still he had thrown over 3,400 innings—not including spring training, postseason exhibitions, and World Series. His 3,432⅔ innings were already more than future Hall of Famers Mordecai "Three Finger" Brown, Don Drysdale, Whitey Ford, Rube Marquard, and Pedro Martinez, among many others, accumulated over their careers. There was also a rumor that marriage was in Plank's near future, and his soon-to-be wife preferred Plank not play baseball. "Plank will not talk on this subject," one news report noted, "but merely says that he thinks he has been in the game long enough."[8]

Connie Mack revealed that Plank indeed told him during the 1912 season that it would be his final one in the majors. "We had a talk about that quitting proposition last season and Plank agreed that he would quit when I thought the proper time has come,"[9] the manager claimed. Nevertheless, Mack started to plan the 1913 season thinking he wouldn't have Plank. He probably didn't relish the prospect. He had only two other reliable starters—Bender and Coombs—to go with a bunch of unproven youngsters. Mack sent Plank a contract and, as the days and weeks went by without it being returned, tried to follow up. January turned to February, and spring training was now just weeks away. The two finally connected in early February, but no deal was struck.

"But you know how Eddie is about these matters. He's never in a hurry to make up his mind," Mack said. "He takes his time and considers a thing thoroughly from every angle. I hope that after he has given the subject every consideration he will send in his signed contract."[10] Mack went on to say that Plank didn't need the money thanks to his previous earnings and his farm. "That is why if he once makes up his mind to quit it will not be a matter of money and nothing will tempt him to return to the game,"[11] Mack

13. Slowing Down

said. Then, of course, Mack tried to appeal to Plank with the promise of more money.

The manager reminded Plank that the Athletics had a good team—a potential World Series team. That meant a sizeable check. Even if the Athletics lost the World Series, each player's take-home check would be more than the average U.S. salary. Mack wasn't wrong. In the past four years, Philadelphia had won 95, 102, 101, and 90 games with two World Series titles. Three of the four members of the $100,000 infield were entering their prime—Collins (.348, 137 runs, 101 walks, 63 steals in 1912) and shortstop Jack Barry would be 26; third baseman Frank Baker (.347, 40 doubles, 21 triples, 10 homers, 116 runs, 130 RBI, 40 steals) turned 27—while Stuffy McInnis (.327, 101 RBI) was just 22. The outfield had Rube Oldring, who had batted .301, and couple of youngsters, Amos Strunk and Eddie Murphy, Mack was high on. Add Plank to Coombs and Bender and have a couple of young pitchers come around, and it was a convincing argument. Mack also had a couple of veterans contact Plank and try to cajole him into returning.

With spring training inching closer, roughly a week away, Mack called Plank. The pair talked for just over 30 minutes—Mack said he was charged $7.75 for the long-distance connection—until finally Plank agreed to return. He got a little boost in pay—up to $5,000—although Mack claimed the prospect of another World Series check was the final determining factor. Plank, however, later said he only returned out of loyalty to Mack.

Continuing to play baseball also meant Plank was able to keep earning a little more income through endorsements. He had the Coca-Cola advertisement, for one. Since 1911, he had also been appearing—in illustrated form—in ads for The Royal Tailors, a clothier based out of New York and Chicago. He was one of a small, exclusive group of notable men who appeared, which included fellow baseball stars Ty Cobb, Walter Johnson, and Christy Mathewson, comedians Eddie Foy and Nat Wills, and author Jack London. In one illustrated ad, an admiring woman in the background cranes her neck to gaze at a nattily dressed Plank, who is facing the reader. The ad is titled "Lady Killer Eddie Plank." While this may or may not have been true, the caption written below the frame might have summed up the pitcher best of all: "Eddie Plank, the youth-eternal."

What no one knew at the time was that Mack and the Athletics needed Plank more than expected. Jack Coombs started the Athletics' first two games at Boston and left early in both. He lasted five innings in the April 10 opener and just one-third of an inning on April 12. Plank eventually was called on in both contests—Chief Bender didn't show much in the first game, allowing four baserunners and getting only two outs, while Herb Pennock rushed in without being warmed up in the latter and walked

New York Giants manager John McGraw and pitcher Christy Mathewson during the 1911 World Series. The Giants wore black uniforms as a nod to—and perhaps a reminder of—their championship in 1905, when they beat the Athletics four games to one (Michael T. "Nuf Ced" McGreevy Collection, Boston Public Library).

both batters he faced. Plank won both, allowing two unearned runs in 3⅓ innings and then pitching shutout ball for 8⅔.

Coombs fell ill—he was diagnosed with typhoid fever—and his season was over. That left Bender and Plank and seven pitchers (10 were the most Mack had kept on a roster to start the season) who were all age 24 or

13. Slowing Down

younger. Plank ended up appearing in 41 games, his most since 1907, with 11 of those coming in relief (to that point in his career he had never had more than 10 relief appearances in any season).

After pitching in four of Philadelphia's first six games—with only one start (in which he lasted only three innings)—Plank showed that at age 37, he still had it. From April 25–June 30, he appeared in 15 games, making 13 starts and completing 11 of those. In that span, he pitched 119 innings and allowed just 77 hits while striking out 73. The Athletics went 12–3 in those games.

On April 25 at Shibe Park, he spun a three-hit shutout over New York and struck out 10. It was the first time since 1905 a pitcher 37 years or older had reached double digits in strikeouts. It wouldn't be until 1927 until someone not named Plank accomplished that feat. He pitched eight shutout innings in his next start against Washington, losing a 2–0 battle to Walter Johnson in part because no one covered second base on a pickoff attempt by catcher Jack Lapp in the ninth inning. Plank struck out 12 and walked just one. "Eddie Plank cannot be passed by without some word of praise," observed the *Washington Times*. "The veteran is pitching as good ball now as he was ever capable of pitching and is due the honors that are coming to him. Of all the Athletics pitchers Plank seems to stand alone as the best of the lot. Always in condition, always willing, he is at top form all the while."[12]

Earlier in the spring, Phillies manager Charley Dooin had proclaimed,

The Philadelphia Athletics take the field before a 1911 World Series game at Shibe Park. Eddie Plank is to the far left, carrying a glove in his right hand (Michael T. "Nuf Ced" McGreevy Collection, Boston Public Library).

"I don't hesitate to declare that Plank is the greatest southpaw in the two leagues, barring perhaps Nap Rucker. The latter is the only one I would rank with Eddie. If I had Plank I wouldn't trade him for six Marquards."[13] New York Yankees manager Frank Chance concurred with Dooin's assessment.

Chance had seen Plank shut out his team already, and on May 5 in New York he handcuffed the Yankees, allowing two hits and walking no one in an 8–1 Athletics win (Philadelphia scored seven runs in the final two innings as Hal Chase, notoriously accused as one of baseball's biggest cheats, made mistake after mistake and "appeared lazy or indifferent from the start."[14]). On June 30, Plank blanked the Yankees again (but not Chase, who was traded to the Chicago White Sox on June 1), 6–0, allowing three hits and striking out seven. "I did see a left-hander this spring, though, who if he always pitches the kind of ball he pitched against us, is the greatest southpaw in the country. That's Eddie Plank of Philadelphia," said Chance, who managed the Chicago Cubs to four World Series and two championships. "I think him superior to anyone I ever saw."[15]

Plank reportedly had a sore arm in mid–May but put any fears to doubt with back-to-back shutouts at Detroit on May 22 and at home vs. Washington on May 27. He allowed just three singles against the Tigers (although he walked five) in winning, 7–0. Against the Senators, he allowed just two hits and faced just 28 batters (thanks to three double plays and a caught stealing) in an 8–0 victory.

When the Athletics beat Detroit, 8–7, in 10 innings on June 6 in a game Plank started, but didn't finish, Tigers manager Hughie Jennings declared, "The Athletics are the class of the league. They will win the pennant."[16] It was quite the proclamation by the Detroit skipper. While Philadelphia was in first place, it was only by a game and a half. In mid–June, the Athletics took three of four games from second-place Cleveland, Plank winning the series opener, 6–1, and the finale, 3–2, on June 16—amazingly, that was his final victory as a starting pitcher at Shibe Park in 1913.

The Athletics reached 30 games over .500–45–15—when Plank won the first game of a doubleheader at Washington on June 26. After Plank's shutout of New York on June 30, the Athletics were 48–17 and holding an 8½ game lead in the American League. Plank was 12–2—both his losses came in 2–0 games—with two saves (by modern rules). There seemed to be little question who would win the pennant. "Begins to look now as though the whole thing had simmered down to a question of whether Bender or Plank will pitch the opening game of the World's Series,"[17] wrote Edgar Wolfe, using his pseudonym, Jim Nasium, all the way back in the June 13 edition of the *Philadelphia Inquirer*.

There was one question which seemed to be prevalent: How could they stop games from taking so long? Games played in under two hours were the norm, but early contests were dragging to around two-and-a-half hours. In the Athletics' first five games, all against Boston, the durations were recorded as 2:20, 2:20, 2:35, 2:35, and 2:10. Writing in *The Sporting News*, Philadelphia-based writer William Weart laid a lot of the blame on Boston's batteries, particularly pitchers Ray Collins and Buck O'Brien and catcher Bill Carrigan. "Time after time Ray stood on the rubber apparently straining his eyes trying to detect the finger motions of Carrigan, while when O'Brien went to the mound, Buck and Bill each left his position several times to hold conferences," wrote Weart. "No slower work by battery men than Carrigan, Ray Collins and O'Brien did, could be imagined."[18]

Umpire Tommy Connolly chimed in that pitchers were throwing to first base far too often. "As soon as they see a runner on first, even if he is the slowest man on the opposing team, they start tossing the ball to the first baseman. The pitchers and catchers are so determined not to have a base stolen on them that they cannot think of anything else but trying to catch the runner off the base. This practice wastes an awful lot of time."[19]

American League president Ban Johnson thought he could help fix the issue by instituting a rule that foul balls were to be left where they were instead of having a fielder retrieve it. The plan didn't work. The *Chicago Tribune*'s I.E. Sanborn had his own theories for the problem. He thought pitchers and catchers were taking their time, mainly to either load up a spitball or feign that action. "If one of the two hurlers is constantly bluffing the spitter that means a waste of 500 seconds between the signal and the delivery of the ball," Sanborn hypothesized. "And 500 seconds is nearly ten minutes. If both pitchers in a game are alleged spitball artists, the aggregate delay will be between 15 and 20 minutes in a game. This idea of time is all inaction."[20] Sanborn also bemoaned the use of too many pinch runners and pinch hitters. "The strategy of the game, or what they love to call the strategy of it, is what is causing the increased inactivity on the diamond."[21]

Interestingly, Plank was not used as an example of elongated games—even though he was accused of doing so throughout his career. Even back in 1901, in one of his first starts against Washington fans were clamoring about the slowness of Plank's delivery, counting as they waited for him to pitch. But not every game Plank pitched went long. In researching this book, times of games, when listed, were noted. Did Plank pitch in games that exceeded two hours? Certainly. But he also had a great number falling under, in the 1:30–1:45 range (not including exhibitions in which he invariably worked faster).

But when he wanted, Plank was the master of movements on the mound. In 1917, a wire story tried to describe what he did before each pitch: "Hitches belt, adjusts cap, walks back to box in half circle, faces batter and stretches arms, steps on rubber with left foot and taps right foot to ground eight times, when ball is delivered to batter, tucks in shirt with every third ball pitched, gazes into sky over third base on every called ball, dislodges imaginary pebble in pitcher's box every time batter has three balls and one strike or three and two."[22]

Umpire Billy Evans added to the imagery, saying Plank shook off the catcher three or four times, clawed at the mound with his spikes and, after pulling on his pants, invariably spit. "It is easy to imagine the mental state of the batsman as Plank went through these mannerisms," Evans wrote in 1926. "I doubt if any pitcher was ever cussed more by the opposing batters than Plank. He merely smiled as they became riled."[23]

An unidentified player from this era groused to *Baseball Digest* in 1952 that "Plank would stand out on the mound so long that your eyes would actually water between pitches. He was the first pitcher I ever saw against whom batters would call time and step out of the box, a practice which was not common in his time."[24]

Not everyone complained, though. Writer John B. Sheridan, who did have issues with part of Plank's delivery—he repeatedly griped over the years that, with the bases empty, Plank took five steps during his windup—defended the pitcher. "Eddie Plank is slower and far fussier than [Roy] Mitchell, but Philadelphians never ask that Plank shall be taken out because he takes his time about delivering the ball," Sheridan wrote in 1914. "The slow pitcher, the man who moves deliberately, especially when batters are in a hurry to hit, is the right man in the right place when the opposition needs hits."[25]

Plank's teammates didn't mind either. Jack Coombs said Plank's style helped make him a better pitcher. "Eddie's greatest strategy was that he always tarried, made the batter wait as long as possible and then let him have it when he wasn't set," Coombs said. "His argument to me for this, was that it made the batter overanxious and he advised me to try the same tactics. I began to do so and found that I had more success. This one point from Eddie was perhaps the foundation of my pitching ability."[26]

Said Eddie Collins: "Plank's style of pitching was unique. To watch his preparations for delivering the ball amused us and aggravated opposing players beyond word. To get his feet properly placed was a task. Then came numerous poses, gyrations and other motions and a change of mind and he would start over. The umpires fussed, the players raved, but Eddie ignored them all. He pitched as he pleased—and won."[27]

But as mentioned, not every game Plank pitched was interminably (for the time) long. Evans brought up the point that "the older he gets the more deliberate he becomes."[28] Which makes sense—as most pitchers age, their stuff lessens. The fastball slows down, and guile must be relied on more often. This was Plank's way of using deception to help the natural reduction

13. Slowing Down

of his stuff over time. After getting a complaint from an umpire that his pace was getting even more leisurely, Plank responded, "Look here, I am nearly 40 years old. I can't go like these young fellows. I have to husband all my strength to go nine innings and I cannot hurry."[29]

Plank was in his "slow" form when he blanked St. Louis on July 20, allowing six hits and striking out nine. It was his 55th shutout, tying Ed Walsh, who was at the tail end of his career, for the American League record. The Athletics scored eight times, which might have accounted for a little longer game, but Plank was at fault as well, according to Louis Lee Arms of the *St. Louis Star*. "Plank has an exasperating way of making batters wait while he goes through a half dozen or more superfluous moves which patently are for the purpose of incarcerating the 'nanny' of the batter," he wrote in his notes of the game. "Several of the wiser batters stepped out of the batting box completely and put the shoe on the other foot by making him wait."[30] Eleven days later, Plank faced the Browns again, this time at Shibe Park, and the 4–3 loss lasted just an hour and 45 minutes.

After his shutout over St. Louis, Plank didn't win a game for over a month (going 0–5 and saving one game in that span) until he passed Walsh for the AL record, blanking the Browns again, 3–0, on August 25. He didn't fare well in his next three starts, though. He lasted just three innings, allowing four runs, against Boston on September 4 at home, then pitched a complete game the next day, giving up six runs. On September 12, against Chicago, he faced only four batters—allowing three hits and a sacrifice bunt—and was pulled.

Plank was going through a slump—he had a 4.61 ERA from July 26–September 12 and completed just four of his 10 starts. Things were going so bad that a report in the *Pittsburgh Press* stated, "Eddie Plank says he is going to quit the game after the season is over. The Gettysburg gattler says he signed up with the Athletics this year merely to please Connie Mack."[31] There had been loud whispers that maybe now he *was* finally nearing the end, wearing down after another long season. Fortunately for the Athletics, even with Plank's downturn, they were able to remain a big lead despite going 14–12 in August and 4–6 to start September.

Mack used him in relief on September 13 and 15. Against Cleveland on September 16, Harry Davis—who had rejoined the Athletics as a coach—made his season debut at the plate, pinch-hitting for Bryon Houck in the sixth inning and doubling in the tying run. Plank, who boarded at Davis' house when he wasn't making trips to Gettysburg, entered in the seventh and pitched four hitless innings, striking out six. It helped quell some fears of how Plank would hold up in the World Series. "In the last game he pitched against us Plank had a better curve ball than he ever had in his life before, while his speed was equal to anything he had ever shown us," Cleveland manager Joe Birmingham later wrote. "He had not pitched three balls before he began to grin and when Plank is wearing that famous grin look out for him. Prior to that time he was a worried man. He was afraid that he would be unable to pitch effectively in the world's series but those three [sic] innings he worked against us showed him he was himself again."[32]

Plank wouldn't pitch again until September 22, when he relieved Herb Pennock after two innings in the second game of a doubleheader in Philadelphia. Mack wanted to give Pennock, just 19, some experience—this was just his second start—and also get Plank a tuneup before the World Series. Inheriting a 1–0 lead, Plank threw seven shutout innings. The score never changed, and with the win Philadelphia clinched another American League pennant, its third in four years.

With the Athletics headed on the road for a week, after one last game against Detroit, Mack gave his two veteran hurlers—Bender and Plank—a break. They were left behind until the team returned for its final series at home against New York on October 3–4. Mack gave the pitchers little instruction. "You fellows have learned to know how to take care of yourselves.... You are at liberty to use your time in any way you want, only show up fit,"[33] he told them.

Bender stayed and worked out at Shibe Park. Plank headed home to Gettysburg before getting in one last preparation against the Yankees, starting the first game of a doubleheader on October 3. On a cold and windy day, he didn't get in a good warmup and allowed three runs in three innings. Mack was going to pitch both men again on October 4, but the conditions were so bad he decided against it. He would need his two big horses in the World Series, no reason to take any chances. He knew exactly what the Athletics were up against. Their opponent in the 1913 World Series was a familiar foe—the New York Giants, who won 101 games (five more than the Athletics) and ran away with the National League pennant. For Mack, Bender and Plank were the key to the Series.

◆ 14 ◆

The Pinnacle and the Mathewson Myth

The Philadelphia Athletics of 1913 weren't the best of Connie Mack's pennant-winning teams, but they still won 96 games and took the American League by 6½ games. This club, more than any of the others, relied on offense. Led as usual by second baseman Eddie Collins (.345, 125 runs, 55 stolen bases) and third baseman Frank Baker (.337, 12 home runs, 116 runs, 117 RBI, 34 steals), the Athletics finished atop the AL in most offensive categories, including batting average (.280), on-base percentage (.356), slugging percentage (.375) and runs (794). Pitching was a different story.

The Athletics finished sixth in ERA (3.19) and dead last in walks allowed (532). Chief Bender went 21–10 with a 2.21 ERA but was used more as a reliever (27 games) than starter (21). Eddie Plank appeared in 41 games with 30 starts—completing a career-low 18—and finished 18–10 with a 2.60 ERA and seven shutouts. He also had a career-high 5.6 K/9. With Jack Coombs ill, Carroll "Boardwalk" Brown had to make 35 starts with mixed results, sporting a 17–11 record, but his 2.94 ERA was roughly league average (2.93) and he walked more batters than he struck out.

Mack liked what he saw from youngsters Bob Shawkey (6–5, 2.34) and Joe Bush (15–6, 3.82) but they were just 22 and 20 years old, respectively. Byron Houck, who turned 22 in late August, showed something in 1912 but regressed. He went 14–6 but sported a 4.14 ERA and walked 122 batters in just 176 innings.

By contrast, the Athletics' opponent in the World Series, the New York Giants, had a stellar pitching staff. The Giants ran away with the National League, winning 101 games. They led the league by at least seven games from August 9 through the end of the season, when they finished 12½ games in front of the Philadelphia Phillies.

New York had a 2.42 ERA, easily tops in the NL. Pittsburgh was next at 2.90, and the rest of the six clubs were all over 3.00, with the league average

Fans line up at Shibe Park before Game 2 of the 1913 World Series between the Athletics and Giants. Over 20,000 people witnessed a great pitching duel between Eddie Plank and Christy Mathewson (George Grantham Bain Collection, Library of Congress).

3.20. The Giants had three 20-game winners in Christy Mathewson (25–11, 2.06), Rube Marquard (23–10, 2.50) and Jeff Tesreau (22–13, 2.17). They also got solid contributions from Al Demaree (13–4, 2.21) and Doc Crandall (2.86), the latter of whom also batted .316. The Giants' offense was steady, with no superstars, but they managed to lead the league in hitting (.273). New York loved to put pressure on opposing pitchers and catchers. The Giants' 296 steals were 70 more than any other National League team.

Seeing what the Athletics were up against—and the limitations of his own pitching staff—it was no surprise that Mack forecast a heavy workload for his two veteran hurlers.

> For the brunt of the battle I intend to rely on my old standbys—Eddie Plank and Chief Bender. This pair of handy twirlers have stood by me in good stead for a number of years, and they are surely not going to throw me down now. I have four good young pitchers—Shawkey, Houck, Bush and Brown—but Plank and Bender will shoulder the brunt of the work on the slab.... Both are at their best in the pinches and in a short series I can recommend them to beat anything in sight. It must be remembered that Plank and Bender are cold weather pitchers and that is why I look to them to carry the Athletics through to another World's Championship.[1]

14. The Pinnacle and the Mathewson Myth

A potential handicap for the Athletics and Mack's strategy was that this World Series would have no off-days. It would begin in New York on October 7, with Game 2 in Philadelphia on October 8, then back to New York the next day for Game 3 and so on, with the lone exception between a potential Game 5 and Game 6, which fell on a Sunday. That wouldn't give either Bender or Plank much time between starts. "It is extremely doubtful that he can pitch more than one good game in a week," Bozeman Bulger of the *New York Evening World* wrote of Plank. "His arm will not stand too much work."[2] Chicago sportswriter Hugh Fullerton, writing in the *New York Times*, predicted Plank would start two games in the series and allow three runs in each.

Cleveland hitting star Nap Lajoie, briefly a teammate of Plank, predicted the Athletics would win and figured his former left-handed pitching comrade would be a big reason why.

> The recent beatings suffered by Plank have almost started a panic among Philadelphia partisans. The Giants should worry about Plank. That old boy will be there when the bell rings. Today I would put a bet on Plank just as quickly as on any man who will pitch in the series. I never saw Plank in better form than when he faced us in the last game at Philadelphia. Two real pitchers in front of a strong, hard-hitting club can just about win a short series.[3]

A crowded first-base grandstand at Shibe Park during Game 2 of the 1913 World Series. Policemen lined the wall, inside and out, to prevent the large crowd from getting on the field (George Grantham Bain Collection, Library of Congress).

Clark Griffith, manager of second-place Washington, also predicted the Athletics to beat the Giants, but based his prognostication on their offense. "There is nothing to this series. The Athletics will walk in," he said. "They hit Walter Johnson harder than any team in the American League this year, and they hit him hard, too. That means that they will hit any pitcher that McGraw puts into the box. The Athletics win their games in one inning.... Mack had the best ball club I ever saw, and that's going some, for I have seen a lot of them. It would not surprise me a bit if the series ended in five games."[4]

Mack had both Bender and Plank warm up before Game 1 at the Polo Grounds before deciding on Bender. Giants manager John McGraw chose Marquard for the opener, saving Mathewson for the road in Game 2. The Athletics jumped on Marquard for three runs in the fourth inning, and Baker hit a two-run home run in the fifth. Marquard was hit for in the home fifth during a three-run inning for New York, which closed the gap to 5–4. But Bender settled in and got a big double play with two on and one out in the seventh inning as the Athletics took the opener, 6–4.

Before the Athletics boarded their train to Philadelphia, Plank told reporters:

New York Giants starting pitcher Christy Mathewson warms up before Game 2 of the 1913 World Series as manager John McGraw (left) looks on (George Grantham Bain Collection, Library of Congress).

14. The Pinnacle and the Mathewson Myth

I expect to be in the box against McGraw's club tomorrow. They say I am "all in" and have nothing left but a wind up and a prayer. All right, let them keep on thinking so. You remember I did not want to play ball this year, but now that I have been in uniform every day, and our club has won the championship, I am anxious to try my luck just once more against the National Leaguers. Perhaps these critics will sing another tune tomorrow night.[5]

Game 2 featured Plank vs. Mathewson, and the former was a big underdog, even at home. The *New York Tribune* previously noted that "even money was placed that the Giants would knock Plank out of the box the first game he pitched."[6] Many fans who lived in the houses surrounding Shibe Park were well prepared for the big matchup, having installed fortified seats on roofs able to accommodate 20–40 people. The attendance at Shibe Park was listed at over 20,000, but that didn't include the estimated 5,000 perched on rooftops. The game lived up to the hype.

Both teams had early chances to score. The Athletics had runners on second and third with one out in the first inning, but Mathewson fanned Baker and got McInnis to fly out. In the third, with one down Fred Snodgrass and Mathewson singled, Snodgrass racing to third but aggravating

Eddie Plank warms up in front of the dugout before Game 2 of the World Series. Plank pitched masterfully, but the game would be known more for manager Connie Mack allowing him to bat in the ninth inning (George Grantham Bain Collection, Library of Congress).

a charley horse he had suffered late in the season. Pitcher Hooks Wiltse replaced him and was tagged out after Buck Herzog hit a comebacker to Plank, with catcher Jack Lapp running down Wiltse. Plank was down 3–1 in the count to Larry Doyle but came back to get him to fly out on a 3–2 pitch to end the inning. Neither team could get another runner to third base until the ninth inning. Plank had kept the game in a scoreless tie by retiring Tillie Shafer and Red Murray on fly balls with two runners on base.

The Athletics quickly got something going in the bottom of the ninth. Amos Strunk led off with a single. Jack Barry pushed a hit past Mathewson which Doyle rushed up to field and then hurriedly threw to first base. His throw was wide, allowing the runners to move up. There later was conjecture that Strunk could have scored as Wiltse, now playing first, hadn't gotten to the ball by the time the Athletics outfielder reached third. The next batter, Lapp, bounced to Wiltse, who quickly threw home as the speedy Strunk raced for the plate. He slid and was called out. Shibe Park fans thought he was safe. The *Philadelphia Inquirer* said he didn't come within a half-foot of home plate. Fifty years later, Strunk insisted the wrong call was made by home plate umpire Tommy Connolly. "I was safe beyond a shadow of a doubt," he told *Gettysburg Times* writer Bill Duncan. "It was a long time ago and my opinion means nothing now. I slid across the plate before Larry McLean, the huge Giants catcher, got the ball on me. McLean was such a large man he blocked the view of the small Connolly and I'm sure Tommy never saw the play and guessed by the timing. He guessed wrong. Our mutual friend, Ed Plank, was waiting his turn at bat and saw the play. Eddie Collins saw it clearly, too. We all knew I was safe."[7]

Mack had a decision to make—whether to let Plank swing the bat or send up a pinch hitter. Reportedly there was much discussion, with a number of players wanting to send someone else up. Rube Oldring even bounced off the bench and waved Plank back to the dugout. But Mack theorized that Plank had swung the bat against Mathewson as well as anyone else in the lineup—he was 1-for-3 and hadn't struck out as Baker, Collins, Lapp and McInnis had—plus no one was warming up; if the Athletics didn't score, a pitcher would have to come in cold. The intuition didn't pay off. Plank also bounced to Wiltse, with Barry tagged out in a rundown. Now with two down and runners on second and third, Eddie Murphy grounded back to Mathewson. Inning over, no runs. According to an article in the Chicago newspaper *The Day*, Collins was among the most upset, and he and Mack "had a wordy war in the clubhouse"[8] which caused the pair to have a rift that didn't fully heal over the next year.

McGraw was faced with a similar decision in the 10th when Mathewson came to the plate with one out and a runner on second. He, too, left his pitcher in to hit, but this one paid off as Mathewson singled home pinch

14. *The Pinnacle and the Mathewson Myth* 149

runner Eddie Grant. An error by Collins (his attempt at a double play hit Mathewson in the head) and a hit batter loaded the bases for Art Fletcher, who drove in a pair with a single. Plank got out of the inning, but the damage was done. Mathewson had more than enough cushion as he retired the Athletics in order to tie the series.

Neither Mathewson nor Plank allowed an extra-base hit. After the game, Plank sat despondently and kept to himself for hours despite the efforts of his teammates to cheer him up. In his ghostwritten, syndicated column, McGraw praised Plank, saying he "would have won against any other pitcher in the country besides Christy Mathewson."[9] Hospitalized, Coombs was on the phone the entire game with Mack's son, Earle, who described each play to him. "Plank was the star for our boys," Coombs relayed. "We all feel proud of him."[10]

Mack was roundly criticized for not sending up hitters for either Lapp (he hit just .227 in 1913, and Wally Schang, a young, hard-hitting catcher who started Game 1, was on the bench; of course, like Plank, Lapp previously had a hit off Mathewson) or Plank. "I would do the same thing tomorrow if a similar situation came up,"[11] Mack said after the game. That wouldn't pacify critics.

The game and situation were brought up over and over to Mack. He talked about it extensively in a story for the *Saturday Evening Post* the following month.

> Why should I want to take Lapp out with this batting record in the game and substitute an untried man? Then again there was his attitude of mind, his strong heart in the emergency. The moment that Strunk singled in that inning Lapp jumped up from the bench, grabbed a bat and exclaimed to me: "Now put your man down to second and I'll win the game for you."
>
> But most of the criticism heaped upon me came because I let Plank follow Lapp ... Let's look at Plank's batting up to that time: He hadn't struck out; he had made one safe hit, and he had knocked a sizzling liner which the Giants' shortstop had caught brilliantly. It is a fact, which few who saw that game apparently remember, that Plank hit that ball harder than any man on our team—'Home-Run' Baker not excepted. "But he's a pitcher!" critics say. That's their whole argument. Plank's batting in the game we're talking about wasn't considered. He was to be taken out merely because he was a pitcher. Who won the game for New York, sending in the only run needed to win? Mathewson, a pitcher! ... The fan is not paid for thinking. I am. It was my business to know this, to be prepared for the emergency, and I was prepared. I did what I thought was right. That night I slept as well as after any game in the series.[12]

The lasting moment of Game 2, however, was something that never even happened. Noted writer Grantland Rice, in his game story for United Press, stated that this was the third time Plank and Mathewson had faced each other, and each score had been 3–0. There was this Game 2, Game 1 of the 1905 World Series, and the time in college when Mathewson's Bucknell nine topped Plank's Gettysburg team. Except the latter contest never happened—Rice made it up to add a little flavor to his story angle.

Unfortunately, it's a story that had legs beyond 1913, oft repeated over the years in newspapers, magazines, and books. In Tom Meany's 1951 book *Baseball's Greatest Pitchers*—and reprinted in a 1952 edition of *Baseball Digest*—it was written that "When Plank was a student at Gettysburg, he often hooked up with Christy Mathewson when the latter was pitching for near-by Bucknell."[13] Noted baseball historians Lawrence Ritter and Donald Honig mentioned in their 1981 book, *The 100 Greatest Baseball Players of All Time*, that the pair faced each other in college.

While research is much easier in the internet age, a little digging would have turned up the fact that Mathewson last pitched for Bucknell in 1898. He pitched in the minors in 1899 and 1900 before being purchased by the Giants in July. As has been described earlier, Plank didn't make his debut for Gettysburg College until 1900. There was no collegiate matchup between the two greats. In 1939, Mathewson's widow, Jane, even tried to put the myth to rest. "I've read in the papers that the World's Series games between Matty and Plank were continuations of pitching duels they had when my husband went to Bucknell and Plank to Gettysburg College," she said in an interview which appeared in *The Sporting News*. "I think this was exaggerated, as Christy always had a great admiration for Plank; they met frequently in the three World's Series between John McGraw and Connie Mack and if he had pitched against Plank in college, I think he would have said something to me about it."[14] Nevertheless, the lie keeps getting reprinted—even by the periodical which ran the quote from Mrs. Mathewson. In 1963, an article in *The Sporting News* referred to Plank and Mathewson facing each other in college.

Plank and Mathewson faced each other one more time. Philadelphia stormed Tesreau in Game 3, scoring five runs in the first two innings, more than enough support for Joe Bush in an 8–2 victory. The Athletics had to dodge things thrown at them—rocks, bricks, cabbage, and the like—as they made their way from the Polo Grounds to their hotel. "If that game was a war, this is hell,"[15] Danny Murphy proclaimed. Back in Shibe Park for Game 4 with Bender on the hill, the Athletics led, 6–0, and held onto win, 6–5.

There was no certainty who would start Game 5. If Plank were to go, he would be working on just two days' rest after having thrown 137 pitches in Game 2 (Mathewson threw 104). Twice during the regular season, Plank had thrown a complete game and started three days later: On June 6, he allowed seven runs on 12 hits in six innings vs. Detroit, and on July 7 in the second game of a doubleheader at Boston, he was bounced after two innings, giving up seven hits and four runs. "Plank cannot possibly be fit

14. The Pinnacle and the Mathewson Myth

for such a grueling duel as that ten-inning battle of Wednesday," Giants catcher Chief Meyers told a reporter for the *Washington Herald*. "One of Connie Mack's colt twirlers will have to fight our best pitcher."[16]

It rained the night before Game 5 in New York, and threatening clouds emerged on Saturday morning before the contest. In part due to the conditions, and the chance of rain with a scheduled day off Sunday, catcher Ira Thomas indicated that Mack would go with one of the Athletics' untested pitchers. "We may give you a chance to look over two new pitchers today," he told reporters. "There are Brown and Shawkey, who have yet to show their pitching wares. Either one will give Matty a run, and we can use Plank if necessary."[17] But somewhere between Thomas' pronouncement and the turning in of lineups, Mack decided on Plank against Mathewson in a rematch of Game 2. There are a myriad of versions of how exactly that came about.

The week after the Series ended, it was written in *Sporting Life* that "Plank warmed up so well and was so anxious to pit himself once more against Mathewson that Manager Mack decided to give Plank the double opportunity of obtaining revenge on his great rival."[18] The *Washington Evening Star* had something similar, claiming, "Mack at the last moment decided to use Plank."[19]

In Eddie Collins' version, which he relayed in 1927, Plank came down with a cold Friday night "which developed immediately into a severe attack of rheumatism, settling in his throwing arm."[20] Plank confided in captain Danny Murphy, who took him to the team trainer, who worked on the pitcher's left arm through the night, trying to rub out the pain. Armed with few hours of sleep, Plank awoke only to have his arm hurting anew—but he didn't tell anyone and took the ball against the Giants.

Writer Jack Kofoed of the *New York Evening Journal* also spun a tale of Plank with an arm injury, although in Kofoed's words, "It was torn with the hot knife of neuritis"[21] and it wasn't Murphy he told but catcher Jack Lapp and pitcher Jack Coombs (who in reality was hospitalized due to typhoid). The pair, according to Kofoed, stayed up with the pitcher through the night, consistently wrapping, removing, and re-wrapping Plank's left arm in hot towels. Still hurting, the trio made their way to the ballpark when Plank insisted on stopping to get some tomato soup—"Eddie positively would not pitch a ball game unless he had eaten a plate of tomato soup for lunch,"[22] Kofoed wrote—and that made him feel better and more confident than the treatment he received in the hotel from his teammates. "It was the deciding factor, the shot in the arm that carried him through. He would have felt weak and ineffectual without it,"[23] explained Kofoed.

Catcher Wally Schang offered a simpler—and perhaps most plausible—explanation in a 1941 article.[24] Schang said Shawkey was scheduled to pitch but Plank went to Mack and made his case to go against Mathewson, saying he wanted one more opportunity to beat the Giants star after failing to do so in his two previous matchups. Whatever Mack's reasoning, Plank did get the nod, and word spread that this could be the left-hander's final game in the major leagues.

Nearly 37,000 fans packed the Polo Grounds for Game 5, and it wasn't long before they were groaning as the Athletics tallied a run in the opening frame on a Frank Baker sacrifice fly. Plank set down New York in order in the first, and after Mathewson held Philadelphia to just a two-out Schang single in the second, Giants manager John McGraw tried to get in Plank's head. As the pitcher strolled to the mound, McGraw complained to umpire Bill Klem that Plank wasn't standing on the rubber when he delivered a pitch from his famous crossfire delivery. Klem had Plank toss a few warmup pitches. After watching a few, he had a few words with Plank and everyone seemed satisfied. Plank went back to the mound, smiled at McGraw, and promptly retired George Burns en route to another three-up, three-down inning.

The Athletics got some more runs for Plank in the third inning thanks to some heads-up baserunning. With one out and runners on second and third, Baker bunted towards first base. Fred Merkle fielded it but Baker, instead of running to first, stopped in the basepath and started going backwards towards the plate. Rather than retreating to the first-base bag for an easy out, a confused Merkle began to chase after Baker—this is when Eddie Murphy, who was on third and creeping down the line, took off for the plate. Merkle threw hurriedly to catcher Larry McLean. The throw was high, and not only did Murphy slide in safely, but also Baker ran to first and had himself a single. The Polo Grounds crowd was merciless, as shouts of "Bonehead! Bonehead!"[25] once again rained down on the infamous "Merkle's Boner" player of 1908. Instead of two outs and no runs in, it was now 2–0, and Stuffy McInnis' fly out accounted for a third run rather than a third out.

Meanwhile, Plank retired the first 13 batters he faced until walking Tillie Shafer in the fifth inning. On a hit-and-run, Red Murray popped the ball up in the direction of the pitcher's mound. Plank looked to settle under it, but Frank Baker rushed over as well—the other infielders shouted, "Frank, have it,"[26] which Plank either didn't hear, ignored or thought they were saying "*Plank* have it." If he figured it out, it was too late. Baker rammed into the pitcher, and the ball dropped to the ground, Murray safe on an error. If the ball had been caught, it would have been an easy double play as Schafer, who had been running on the pitch, was down near second base. McLean then lashed a single to left-center field, scoring Schafer, but poor Merkle hit into a double play and the threat was quashed. Plank made no more mistakes after that.

14. The Pinnacle and the Mathewson Myth 153

Eddie Plank tosses a warmup pitch in front of a packed house at Shibe Park during Game 2 of the 1913 World Series. Plank's last win as a starting pitcher at Shibe Park came in mid-June, but perhaps the biggest win of his career came days later in Game 5 at the Polo Grounds (George Grantham Bain Collection, Library of Congress).

The Giants got only one more hit off the veteran Athletics pitcher—a Mathewson single to lead off the sixth, but he was quickly erased on a Buck Herzog double play grounder, Barry to Collins to McInnis. No one else reached base against Plank, and when Doyle flied out to Murphy in right field for the game's final out, Plank had his win against Mathewson—and a World Series–clinching victory. Plank's effort was outstanding, especially considering going on short rest after pitching 10 innings. He was efficient, walking only one but also striking out only one. Doyle's final out was Plank's 100th pitch of the game, which was played in a swift one hour, 39 minutes. Plank later called it "the greatest game I ever pitched."[27] Mathewson, as expected, was magnanimous in defeat. "Plank beat me by pitching wonderful ball, and I take my hat off to him," he wrote in a syndicated article. "I would rather be beaten by Plank than some youngster with lots of 'pep' and dash. There is something in losing to an old bird like Eddie Plank."[28]

As Plank walked off the field, the crowd at the Polo Grounds, recognizing the accomplishment of the veteran Athletics pitcher, "rose and greeted him with an ovation such as only Mathewson gets in Manhattan."[29]

Many fans, presumed to be Philadelphians, made their way onto the field and hoisted Plank upon their shoulders. Later, after leaving the clubhouse, Plank was surrounded again—but this time by those wanting memorabilia. A fan took his cap, which Plank tried to retrieve. When he did that, his glove and spikes were swiped. There was no mention of anyone taking the ball which resulted in the final out. Plank had made sure he got that himself from Murphy, the man who caught it.

Back at the team hotel, Plank was greeted by a traveling group of Philadelphia fans sponsored by one of the local papers known as "The Inquirer's tourists" with "Three cheers for Eddie Plank."[30] Plank was humbled by all the attention and gave much of the credit for the win to his teammates. "I don't deserve all this," Plank said at one point during the Athletics' celebration as he garnered much of the attention. His words belied his smile. As *Sporting Life* reported, Plank "was the happiest man in the exceedingly happy Athletic party after the game."[31] He also wasn't ready to retire.

◆ 15 ◆

Holding Out and Helping Out

On the morning before his victory in the Game 5 of the World Series, Eddie Plank reiterated that he was through with baseball. Twenty-four hours later, however, after some thought, he reconsidered. "Well, I did say last year that I was going to retire," Plank said the day after his big win. "But this year, I have not spoken of it, and have no idea where the news started. I feel in fine shape and could pitch again tomorrow if Mack wanted me to do so. I am not going to quit the game and you can gamble on just one thing: When the team leaves next spring on its training trip, I will be on hand."[1]

That was big talk in October, and by the time the calendar flipped to 1914, he wasn't in such a willing mood to sign. But one of Connie Mack's lures to Plank in getting him to re-sign with the Athletics in February 1913 had in fact become a reality when Philadelphia won the World Series, and each member of the team took home $3,246.36 (they also allotted $500 to Louis Van Zelst, the team's batboy and mascot who had a humped back; Van Zelst promptly gave the money to his parents). "I'm going to put my money in the bank," the ever-frugal Plank said. "If I see a good farm down my way later on I'm going to buy it."[2]

Plank had the chance for even more money. Along with pitcher Joe Bush and catcher Wally Schang, the trio were offered $1,000 a week each for 10 weeks to perform on vaudeville. Plank, as well as the other two, turned down the offer, which came as no surprise to anyone who knew him. "It would require a mighty pile-driver to push Plank before the footlights,"[3] said the *Philadelphia Inquirer*.

A celebration was scheduled for Plank back in Gettysburg, but tragedy delayed the ceremony. Plank and little-used infielder Billy Orr boarded with the family of Harry Davis. The team arrived back in Philadelphia on Saturday night and were met by a reported 15,000 people at the train station, many of whom had "watched" the game at Shibe Park, where plays as they happened were reproduced on an electronic scoreboard. Early Sunday morning, Plank was awakened by cries of pain from Davis' eldest son, Harry Jr. The 13 year old was a frequent visitor to Shibe Park—he would play catch with Athletics players and work as an usher during games; when his father wouldn't take him to New York for the World Series, such as in Game 5, he went to the park so he could find out the immediate result. But Davis Jr. also had what was reported as a "distended liver, a complaint of long standing. This physical condition, made worse by the excitement brought about his sudden collapse."[4] Plank went to get a doctor while Harry Davis and his wife tried to comfort their son. It was too late; Harry Davis, Jr., died before the doctor could get to the house.

"The boy never presumed on his familiarity with the members of the club," said Plank, who by all account had a great relationship with Harry Davis, Jr. "Most youngsters get fresh if the players are friendly with them, but Harry Davis wasn't that sort of boy. He was always the same—smiling, pleasant and decent. He never played smart tricks and never picked up the bad talk and mischief that most youngsters around a ballpark do. His death has taken a great deal of the pleasure out of our victory for all of us and we are all terribly sorry for his mother and father."[5] Plank, Frank Baker, Jack Barry, Chief Bender, Eddie Collins, and Stuffy McInnis served as pallbearers at the funeral.

Despite the death of Davis' son, the celebrations would go on. On October 28, a parade was held followed by a dinner—replete with speeches and toasts (Plank, as his custom, did not speak) at the Bellevue Stratford Hotel. The next night the team was feted "by a prominent moving picture concern at their uptown manufacturing plant,"[6] with actor John Ince acting as emcee.

Plank headed back to Gettysburg after the event, where the ceremony in his honor was moved back to November 6. Before that, though, he headed to Carlisle to watch Gettysburg College play Dickinson in a football game (Gettysburg lost, 39–13) as well as pick up a free Stetson, courtesy of the company, for winning the World Series, at a local hattery.

Connie Mack arrived in Gettysburg earlier in the day on November 6 bearing a gift—a gold pocket watch from the E. Howard Watch Co. in Boston. On the back was engraved WORLD'S CHAMPIONS * 1913 * in a circle with 1913 on the bottom, "WORLD'S" above left, and "CHAMPIONS" above right. In the middle was a baseball diamond with second base slightly askew. All of it was enclosed in a circle with leaf design around. On the inside was engraved Edward S. Plank. In 2014, the watch fetched nearly $40,000 in an auction. Plank took Mack and three other dignitaries to the Gettysburg battlefield. The quintet stopped and had their picture taken at Devil's Den and the 12th and 44th New York volunteer infantry regiments

15. Holding Out and Helping Out

monument on Little Round Top while they were seated in a car—a 1914 Oakland Model 43—which was draped in a large pennant with a white elephant and the word "CHAMPIONS" written vertically, as well as a small Athletics pennant attached to the windshield.

Teammates Collins and Davis were in town—they spent the weekend at Plank's house—for the ceremony, which began at 9:30 p.m. Originally planned for 150 attendees, the demand was so large that it was increased to 200, the maximum capacity at the Eagle Hotel. A program for the night included a quote from Mack, "We won chiefly because of Plank's great work," as well as several espousing Plank's pitching greatness and/or relationship with his hometown, such as "Gettysburg's Great Southpaw," "The Great Cross-Fire Artist," "The Gettysburg College Man," "The Gettysburg Farmer," and "Plank, the Old Master."[7]

Judge Samuel McCurdy Swope, one of a myriad of speakers on the night, summed up the feeling of the townspeople and their relationship with the great pitcher.

> Eddie, we are glad you were born here. You are a credit to the town. There is not a hamlet in these United States however small that does not know the name of Eddie Plank and where he is from. Gettysburg has been enjoying a world fame for many years.... Again we stand in the limelight of the world as the home of Eddie Plank, the great baseball pitcher, and we are honoring tonight not simply his baseball prowess but because he is a clean, sober and honorable man.[8]

Swope was also charged with presenting Plank a gift, a scarf pin which had a big diamond in the middle and eight smaller diamonds circled around it. "This is a case of diamond meeting diamond, both typical of purity, virtue and worth,"[9] Swope said as he made the presentation.

Plank, never one for a lengthy speech, stayed true to form even at a ceremony in his honor. After receiving the pin, he remarked, "It is quite a job for me to say a few words and I want to say they will be very few. We have others here who will talk to you about baseball and I will simply thank you from my heart for this beautiful gift."[10]

Mack and Collins spoke as well as Charles S. Duncan, who served as toastmaster, and Gettysburg College president Dr. W.A. Cranville. A running theme was, as summed up by Mack and paraphrased by the *Gettysburg Compiler*, how Plank's "clean and sober life had helped to make him the great pitcher that he is, and that he was a man without vices, a model for the young men and boys of present day."[11] Davis, a teammate of Plank's since 1901 who also spent plenty of time with the pitcher at his own home in Philadelphia, concurred with the characterization. "Everything that has been told here tonight about him is absolutely true," Davis remarked. "I know it."[12]

One other thing which came out the ceremony, which finally broke up just before 2 a.m., was another rumor of an impending wedding for Plank. That caused an eyebrow to be raised when Plank, along with his brother Ira, visited the Rev. Fred Goltwalt, the secretary of the Board of Education of the Lutheran Church in nearby York, in the middle of November. But Plank left town not with a marriage certificate but rather a date for a bowling match between teams from Gettysburg and York.

It was reported that Plank would be heading to Harrisburg with Mack to speak on November 25 at a luncheon for the Board of Trade. However, Ira Thomas instead showed up and gave the speech. Neither Plank nor Mack attended, but they'd have plenty to talk about in the coming months.

While Plank had stated his intention to return for the 1914 season, shortly after the Athletics won the World Series, when Mack sent him a contract in early January, he did nothing with it until returning it—unsigned. Perhaps for the first time, Plank realized he might have some leverage. In this era of the reserve clause, which allowed teams to renew a player's contract in perpetuity, Plank, like any other player, didn't have many options. It was sign, retire (and find some other line of work), or perhaps sign with some minor-league team not affiliated with organized baseball.

In 1914, however, Plank had some choices. First, there was the upstart Federal League, which was trying to establish itself as a third major league. Cincinnati's Mordecai Brown and Joe Tinker, both, like Plank, on the wrong side of 30, had signed with the circuit in December. A few others here and there, but no one too notable, also jumped to the Feds, and the worry of losing their stars eventually helped drive up salaries for American and National League players. Plank had overtures but was loyal to Mack.

It wasn't just the Federal League that was after the veteran pitcher. There was talk of him becoming part-owner of a team in Lancaster, which was trying to re-enter the Tri-State League, after moving its franchise to Atlantic City during the 1912 season. Another team which was returning to the Tri-State league was the Reading Pretzels, when the Atlantic City team transferred to their city (Reading had been in the league from 1909–1911, moving to Altoona in June 1912). They were looking for a manager and had targeted Plank after their first choice, former Chicago Cubs outfielder Jimmy Sheckard, took a similar job with the Cleveland Bearcats in the American Association.

"Reading backers would like to land Eddie Plank as manager. It is said the signing of the Athletics' twirler depends on the decision of Connie Mack," reported the *Harrisburg Telegraph*. "Plank wants to break into the minor league game as an owner and this may be his chance."[13] The *Reading Times* reported that Plank was one of three final candidates, with Izzy Hoffman, an outfielder who also played for the team, eventually chosen.

"Hoffman was secured as the team's pilot through the efforts of Connie Mack,"[14] the paper disclosed. Mack also later sold outfielder George Brickley and infielder Albert McInnis (brother of Stuffy) to the Pretzels. Both were in camp with the Athletics in 1914 before being transferred to Reading.

Mack got involved in Plank's other possible venture as well. He was outspoken in his disapproval. "There's nothing to it because Plank is needed more in Philadelphia than in Lancaster," Mack spouted. "Plank isn't ready for the minors. He pitched better ball last season than he did in all the years he has been with me. I would no more think of letting him go than I would Collins or Baker. I think that Plank is the marvel of baseball, and I wouldn't be surprised were he pitching good ball for me five years hence. He isn't thinking of any minor league berth. He knows that he is far from being through with the majors."[15] In the end, Mack's words made no difference—York got the Tri-State franchise instead of Lancaster (although it wouldn't stay in York long, and eventually Lancaster got the team when it relocated in early July).

That left the impasse between Plank and Mack whittled down to one thing: money. Plank wanted an increase from the $5,000 he earned in 1913, while Mack was offering the same contract, claiming his budget was set and the Athletics could incur no higher salary. The standoff continued throughout February and, once again, with spring training (this time in Jacksonville, Florida) approaching, Plank was Philadelphia's lone holdout. Both men were holding their ground. "It is now up to Eddie," Mack said. "If he wants to sign at the club figures, well and good. If not, then he will have to fulfill his threat of tilling the soil, for I have gone my limit financially."[16]

"I wanted to quit at the beginning of last season but Connie felt that he wanted me with the team and he feared that the injury to Coombs would hurt his pitching staff," Plank said. "I no longer am a young man as pitchers go, and it is not an easy matter for me to get into condition. When I pitched my last game during the last world's series I said that I was done. I meant what I said. I want to retire before people can class me as a has been."[17]

Either something changed or Mack bluffed, but on February 21, when the Athletics manager sent out his list of players who would attend spring training with the club, Plank was a surprise addition. Mack, though, did not reveal whether Plank had signed—he hadn't—but the pitcher confirmed he would head to Jacksonville by train with Mack. "Some of the boys are going by water, but I took that trip once and will never do it again,"[18] said Plank, who probably chuckled at the news that Albert McInnis and Bob Shawkey, as well as the wife of pitcher Weldon Wycoff, got seasick on their boat journey.

Plank boarded the train with Mack (along with a Father McCloskey from Camden, New Jersey, one of the team's chaplains) and headed down to spring training. At a stop in Savannah, Georgia, Mack told reporters there was no animosity between him and the pitcher. The manager's plan was likely just to get Plank down to Florida and around his teammates. Get him smelling baseball, living baseball again. Just two hours into his first workout on February 28, Plank signed his contract for the 1914 season. He did not get any pay increase.

With Plank back in the fold, Mack's Athletics of 1914 was nearly identical to the team that won the World Series the previous season, with a few exceptions. Jack Coombs remained sidelined and was expected to remain so until at least June (he would return in late July, saying he was 20 pounds lighter than his usual weight, and pitch only in a handful of exhibitions before making two starts at the end of the season, totaling eight innings). Catcher Ira Thomas had transitioned to full-time coach.

Then there was the matter of Danny Murphy. The one-time team captain had been used sparingly in 1913, making only nine starts plus pinch-hitting appearances. Mack decided in the off-season to drop the 37-year-old outfielder. He tried to pawn him off to the St. Louis Browns, to no avail. Mack reached a deal with Baltimore of the International League— the Orioles were going head-to-head with a Federal League team and this could hurt the new league as well. As part of the deal, the Athletics agreed to pay Murphy an additional stipend each month, an additional $1,000 on top of his $2,000 Baltimore salary.

Murphy made $4,500 with the Athletics in 1913—boosted to $5,000 after Brooklyn of the Federal League came calling—and while he wasn't pleased by this transaction, he asked if it could be kept under wraps until he sold a café he owned in his hometown of Norwich, Connecticut, called "White Elephant." If potential buyers knew he was no longer with the Athletics, it could potentially hurt his market. It also gave him time to work out another deal. Instead of reporting to Baltimore, Murphy signed with the Brooklyn Tip-Tops of the Federal League, a move that eventually proved even more costly to Mack.

At 38 years old, Plank was one of the oldest players in the major leagues, and the eldest pitcher. Those older than Plank were either player-managers or coaches who got into a token game or two (including Washington's 44-year-old Clark Griffith, who put himself on the mound for one inning on the final day of the season), part-time players, such as shortstops Bobby Wallace (St. Louis Browns) and Kid Elberfeld (Brooklyn Robins), or a couple of future Hall of Famers who had career-worst seasons (Cleveland's Nap Lajoie and Pittsburgh's Honus Wagner). Meanwhile, Mack was counting on Plank once again to be one of the anchors of his pitching staff.

Plank was used sparingly in spring training. One such instance was in

15. Holding Out and Helping Out

Richmond on March 27, when he entered in the sixth inning. In the ninth, with the Athletics ahead, 9–3, he turned around and ordered his outfield to come in—just as his former teammate Rube Waddell used to do during exhibitions. He then struck out all three batters he faced, just like Waddell. This was perhaps a tribute to Waddell, who was hospitalized in a sanitarium with tuberculosis (the players likely would have known about this from reading newspaper reports or from Mack, who was fronting part or all of the hospital bill). Waddell died on April 1 at the age of 37. His longtime batterymate—and drinking partner—Ossee Schrecongost, upon hearing the news, reportedly said, "The 'Rube' is gone and I am all in. I might as well join him."[19] The man better known as Schreck during his playing days died on July 9. He was 39.

The death of Waddell once again called into contrast the differences between Mack's two most famous lefties. The enigmatic Waddell, who liked to imbibe (and often) alcohol, and the tee-totaling, straight-laced Plank. Preacher Billy Sunday used Waddell's passing—ignoring that the former pitcher died of tuberculosis—to extol the virtue of leaving a good, clean life, using Plank and Christy Mathewson as his examples. In a temperance speech he entitled "Your Sins Will Find You Out" which he gave in Scranton on April 5, Sunday told the large gathering:

> The "Rube," Matty, Plank and "Bugs" Raymond started in baseball at about the same time. All were pitchers. Two started on the wrong road and two on the right road. Two are dead, "Bugs" and "Rube." ... Plank, grand old man, steady and earnest, is getting along, but he can pitch a great game. Yes, he sure can. And Plank and Matty are honored by the men on the field and by men in every walk of life. They followed the right path. "Rube" and "Bugs" are dead. Does it pay? Your sins will find you out.[20]

In 1914, Plank himself gave a speech called "How to Last" to boys at a Philadelphia YMCA on how "a number of well-known pitchers have played out because of intemperate habits."[21]

Plank prided himself on always being in good shape, especially late in his career, but Mack continued to play it cautiously with not only the left-hander—who made only four relief appearances in April (although he was scheduled to start a couple of games and Mack decided against it)—but also veteran right-hander Chief Bender, who started only once in the opening month, and that didn't come until April 27. Mack instead relied on his bevy of youngsters, such as Joe Bush, Herb Pennock, and Bob Shawkey. Another, Boardwalk Brown, had been unhappy that he didn't get a pay increase and let it affect his pitching (4.09 ERA in 66 innings) before being sold to the New York Yankees in July.

After pitching five scoreless innings in four relief appearances, Plank's first start came May 2 at home against Boston. He allowed 10 hits and was in trouble in both the first and third innings, causing Mack to warm up *three* pitchers at once, but Plank worked out of jams all game ("Eddie never exerted himself until they got somebody on, then he threw on the emergency brake,"[22] reported the *Philadelphia Inquirer*) in a 5–2, complete-game victory. Plank walked none and struck out five.

When Plank wasn't pitching, Mack had him and Coombs scout a young pitcher for Ursinus College, Russell "Jing" Johnson, when that school played Gettysburg College. Johnson pitched all 17 innings of a 1–1 tie, striking out 17. Johnson joined the Athletics in 1916.

Plank could still pitch extra innings, too. On May 14 he beat Cleveland, 1–0, in a 13-inning affair, allowing just five hits and one walk while striking out nine. He was partly saved in the top of the 13th when left fielder Rube Oldring jumped up to snag a likely home run away from Lajoie. Fans then rained down upon Oldring pouches of tobacco, which had been handed out as a promotional item by an ambitious salesman. Dubbed "the idol of the left-field fans,"[23] Oldring was indeed extremely popular. When Sweet Caporal Sweets, a cigarette, held a contest during the 1914 season to see which Athletics or Phillies player was the most popular, Oldring easily won, despite the presence of such stars as Plank, Eddie Collins, Frank Baker, Chief Bender, and the Phillies' Grover Cleveland Alexander (the latter finished second, more than 20,000 votes behind Oldring). In September, Oldring received as a prize a brand-new Cadillac. Later in his life, Oldring would remark, "I didn't know what to do with the machine, because I couldn't drive."[24]

The 30-year-old Oldring was on the downside of his career but was still steady if unspectacular. The Athletics didn't need him to do anything other than be steady. They had enough strong hitters in their lineup. That combined with a young pitching staff performing well, and Philadelphia recovered from a slow start to eventually take charge of the American League once again.

On May 28 at Shibe Park, Plank shut out St. Louis, 3–0, striking out eight. It was the 57th shutout of his career, once again passing Ed Walsh for the most in American League history (Walsh picked up No. 57 in 1915 and ended his career with that number). "It used to tickle me every time the Browns came to Philadelphia. The first fellow I would see would be [outfielder Burt Shotton," Plank recalled to a reporter in 1917. "He always came up over to our bench and looked me up. 'Well, old crooked arm, are you going to pitch today?' he would ask. I always had good luck against the St. Louis club."[25]

In his career, Plank tossed 13 shutouts against the Browns, the most he had against any team (next was 11 vs. Detroit). He got one of those 13 in his next appearance against them in St. Louis on June 22, another 3–0 win.

15. Holding Out and Helping Out

When Plank threw his next shutout, at home against Detroit on July 8 and another 3–0 game, it was his fourth in his last eight starts.

Plank didn't spin another shutout in 1914, but he played a big part in another. One of the surprises of the season was 19-year-old left-handed pitcher Rube Bressler. In his rookie season, Bressler was used exclusively as a reliever in the first half of the season. Mack didn't give Bressler his first start until July 21, on the back end of a doubleheader with the Athletics already six games in front in the American League.

On August 25, in the first game of a doubleheader at Shibe Park against St. Louis, in his 20th appearance and fifth major-league start, Bressler twirled a three-hit shutout, walking one and striking out 10. That lowered his ERA on the season to 1.82. Bressler's style was very much patterned after Plank—and that was no accident. The veteran had taken the pitcher who was literally half his age under his wing. "If Plank and Bressler were father and son, the younger twirler might be called 'a chip off the old block,'" said the Sports Magazine of the *Sunday Philadelphia Ledger*. "Every move, every curve, of the instructor has been so carefully copied by the pupil that one can easily imagine he sees Plank flinging when Bressler is on the mound."[26]

Ira Thomas was given a lot of credit in the development of Bressler,

Raymond "Rube" Bressler joined the Athletics in 1914 and had the best pitching season of his career as Eddie Plank took him under his wing (George Grantham Bain Collection, Library of Congress).

which one unnamed Athletics player scoffed at in speaking to the *New York Times*. "Every time the Athletics saw that statement in print they laughed," the anonymous player said. "Why? Because Bressler hated to have Thomas warm him up. If there was ever a chance to spoil Bressler, Thomas would have done so. Bressler is a pitcher because Eddie Plank took an interest in him."[27]

Bressler was just the latest left-hander brought to the Athletics to be the next Plank, and also the latest Plank served as a mentor. In 1908, Harry Krause had his impressive streak of 10 straight starts to open the season with at least seven innings and allowing two or fewer runs. Questioned on what factors led him to have such a run, Krause said, "That's easy. A capable manager in Connie Mack, one of the best pitching tutors in the world in Ed Plank, fairly good control on my part and lots of luck."[28]

Dave Danforth, who appeared in 17 games for the Athletics in 1911–1912 and had a modicum of success with the Chicago White Sox (1916–1919) and St. Louis Browns (1922–1925), copied Plank's mannerisms on the mound. According to St. Louis sportswriter Sid Keener, Danforth "fusses around the hill, adjusts his cap, hitches the belt, wets the tips of his fingers a bit, nods the head when he has received the signal from the catcher, and then—just at the moment when the batter is fretting, nervous and excited—he pitches."[29] Danforth said the lesson he learned from Plank was to "Get the batter nervous and you have him down."[30]

Dave Davenport, a future teammate of Plank, relayed the advice he was given—and followed. "I shall never forget the first instructions I received from Eddie Plank. Eddie said: 'My boy, don't forget that there are corners on that plate and the strike territory measures from the knees to the shoulders.' I followed that advice with study and practice and I soon learned that having control was not to whip the ball through the center waist high."[31]

Plank, of course, wasn't just about guidance. He threw three straight complete-game wins from August 9–24, and on September 9, just nine days after turning 39, he went 11 innings in a 2–0 loss to Boston. Both runs were unearned as Eddie Murphy dropped a fly ball to open the inning (and both runs scored on controversial, at least from Mack's point of view, ball four calls on 3–2 pitches). He allowed only six hits and struck out 11—no 39 year old whiffed that many in a game until 1930.

The Athletics won 99 games, easily taking the American League flag for the fourth time in five years. Philadelphia led the league in runs, hits, batting average, on-base percentage, slugging percentage, and total bases. Eddie Collins led the way with a .344/.452/.452 slash line, 122 runs, and 58 steals. But it was a solid, all-around lineup. Jack Barry (.242) was the only starter to hit lower than .272.

15. Holding Out and Helping Out

The pitching was good, but not up to the usual Athletics snuff. The team had a 2.78 ERA, fourth in the AL and above the league average of 2.73. The majority of pitchers had an above-average ERA—though all had winning records, none had more than 17 wins. Chief Bender (17–3, 2.26 ERA) and Joe Bush (17–13, 3.06) led in victories, with Plank (15–7, 2.87) and Bob Shawkey (15–8, 2.73) right behind.

It was Plank's fewest wins since he had 14 in 1908 and his highest ERA since 1902—when foul balls weren't counted as strikes. Nevertheless, F.C. Lane of *Baseball Magazine* included Plank on his American League All-Star team. "We believe Plank ... was a far more valuable man than Bender, though he lost more games. The records show that he was hit less freely, gave fewer bases on balls, and was an almost certain winner, truly one of the prodigies of the diamond, considering his age,"[32] Lane wrote.

The Athletics had a new opponent in the 1914 World Series, the Boston Braves, who came back from down 15 games on July 4 to win the National League pennant. Chicago Cubs manager Hank O'Day didn't see much of a challenge for Philadelphia.

> I do not think the Braves will take a game from the Athletics. They are so weak a squad that I do not see how they can do it, despite their having succeeded in winning the National League title. Stallings will not get a game, because he does not possess the hitters to beat Connie Mack's twirlers. And it will be Bender and Plank who will star again.... The Braves are a bunch of young fellows who do not know what it is to go through a nerve-wracking series. They have been under a strain all summer and have held up well under it, but in these last few games they have shown a tendency to break, although they did beat us.[33]

Philadelphians were confident of another championship as well. In years past, the city's fans hadn't been as optimistic with the Athletics' chances, especially against the New York Giants. But this year was different. The Athletics were a dynasty. But the wheels of this American League regime were about to fall off.

♦ 16 ♦

Making a Federal Case

In the short history of the World Series, no team had completed a four-game sweep until the Boston Braves took four straight from the Philadelphia Athletics (in 1907, Detroit didn't win a game against Chicago, but the two teams played to a tie in Game 1). In 1950, in his book *My 66 Years in the Big Leagues*, Connie Mack proposed that his team lost so badly because of in-fighting due to some players being recruited to play in the Federal League.

> Our team was divided into two factions: One for jumping to the rich Federal League, and the other for remaining loyal to the American League. Even with this split, we had won our sixth pennant. But during the World Series our team fell apart. The Boston Braves slaughtered us. I felt this keenly, as I knew we could walk away from the series if only we had been united. It was the proof of the slogan: "United we stand, divided we fall." And we fell.[1]

This reasoning has been repeated over the years, but the claims seem dubious, a revisionist history.

Chief Bender reportedly refused to scout the Braves late in the season when they were playing in New York, saying "he didn't propose to waste any time on a bush league team."[2] Bender was the Game 1 starter yet didn't show up at Shibe Park, which hosted the first two games, until 20 minutes before the start of the contest. After allowing a two-run triple and RBI single in the sixth inning to give Boston a 6–1 lead, Bender was pulled. As he made his way to the clubhouse, Mack supposedly said to the pitcher, "Pretty good hitting ... for a bush league team."[3]

The Athletics lost that game 7–1, but Philadelphia fell by a combined four runs in the other three defeats. Eddie Plank started Game 2 against Boston's Bill James, and the two remained locked in a scoreless duel through eight innings with neither hurler allowing a runner to reach third base. With one out in the ninth, Braves third baseman Charlie Deal lofted a fly ball to center field which Amos Strunk camped under. However, the sunglasses-wearing Strunk still lost the ball in the glare as it made its descent, and it landed behind him, Deal ending up on second base with a double. Pitcher Bill James tried to bunt—but the Athletics called a pitchout. Deal was caught off second and made a move back to the bag. As soon as catcher Wally Schang threw down, Deal reversed direction and bolted to third. Shortstop Jack Barry got the ball caught in the webbing of his glove, and Deal was safe. After James struck out, right fielder Les Mann blooped a hit just past the outstretched glove of second baseman Eddie Collins, the ball landing safely in short center field as Deal crossed the plate.

The Athletics put two men on with one out in the ninth inning—this time Mack did hit for Plank, who had gotten standing ovations from the crowd every time he stepped to the plate, and Jimmy Walsh walked—but Eddie Murphy grounded one to shortstop Rabbit Maranville, who stepped on second and threw to first to complete a game-ending double play. It was the fourth World Series game Plank lost as a starting pitcher—and each time the Athletics were shut out. "Plank ... demonstrated that he is still one of the greatest pitchers in the game," Braves manager George Stallings said. "He gave us more trouble than any left-hander we have faced since the Fourth of July."[4]

Plank perhaps knew this might be his final game in an Athletics uniform. Years later, Joe Bush described the scene in the clubhouse afterwards. "After the game we all felt gloomy and it was very quiet in the clubhouse as we took our showers and dressed," Bush recounted to the *Saturday Evening Post* in 1929. "I was one of the last to leave. Good old Eddie Plank hadn't even started to take off his uniform. He was sitting in front of his locker with his head between his hands as downhearted as any man could be. We all were genuinely sorry for him. It took him some time to get over losing that game."[5]

The Athletics lost Game 3, 5–4 in 12 innings. Philadelphia scored twice to take the lead in the top of the 10th inning, but Bush allowed a pair of runs in the home half, then made a bad throw to third after a bunt attempt in the 12th to allow the winning run to score. The Braves completed the sweep the next day with a 3–1 victory.

The Athletics scored just six runs and batted .172 with 28 strikeouts in 128 at-bats (Murphy had led the team during the regular season with 46 strikeouts in 573 at-bats) in the four games. "We knew that the Athletics loved speed and Stallings cautioned us before every game and threatened to do a lot of things to us if we slipped up any fast ones, especially in a pinch," said James, who also pitched the final two innings of Game 3, of the Braves' pitching strategy. "Therefore, I relied almost entirely on my slow ball and 'spitter.'"

Plank had another theory. The pitcher ran into Stallings in Chicago in late November and told him the manager found a way to curtail the

Athletics' sign stealing—which they had been very good at doing for a number of years—and that led to Philadelphia's downfall. "The Athletics profited a good deal from signal tipping. It was specially useful to the batter to know whether he could expect a curve or a fast ball. Stuffy McInnis, who was not naturally a good hitter, was able to hit over .300 solely through the benefit he gained from this inside dope on the pitcher's stuff,"[6] Plank later noted.

Ty Cobb espoused this as well in a syndicated article after Game 1, when the Athletics had just five hits off Dick Rudolph:

> A great trick of the Mackmen is for the batter to pull out of the box when the catcher is giving his signals to the pitcher so that the coachers at first and third bases have a better chance to get a glimpse at what is going on. They tried this old trick yesterday, but Stallings knew it well as the Philadelphia team did, and [Johnny] Evers could be heard shouting from second base: "Take your time, Dick. Wait till he gets back in the box." As a result no signs were given while the batter was out of the box. As soon as Evers shouted his suggestion to Rudolph, [catcher Hank] Gowdy would stop all signs. All this was a big surprise to the Athletics. The Mack team would probably have done much better if they had gone out here and tried to hit the ball as they saw it.[7]

Boston Braves second baseman Johnny Evers shakes hands with Eddie Plank before Game 1 of the 1914 World Series. Evers was 7-for-16 in the series, including 2-for-4 off Plank in Game 2 (George Grantham Bain Collection, Library of Congress).

16. Making a Federal Case

Plank went into great detail about the Athletics' system of sign stealing in talking with *St. Louis Post-Dispatch* writer W.J. O'Connor during spring training in 1916:

> The co-operation of batter and base runner with the aid of the coacher who transmits the signals, is everything. With men such as Coombs, Bender and Davis we had lots of fun. I give these men credit for making .300 hitters out of kids who didn't figure to bat better than .200. I say Collins is the greatest infielder of all time in baseball. He knows the game from every conceivable angle, can sense in advance any play that may come up. I'll tell you how far this system went. Chief Bender has the keenest eye I have ever known. I know that he has gotten the signal of a catcher by seeing from first base or third, the muscle move in the hand above the finger. That's almost incredible but it is true.
>
> To my mind the greatest advantage in signal tipping is to know when they're going to pitch out. Can't you appreciate that? Say, for instance, there's a runner on first and he's taking all the lead he can get. If the other fellows waste one and we know it, look what we gain. The runner doesn't move, the batter has the advantage of having a ball called and the enemy is slowly getting into the hole. I remember that Joe Lake for two years had the Athletics' number. We couldn't solve his delivery. He had a spitter, fast one and curve. One day I noticed that when he spit on the ball he put his first two fingers over his mouth. When he "faked" a spitter he kept the two fingers on the ball and went through the rotary motions of moistening the pellet. Now our detection board did this: It eliminated the spitter from Lake's repertoire. We could always spot the spitter. We had to guess when the curve or fast one was coming. But from that day on Lake never won a game from us.
>
> Sometimes we got our signals from the enemy catcher. If he covered up so we couldn't get them from the coacher's box, we worked a wise head to second and kept him there as long as we could. These signals are transmitted to the batter by word signs. That's why some of those apparently insane remarks of the coacher are often so repeated. They mean something to the batter.[8]

This is not to say that Mack's fear of the Federal League wasn't real. It was later reported that he was so sure Plank was headed to that league that after Game 4 he didn't even say goodbye to his longtime pitcher as he left the clubhouse. "Maybe I should have stopped him," Mack would later regret. "But I was too upset by what I knew was going on."[9] Plank hadn't signed with the Federal League nor had he come to any agreement. But the seeds had been planted months earlier.

. . .

The rumors started early. In November 1913, Eddie Collins was reportedly approached with a three-year, $50,000 offer by the Federal League, a report which the Athletics second baseman denied. Pitchers Joe Bush and Herb Pennock and outfielder Rube Oldring had supposedly also received offers.

The first mention of Plank and the fledgling league came in January 1914 when a wire story reported that the Feds tried to start up negotiations with the veteran Philadelphia pitcher. "Plank, always polite as a gentleman should be, replied that it was a waste of time to talk to him about a berth as he would refuse if the Federals gave him $50,000 a season. He wished the newcomers well, but added that aside from that he could not see the percentage in jumping away from the organization,"[10] stated the report.

It was around this time when opportunities with Lancaster and Reading of the Tri-State League were still on the table. However, even when those lapsed and he engaged in a stalemate in contract talks with Mack, Plank did not bring up the Federal League as leverage. Still, the upstart league kept trying.

Brooklyn Tip-Tops business manager John Montgomery Ward, a player of renown in the 19th century, visited Plank at his home in Gettysburg. The two chatted, and Plank revealed the offer Mack had made him—the same $5,000 he had earned in 1913. Ward was aghast, said a player of his tenure should be earning a higher salary, and offered Plank $7,500 to switch leagues (Ward also claimed he was willing to go to $10,000). Plank mulled it over, but in a letter to Ward rejecting the offer, he said it had nothing to do with the money, which he admitted was fair (and well above what he would sign for with Mack), but loyalty to Philadelphia, as well as worrying that he wouldn't pitch as well outside of the Athletics, led him to decline.

However, Plank might have been closer to accepting than he let on. While on the train ride to Jacksonville for spring training, Plank shared with Mack the offer which had been presented to him. He decided to get to camp and see what his teammates were doing. If others jumped to the Federal League, he would give it more consideration. But the Athletics remained intact.

Danny Murphy was gone, but not by his choice. Mack had tried to keep him from the Federal League—in fact, sending him to Baltimore to try and weaken it—but Murphy ignored the transaction and signed with the Tip-Tops. While he could still hit, at 37 years old, Murphy wouldn't be counted on to fill a regular spot in Brooklyn's lineup (he would play in just 52 games with 43 starts, but still hit .304 with 32 RBI in 161 at-bats) but rather act as agent for the league, trying to get players to jump to the Feds. And who better would he try to convince than players he knew from the Athletics? Among Murphy's friends on the Athletics were Jack Coombs and Plank, with whom he went hunting. Coombs, though, was still recovering from his bout with tuberculosis. Plank would be a year-long project.

Murphy perhaps helped land his new team one former Athletics player. Byron Houck, a 22-year-old right-handed pitcher who had won 14

16. Making a Federal Case

games the previous season, was sent by Mack to Baltimore in mid–May after posting three subpar starts in April. Houck refused to report, saying "I'll quit playing ball first"[11] before heading to the minor leagues. A few days later, he signed a three-year contract with Brooklyn. It's not hard to imagine Murphy playing a role either in contacting the pitcher or offering a recommendation.

Federal League commissioner James Gilmore was based out of Chicago, so when Philadelphia visited the Windy City in mid–June, rumors again began swirling about Athletics players considering offers from the Federal League. Collins now admitted Brooklyn had contacted him and made an offer for the 1915 season. Frank Baker and Stuffy McInnis reportedly were among the Philadelphia players contacted, although the pair didn't acknowledge the veracity of the report.

Publicly, Mack acted nonchalant. "Manager Mack wires that he knows nothing about the matter," wrote F.C. Lane of *Sporting Life*, "that his players have not taken him into their confidence, and that he is not worrying about the matter at present."[12] Privately, though, Mack ensured his star players wouldn't be going anywhere. "We tore up some contracts in midseason, wrote new ones, entered into three-year agreements with Eddie Collins, Frank Baker and other key players,"[13] he revealed in Fred Lieb's book, *Connie Mack, Grand Old Man of Baseball*, which was published over 30 years after the fact.

Plank was not among those to get a revised, more lucrative deal in mid–July. Turning 39 later that summer, he was not the kind of player to whom you handed out a three-year contract. But he still had some star power. On August 3, several high Federal League officials—Gilmore, Brooklyn owner George Ward, Chicago owners Charlie Weeghman and William Walker, and league attorney E.E. Gates—came out to see the Athletics play the White Sox in Chicago. On the mound that day were Plank and Chicago's 25-year-old right-hander, Jim Scott.

As summer turned to fall, the Federal League rumors quieted. But once the World Series ended, they sprung up anew. The Feds held their league meeting in New York City, and Plank and, of all people, 41-year-old Harry Davis, who was now relegated to coaching and a ceremonial plate appearance here and there, were reportedly spotted at in a hallway at the Hotel Biltmore, where the meetings were taking place, although, as one story noted, "no one could be found who [had] actually seen the pair."[14] Plank also shot down reports that he had signed with the Federal League's Chicago Whales. "Plank said that he had no intention of signing with the Feds, and in fact had received no offers from them since last spring, when he turned down their inducements,"[15] reported the *Philadelphia Inquirer*. Connie Mack, cornered while watching a football game between Carlisle and Penn at Philadelphia's Franklin Field, said he hadn't heard of anything relating to Plank and the Federal League.

But Mack might have gotten wind of some other news. Plank said he was in New York because he was making his way to Maine for a weekend hunting trip—with Danny Murphy. In addition, fellow pitchers Chief Bender and Jack Coombs were on their way to that expedition. A week later, none of those players would be members of the Philadelphia Athletics.

While Mack said he knew nothing of the goings-on between Plank and the Federal League, the truth was that the pitcher did inform him that the circuit had made him a substantial offer, but he had not accepted anything. On the Tuesday after the trio of pitchers went hunting with Murphy, Mack put them all on waivers. Although Mack hoped to keep that news quiet, Detroit manager Hughie Jennings let it slip (perhaps intentionally), which infuriated Mack. "When a waiver is asked on a player it is supposed to be treated in confidence by owners and club managers, but this much could not be expected of Jennings, who devotes six months of the year to baseball and the other six months to his vaudeville act,"[16] he told reporters.

Mack explained that the Athletics lost money in 1914 and these were just the first of his moves, with bigger ones to come (he lived up to that promise when he sold Eddie Collins to the White Sox on December 8). He said he no intention of bringing any of the three pitchers back in 1915; they were waived with the purpose of releasing them, but perhaps someone wanted to pay the $1,500 claiming fee.

"While I had no intention of retaining the three players named for the season of 1915, I would not have asked for waivers on the players at this time but for the fact that one of the three had told me that he was talking business with the Federal League," said Mack, referring to Plank. "He told me that he had been offered big money and did not suppose that we wanted to meet the offer. I suggested to this player that perhaps some of the other clubs in the league would meet the demand. I want it strictly understood that I am for the American League in victory or defeat."[17]

Plank, back in Gettysburg, only knew he had been waived because a friend of his in Philadelphia read about it in the newspaper and telephoned him. Saying it was a "complete surprise,"[18] Plank turned his frustration to his now-former manager.

> I should have thought Connie would have told me something about it, particularly since I told him a few days ago that I had received a strong offer from the Federal League. I was man enough to do that, and Connie might at least have done the same towards me. I gave the best I had to the Athletics and would like to be able to say the club treated me as well in return. I feel that I have at least a couple of years more good pitching left in my old wing, and the fact that the Athletics want to release me will not make the Federals believe that I am all

in. If the Feds think that way, I don't have to worry, for I have got mine stowed away in farms and the bank, and I don't have to play ball anymore unless I want to. Even now I am not sure that I shall play ball with the Federals, but if I do, you can bet that I shall get a fat salary and I shall give them the best I have in return. So far as Coombs and Bender are concerned, I don't know anything about them, and their business is their own.[19]

Plank wasn't the only one who was surprised. Athletics fans were in a tizzy, seeing three longtime pitchers, catalysts for a dynasty ("The Athletic team from 1909 to 1914 was the strongest that ever played in baseball. I feel proud to think I belonged to it,"[20] Plank later said) let loose. "The loss of Plank seems to have touched the hearts of fans, who regret it deeply," wrote *Sporting Life*'s Chandler D. Richter. "The fact that Plank was one of the original team that entertained this city under the name of Athletics has endeared him to the fans. For years it has been predicted that Plank, because of his age, was all in, but each season Eddie bobbed up serenely with a great percentage. This refusal to weaken threw the spotlight on Plank at all times, and his clean living off the field strengthened him in the eyes of the fans."[21]

Each American League team had a chance to claim Plank, as well as Bender and Coombs. If none did, and after going through waivers in the National League and passed through there, they would be released from their contracts and be free to sign with any club—in any league.

The Chicago White Sox were the first to speak up. Owner Charles Comiskey and manager Jimmy Callahan intimated they wouldn't claim Plank because they already had enough lefties on their team—one to be exact, Reb Russell. St. Louis Browns manager Branch Rickey also said he felt his pitching staff was just fine as is and didn't need the addition of Plank (the Browns finished sixth in the AL in ERA in 1914). Boston Red Sox manager Bill Carrigan stated publicly that "with Plank winning twenty games for the Red Sox in 1915, the world's title will be featured between the Braves and Red Sox next fall."[22] However, there's no indication that beyond this the Red Sox showed any interest in bringing in Plank.

Detroit owner Frank Navin at first said he was going to let all three pitchers pass through waivers but a day later made it known he would claim Plank. "I would not pay any big money for Plank, but if I can get him to come here, I will hand him a contract for one year," Navin said. "I couldn't afford to take a chance on him with a long contract but would be willing to pay him just as long as he delivered the goods. You never can tell how long one of those old fellows is going to last."[23] Navin, though, expressed more of an interest in trading for Plank or signing him as a free agent, than in letting Mack get all the money, which might give Plank less motivation to do well. When he tried to deal for Plank, Mack refused, telling the owner "You have a good enough club as it is, Frank, and so has Boston. I want Plank to go to some team that needs strengthening and to which Eddie will not add enough to make it a pennant contender."[24]

But the New York Yankees emerged as Plank's biggest suitor. On November 12, Yankees team secretary Tom Davis made public that only they had made a claim on Plank, the other American League teams passing on him to better keep him in New York and the American League (AL president Ban Johnson said both Boston and Cincinnati of the National League put a claim in on Plank). "We refused to waive on Plank and I will do all I can to land him for my club,"[25] New York owner Frank Farrell declared.

Yankees scout Arthur Irwin was quickly dispatched to Gettysburg to find out if Plank had already signed a deal with the Federal League and, when finding out he hadn't, to offer him a sizeable salary for the 1915 season. Neither Irwin nor Plank discussed the details of the meeting—length or term of a contract or even if he signed (he hadn't).

On the heels of Irwin's visit, a week later Joe Tinker, player-manager of the Federal League's Chicago Whales, was the next to arrive in Gettysburg. Despite rumors of Plank having already signed with Chicago, those reports were baseless. Tinker had come to make an offer and reportedly extended Plank a contract for $6,000, but the pitcher wanted more (he was reportedly seeking between $7,500–$10,000 a season). Tinker headed back to Chicago with this information, which he relayed to Charles Weeghman. The Whales owner proclaimed, "I would like to see Plank in a Chicago Federal uniform but his terms are too strong and I have practically ended all negotiations."[26]

With the Federal League prospects apparently fading, the Yankees remained confident. "I didn't get Plank—at least, I haven't so far," Irwin said, "but it's a long time till reporting for spring training."[27] Irwin wouldn't have to wait nearly that long. A week later and Plank was officially with the Feds.

While Weeghman might have balked at Plank's salary demand, it was clear the league wanted to sign him. It was reported that Brooklyn offered him $10,000 for one year, but Plank wanted a two-year deal. In the end, the league sent Baltimore Terrapins treasurer Harry Goldman to Gettysburg to seal the deal, which he did. Plank signed a contract not with Baltimore, or any specific Federal League team, but rather a general contract which could see him sent anywhere, although Chicago and Brooklyn were the favorites. Plank confirmed the signing and wouldn't reveal any details about the contract. Speculation had his contract being two or three years, but in actuality it was for only one. His salary reportedly paid him $8,000, and he might have received a signing bonus (Bender, who visited Plank a few days earlier, signed a two-year contract with the league on December 5, reportedly worth $8,500 per season with a $5,500 bonus). Plank finally got his money, although his negotiations with the Yankees would come back to haunt him in a couple of years.

There were other big names and established stars the Federal League was going after, and one, Walter Johnson, provided Plank's fate for his next ballclub. Phil Ball of the St. Louis Terriers was after Johnson but was unable to secure a deal. Chicago's Weeghman was then allowed to make a run at the Washington Senators pitcher with the understanding that if he signed, Ball could get another pitcher who was in the Federal League's control. Offered a two-year deal worth $17,000 per year and given a $6,000 advance on his salary, Johnson signed. The Feds had their big coup, and Ball, with his pick of the litter, chose to add Plank, who had been earmarked for either Chicago or Brooklyn.

The plan would blow up in the Federal's face, though, as the American League pitched in to get Johnson back, helping Washington give him a $12,500 contract while also paying back the $6,000 advance, which Johnson got to keep. Plank, meanwhile, was still stuck in St. Louis, which was fine for 1915. But down the line his attitude would change.

Eddie Plank (middle) and Chief Bender (right) in 1911. The pitchers were teammates on the Athletics from 1903–1914, and both headed to the Federal League in 1915 (George Grantham Bain Collection, Library of Congress).

Gettysburg Eddie Plank

Only a gap in baseball nine—
A few players missing, so why repine?
Other heroes will take their place
And respond to our cheers through the pennant race.
But Reader, if sentiment is not yet dead,
You'll brush off a tear and bare your head
As you see no more in the same old rank,
Collins and Bender and Coombs and Plank.
Collins and Bender and Coombs and Plank;
What thrills ye gave us! What joys we drank,
As bravely ye fought when the battle was on
And hurled back the foe with your mighty brawn.
Year after year we have looked to you
To lead in the charge of our flag-winning crew.
Always in the van of the valorous rank
Were Collins and Bender and Coombs and Plank.
Collins and Bender and Coombs and Plank;
Of your best ye gave us; no duty ye shrank.
Yours was the place where the blood grows hot—
Where the less brave trembled, and nerves stretched taut.
But the time comes to all, as it has to you,
When we've got to move on for another crew;
And when our time comes let us hope that we'll rank
With Collins and Bender and Coombs and Plank.[28]
                    —Jim Nasium, *Philadelphia Inquirer*

◆ 17 ◆

One Year with the Feds

A new league wasn't the only change in Eddie Plank's life. On January 30, 1915, at a church in Ridgewood, New Jersey—over 200 miles from Gettysburg and out of the public eye—Plank married Anna Cora Myers. In true Plank fashion, he didn't tell anyone, including his closest confidants, until three weeks later, just as the couple were readying to leave for Havana, Cuba. "Yes, I am married," Plank confirmed on February 22 after his new mother-in-law issued an announcement. "I suppose you will hear all about it tomorrow, but I wanted to keep it a secret until I left for spring training. Mrs. Plank will go along south, where we train."[1]

There were clues, if you were looking for them. It was later reported that Plank and his new bride had been seeing each other off and on for 13 years and Plank had "been a frequent visitor to the Myers home during his vacations after the playing seasons"[2]—hence the rumors of marriage which occasionally cropped up. It was reported at the end of January that Plank "is preparing to join the Presbyterian church"[3] in Gettysburg. The couple were indeed married in a Presbyterian church in that small New Jersey village (their son would be married in the same church 21 years later).

The sudden betrothment was a shock, even to locals in Gettysburg and New Oxford, Myers' hometown. "It came as a distinct surprise to the many friends of both the bride and bridegroom,"[4] stated the *New Oxford Item*. The *Gettysburg Star and Sentinel* said, "The announcement of the wedding came as a surprise to all the pitcher's friends and acquaintances in Gettysburg and throughout the country. In every place but his home town 'Eddie' has been regarded as a confirmed bachelor. He escaped the charms of many a girl during his 14 years on the diamond, only to have his heart pierced by Cupid's arrows from his native county."[5]

The information on Anna Myers was scant as well. One report had her as being 26. In actuality, Myers was 32—she would turn 33 in early March. She lived in New Oxford with her mother but was hardly a stay-at-home spinster. She enjoyed throwing parties for friends at her home during holidays—there were notices in the local paper about celebrations she had surrounding St. Patricks' Day in 1911 and Valentine's Day in 1914. There were also trips to Gettysburg to visit her aunt (and perhaps Plank), among other excursions.

In 1914, at least, she was a corsetiere, advertising often that they were "Made to measure and guaranteed not to rust or break for one year."[6] Later that summer she got together with a friend, Mabel Roth, and got into millinery, apparently setting up a hat shop in New Oxford.

Even with his new wife and about to make more money playing baseball than he ever had in his life, not all was rosy for Plank. A report—coming out of New Oxford, which lends to the source and the validity—had asked Federal League boss James Gilmore to assign him somewhere closer to his home, perhaps Pittsburgh or, preferably, Baltimore. St. Louis was the furthest locale that could be chosen, but that wasn't a matter of choice for Gilmore but a matter of politics with owner Phil Ball. Plank didn't want to make waves, so he quickly gave up his protest.

He also initially claimed he wouldn't go to Cuba—professing he didn't like the weather there, nor was he fond of boat trips—then said he would take a train to Jacksonville before going to Havana, but in the end after Anna joined him at a stop in New Oxford, the pair set sail from Philadelphia to the island, making a stop in Key West first, where Plank met up with some of his new pitcher and catcher teammates for a pre-training camp.

In Havana, as the team checked into the Hotel Gran American, Plank met his first professional manager other than Connie Mack. Fielder Jones had a history with Plank as well—as an opponent. Jones jumped to the American League's Chicago team in 1901 after playing five years in Brooklyn. An outfielder, Jones was named manager of the White Sox during the 1904 season and remained there until quitting the game in 1908. He led Chicago to four straight winning seasons, including a World Series title in 1906, and was considered a coup for the Federal League when he took over for first-time manager Mordecai Brown, a future Hall of Fame pitcher who jumped to the Feds from the National League but sported a 50–63 record when Jones was hired.

The 1914 St. Louis Terriers—in the papers the team was called the "Miners" or "Brownies," both takeoffs off Brown (one of his nicknames was Miner)—finished in last place in the eight-team Federal League. Ball, who was not afraid to spend money to improve his baseball team, vowed the team would be better in 1915. At first, Jones wasn't sold on the league adding Plank, but it was partly due to his recommendation of the pitcher to Harry Goldman that the Baltimore treasurer went to Gettysburg and eventually sealed a deal.

If he ever had any doubts, Jones was a full Plank backer before spring training even started. "I regard Eddie Plank as the best pitching bet in the league," he said. "Plank's peculiar motion—you know he faces first base when he pitches—and his eagerness to win, will make him a headliner. You can't solve Plank's delivery in a season; I couldn't in three, and during my stay in the American League I feared him more than any other hurler—and for that reason I expect him to win."[7]

Plank wasn't the only addition for St. Louis. Third baseman Charlie Deal, who scored the only run in Plank's 1–0 loss to Boston in the 1914 World Series, made the jump to the Federal League, as did three minor-league infielders: Babe Borton, Ernie Johnson, and Bobby Vaughn. The latter allowed pitcher Doc Crandall, who had made over 60 starts at second base for the Terriers in 1914, to be a full-time moundsman. The outfield of Delos Drake, Ward Miller, and Johnny Tobin remained intact, although the club hoped to regain the services of Cuban outfielder Armando Marsans, who played nine games with the team after jumping from Cincinnati during the previous season. However, the Reds took the Federal League to court over the issue, and an injunction prevented Marsans from suiting up for St. Louis until August (he still played ball in Cuba and acted as the team's tour guide, with certainly more than one stop at the cigar shop he owned).

Besides Plank (and now a full-time Crandall), the pitching staff remained relatively the same, with Dave Davenport, Bob Groom, Ed Willett, and Doc Watson, who had moved from the Chicago Whales to St.

Philadelphia Athletics players sit in the dugout at a crowded Shibe Park during Game 2 of the 1914 World Series. Eddie Plank lost a 1–0 heartbreaker—his fourth World Series start in which the Athletics did not score (George Grantham Bain Collection, Library of Congress).

Louis after Mordecai Brown was sent to Brooklyn. The pitching mostly held up in Cuba as the Terriers won nine of 11 games—Willett beat the heralded Jose Mendez twice—and the trip was a success. For the most part.

Upon arrival, there was an issue with the Habana Reds, who postponed their games with the Terriers upon orders of the Philadelphia Phillies, who were training in in Cuba as well. Instead, the St. Louis players walked five miles to witness boxer Jack Johnson train for his fight against Jess Willard. The players were excited to watch the bout, but after it was postponed from April 4 to April 5 (the former being Easter) they had to skip it or risk missing a boat back to the United States.

After pitching five shutout innings on March 20, Plank sent a letter to his brother Ira declaring he had "The same old stuff. Never felt better or came around better in my life."[8] However, he would later grouse about the lack of fans at games. "There was much novelty connected with watching an American team then [with the Athletics in 1910 and 1912], while now, the trip has become a regular occurrence, and the natives are not so anxious," he said. "Spring is a bad time for a club to come here. It corresponds to our fall in that the people have grown more or less wearied of watching ball games. The Cuban season has just closed, and, as is true in the States, ball games are a drug on the market."[9] At least Anna Plank had a good time. In her letters to her mother, she remarked on the beautiful weather conditions (especially compared to Key West).

The Terriers arrived back in St. Louis full of bluster. "The fans back in old St. Louis might think it is a joke when I say that the Terriers will be the runners-up for the pennant this season, but when they see my squad they will be surprised," Jones declared as they made the trek back to the Midwest. "Eddie Plank, the veteran twirler, is going to win a good many games this season for us, and his knowledge of the game is going to be a great help to the younger men on the team. Plank was good enough last fall to be picked by Connie Mack to pitch in the world's series, and if Ed is good enough for a world's series he will be good enough for the Terriers."[10] Owner Ball challenged the American League's St. Louis Browns to games with a bet of $2,500 by each club (he also said he would give any gate receipts to charity if and when his team won). The Browns didn't respond.

On a cloudy day with rain threatening, the Terriers opened their 1915 season at Chicago's Weeghman Park, recently renovated with the addition of bleachers in left field (the park would later be known as Wrigley Field, home of the Cubs). Jones hadn't decided who would start between Groom or Plank, but eventually went with Plank. Dressed in his new digs, an all-blue uniform with a white cap and white socks, Plank faced spitballing right-hander Claude Hendrix, who led the Federal League in games (49), wins (29–10), and ERA (1.69) in 1914.

17. One Year with the Feds

He had the 16,000 opposing fans cheering for him early on after fanning four batters in the first two innings. Plank receiving enthusiastic ovations early in the season became the norm, even more so in cities whose fans had never seen him pitch. He tossed seven shutout innings before faltering in the eighth, allowing three runs and losing, 3–1. Plank scored St. Louis' only run, doubling in the fifth and coming home on Jack Tobin's triple.

Plank pitched 1⅓ innings of relief on April 15 in Kansas City, then was shelved with a sore arm—the *St. Louis Post-Dispatch* dubbed it "the worst he has ever owned"[11]—and wouldn't pitch again until starting in Pittsburgh on April 27. By that point, St. Louis was 3–8 and had lost the first three games of the series to the Stogies, coming off being shut out in back-to-back games. It was early in the season, but the Terriers desperately need a win. Plank delivered.

"It was with a sort of awe that the spectators watched Eddie Plank take charge of the rubber," the *Post-Dispatch* reported. "He justified the reputation that preceded him to Pittsburgh at the start."[12] Plank took a shutout into the seventh inning before allowing a run in the eighth and another in the ninth before loading the bases with two out. Jones had Bob Groom warming up and went to the mound, where Plank either argued his case to stay in or insisted he wouldn't leave. Either way, he remained and got the final out to record his first Federal League victory, the 285th of his career. James J. Long of the *Pittsburgh Sun* wrote:

Fielder Jones was Eddie Plank's manager with both the St. Louis Terriers and Browns (George Grantham Bain Collection, Library of Congress).

Any fan who doubted the right of Eddie Plank to be classed among the greatest wonders in the history of base ball must have been convinced by the old man's performance at Exposition Park yesterday. After Plank and Bender had been enlisted under Federal colors Connie Mack told friends that both hurlers were all in and that he had advised them to accept any big offer the insurgents might make, but from yesterday's developments he had the wrong dope, at least as far as Plank is concerned. Eddie is 40 years old and has 14 years of major league service behind him, but he can still pitch big time ball occasionally, though his ability to keep it up all season remains to be demonstrated.[13]

In his next start, Plank blanked Newark, 1–0, but the arm problem cropped up again as he removed himself after one inning in his next outing and missed a week. He returned and tossed three straight complete games. Plank's shutout at home against Brooklyn, an 11–0 win in the first game of a May 29 doubleheader, evened the Terriers' record at 16–16. However, only roughly 500 people saw it as attendance for all three teams in the city—Terriers, Browns, and Cardinals—took a hit. "You fans have complained because the newspapers have not supported the Federal League, since the St. Louis club has been playing such wonderful ball. What have you done? How many times have you been out to see Fielder Jones' aggregation of speed marvels?"[14] *St. Louis Star* reporter Billy Murphy wrote.

Three days later, Plank won, 2–1, at Chicago, topping Mike Prendergast, who had been 5–0. Plank retired the order in six of the nine innings and set down the final 12 batters. He allowed just five hits and walked no one, while striking out five. His performance prompted this poem from the *St. Louis Post-Dispatch*'s L.C. Davis:

> The Terriers met up with the Whales
> And gave them quite a whaling;
> Those Whales found they were up against
> The toughest kind of sailing.
> As fast as they came up to blow,
> Old Eddie Plank harpooned 'em;
> They couldn't clout,
> For some struck out
> And others still ballooned 'em.[15]

The win pushed the Terriers to 18–17 and 2½ games out of first place. However, St. Louis had four teams ahead of it. Kansas City and Pittsburgh were tied for first at 23–17. Newark (22–17) and Chicago (23–18) were tied for third. Even Baltimore at 18–19 was only 3½ games behind the leaders. "That means the Feds are putting on one of the closest races ever staged in any circuit,"[16] the *Chicago Tribune* declared.

Plank's win on June 12, 4–1 over Pittsburgh, started St. Louis on a 12-game winning streak—Plank missed the tail end of it due to a bout with

17. One Year with the Feds

food poisoning—which lifted the Terriers into a tie for first place with Kansas City. The streak ended June 24 in Baltimore, dropping St. Louis back to second place. But a win the next day put the Terriers back in a tie for the league lead.

In contrast to St. Louis, Baltimore was struggling. The Terrapins entered a June 25 doubleheader 11 games under .500 and 12 games behind the co-leaders. Yet there was palpable excitement in the city as former teammates Plank and Chief Bender were set to face off against each other for the first time. A previous scheduled meeting in St. Louis in late May had been rained out, so this anticipated matchup was months in the making (and it nearly never occurred at all as St. Louis was offered Bender's contract after he signed but declined). Even the *Philadelphia Evening Ledger*—which had no Federal League team in its city—declared it a—"much advertised pitching duel."[17]

It was declared "Plank Day" at Terrapin Park, and Plank's parents and his brother Howard, a policeman, came down from Gettysburg to witness the event. It was only the second time Howard Plank had watched his younger brother pitch as a professional. Before the game started, both pitchers were asked to approach home plate, where each received flowers, courtesy of the Terrapins.

The park was filled, with 12,000 fans eventually cramming their way in. "There was no room for the band in the grandstand," the *Baltimore Sun* noted, "so the musicians were placed in back of third base."[18] During the fifth inning, fans started exiting the bleachers and onto the field, calling for the ground-rule double rule to be instituted for any ball which landed in the crowd. That wouldn't be an issue for Plank, who was pitching like he was 29, not 39.

Plank allowed only three hits in the game. George Zinn doubled with two outs in the first inning but was gunned down trying to stretch it into a triple. Jimmy Walsh doubled off Plank twice—with one out in the fifth inning (Plank then struck out Otto Knabe and Mickey Doolin) and to lead off the eighth. Plank didn't walk a batter and struck out nine. He also drove in a run in the seventh inning on a single off Bender, who gave up 10 hits without a walk, striking out four. Plank faced only 29 batters as St. Louis won, 2-0. The big crowd was loud all game and in the ninth stood and cheered Plank on as he recorded the final outs. "It was a well-deserved tribute for the veteran,"[19] said the *St. Louis Post-Dispatch*.

That wasn't Plank's only memorable game of the season. Plank often spoke of wanting to throw a no-hitter. On July 13, he did. Well, sort of. Plank had pitched only three innings since July 5 as Jones was saving him for this particular contest, the opener of a four-game series in St. Louis against Chicago, an encore of the Opening Day matchup against Hendrix.

With two down in the third inning, Hendrix doubled to right field off Plank. After that, he had Chicago hitters as his mercy. Through nine innings he allowed just the lone hit—the problem was St. Louis couldn't score off Hendrix. The Terriers had a couple of chances but catcher Art Wilson, who was on the New York Giants teams Plank and the Athletics had faced in the 1911 and 1913 World Series, picked runners off second base in the second and fourth innings. In the fourth, the Terriers loaded the bases with two out but Babe Borton struck out.

The game went into extra innings, and despite the hot temperatures—it hit 100 degrees at the day's hottest point—the trend continued: Plank set down the Whales while St. Louis couldn't push across a run against Hendrix. Finally, in the 14th, Plank wilted, ever-so-slightly. First baseman Bill Jackson opened the inning by walking on a 3–2 pitch. It was the first walk issued by Plank, and the deciding pitch was close enough that both the *Chicago Tribune* and *St. Louis Star* called into question the ball four call by umpire Bill Finneran, as did Plank, who argued to no avail.

Up stepped Les Mann—he of the 1914 Boston Braves who drove in the run which sent Plank to a defeat in his final game with the Athletics—and he singled. It was the first hit for Chicago since Hendrix's double—Plank had gone 10⅓ hitless innings. The only baserunner, besides Jackson, during that span reached by an error. Plank retired the order in 11 of the first 13 innings.

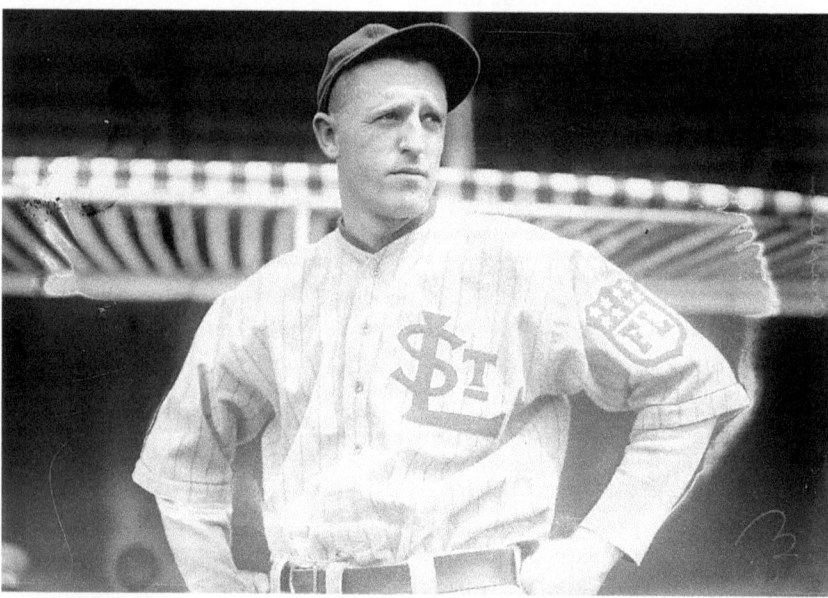

Harry Chapman was Eddie Plank's Doc Powers of the Federal League. Chapman hit only .199 in 1915 but Plank had five shutouts in the 15 starts when Chapman was the catcher (George Grantham Bain Collection, Library of Congress).

Now he faced two on with nobody out but got eighth-place hitter Jimmy Smith to pop out to second baseman Vaughn. Hendrix stepped in and lofted a fly to left field. The game was roughly three hours long, and the left fielder, Ward Miller, had ditched his sunglasses as the sun began to set. As a result, he lost the ball and it fell for a double, both runners scoring. St. Louis filled the bases in the home 14th but a strikeout and double play sealed Plank's fate: a 2–0 loss. "[Miller] lost Eddie Plank the greatest game this hero of world's championships has ever pitched,"[20] the *St. Louis Star* ruminated.

Plank was matched up with Bender in his next start, but it was called off due to rain after one inning. The teams agreed to have them face off in two days, in the first game of a doubleheader. Plank bested his old teammate again, 4–1. He allowed just four hits and walked no one. In Plank's last 23 innings, he had given up just seven hits and one walk while letting just three runs cross the plate. Bender, who was tagged for three earned runs, allowed seven hits and also didn't walk a batter. "It was the hardest game I ever umpired," said home plate umpire Bill Brennan. "Neither pitcher grooved a ball the entire game. They were cutting the corners in an uncanny manner and when pitchers are pitching that way it is hard to umpire. I can easily see why Plank and Bender have been leading pitchers for so many years."[21] Said Baltimore manager Otto Knabe: "There's no greater pitcher than Plank. And he is just as good as he ever was. We were lucky to get a single hit off him and so is anyone else when he is going as he is at present."[22]

Plank had the Terrapins' number. In early August, he shut them out twice in a four-game series in Baltimore (neither time did he face Bender, who was losing favor in Baltimore and would be unconditionally released at the end of the month). On August 5 he won, 1–0, and four days later, 3–0, in a game shortened by rain after eight innings. "I like a pitcher like Plank, who will come to you occasionally with the suggestion: 'Get me one run today and I'll win this ball game,'" Jones said while reflecting in 1916. "Eddie said that on several occasions last season and we usually did as he bid."[23]

He won his next two starts to push his record to 14–7. Then Plank's career—and life—nearly ended. As he often did, Plank headed to Gettysburg during some off-time. He had to drive to Harrisburg to catch a train to Chicago, where St. Louis next played. But there had been a big rainstorm and he had to find a way to drive through four streams as bridges hadn't survived the onslaught of wind and rain. After crossing the fourth, the car stalled on train tracks. He barely got himself, and the car, out of the way before a train rushed past. Plank had to carve out a path to get back to the main road. He made the train to Chicago. No word whether he told Fielder Jones or the manager read about it in the papers.

A little over a week later, Plank turned 40. When he pitched against Pittsburgh on September 4, he became just the third major leaguer in the

20th century to pitch in a game at that age—and one of those was Washington manager Clark Griffith, who put himself in to pitch in one game from 1912 to 1914. The other: Cy Young, who pitched regularly until he was 44 years old, when he made 18 starts in 1911. Besides Plank, a 40 year old, wouldn't make a regular turn in a rotation until Babe Adams in 1922.

Plank lost the first game he pitched after his 40th birthday, but the Terriers were sticking around the pennant race. St. Louis opened the month in fifth place, 5½ games out. When Plank beat Kansas City, 3–2, on August 28, the Terriers were still fifth, but 3½ back. Slowly, the pack began to separate. Pittsburgh emerged in first place, with St. Louis inching its way to second and Chicago in third. Newark and Kansas City were falling off the pace.

On September 11, Plank was given a big lead and easily beat Newark, 12–5 at home. The nearly 4,000 in attendance didn't know it—there was no mention of it in the newspapers—but the win was the 300th of Plank's career. He was just the eighth pitcher to reach the milestone and only the third since 1901, when the American League came into existence and Plank began his career. Cy Young got his 300th in 1901 and Christy Mathewson in 1912. It's still an exclusive club to this day, with only 24 members.

The win also meant St. Louis was just one game out of first place. With his team in hot pursuit of a pennant, Jones started using Plank more and in different circumstances. From September 14–19, he made five appearances, all but one in relief. After lasting only two innings in a September 14 start, Plank pitched two innings vs. Brooklyn (and lost) on September 16, then toiled in both ends of a September 18 doubleheader, 6⅔ innings in all, winning both games against Baltimore. The next day, Jones used him again against the Terrapins, this time going the final 4⅔ innings and picking up a loss after allowing five runs (only one earned), although he did strike out six with no walks.

While the *St. Louis Post-Dispatch* thought "It showed clearly that Davenport, Crandall and Plank are cracking under the strain of working too much,"[24] Fielder Jones doubled down. In the final week-and-a-half of the season, in which the Terriers played 12 games, those three pitchers were the only ones to take the mound for St. Louis, with the exception of one inning when Ed Willett relieved Plank in a 10–2 win over Baltimore.

The strategy, however, worked. After beating Baltimore on September 21, St. Louis was in third place and four games out. The Terrapins won their next eight games as well, including Plank's 5–0 shutout of Buffalo in the second game of a September 26 doubleheader. St. Louis was off September 28 and fell half a game behind Pittsburgh. Chicago lurked as well, just 1½ games back in third place—and the Whales finished with five games against Pittsburgh, three on the road and the final two at home. The Terriers closed with four games in St. Louis against Kansas City.

St. Louis lost a heartbreaker in the opener, 1–0, as Gene Packard outdueled Dave Davenport and accounted for the only tally of the game with a home run. Meanwhile, Chicago beat Pittsburgh to make things even more interesting. Plank pitched on September 30 and beat Chief Johnson, 4–2, while the Stogies bounced back with an 8–4 victory. All three teams were off Friday, October 1. Chicago and Pittsburgh would play a pair of doubleheaders on Saturday and Sunday, while St. Louis and Kansas City had single games. One thing was clear for the Terrapins: They had to win both games to have a chance to claim the pennant.

Jones decided to start Davenport on Saturday and save Plank for Sunday, when a win could potentially clinch a pennant instead of just keep the hopes alive. This would be Davenport's 46th start and 55th appearance overall. St. Louis led 1–0 early, but in the sixth inning Kansas City put two men on. Jones had Davenport walk light-hitting shortstop Johnny Rawlings intentionally to load the bases for pitcher Nick Cullop, who proceeded to smack a two-run double. The Packers scored another run in the inning, but it didn't matter as Cullop kept the Terriers off the board. Final: 4–1 and St. Louis' dreams of a pennant quashed. Jones later recounted:

> [Cullop] has his groove, anything high and outside. That's exactly where Davenport pitched. A fast one outside, with nothing on it, Dave thought he could get it far enough away to keep Cullop from getting hold of it. But that's the difference between Davenport and Plank. Had Plank tried that, the ball would never have been touched. He has perfect control, especially in the pinch. However, that one pitch beat us out of the pennant. I'm sure we would have won the flag had I had two Planks, one to go Saturday and another Sunday.[25]

The players were disconsolate after the game, as was St. Louis management. The team had planned on putting up more bleachers through the night to account for what was expected to be a large turnout for a potential pennant-winning finale. The new seating would have provided for 35,000 fans. Still, with nothing to play for but pride, between 7,500–10,000 (depending which newspaper you read) showed up for the finale. Plank didn't start, but he did come into the game in the third inning and threw seven shutout innings to pick up his 21st win (against 11 defeats) of the season.

Chicago took the flag by winning three of the last four games against Pittsburgh. The Whales finished with a record of 86–66 (.566). St. Louis was 87–67 (.565) and Pittsburgh 86–67 (.562). The Terrapins lost the Federal League pennant by .001 percentage point, the closest race in major league history. Chicago played two fewer games (actually four if ties are included), but no one from St. Louis complained about the disparity. The Whales were the champions. There was always next year. Except there wasn't. This was the end of the Federal League. Eddie Plank hoped this also meant a new beginning for him.

◆ 18 ◆

Meet Me in St. Louis (Again)

Eddie Plank's first season away from Connie Mack and the American League went about as well as could be expected, with the exception of just missing out on capturing the Federal League pennant. Pitching in 268⅓ innings—his most since 1907—he led the league in WHIP (0.99), was second in ERA (2.08), tied for second in shutouts (6), finished fourth in strikeouts (147), and tied for fifth in wins (21).

The St. Louis Terriers had a post-season banquet, but Plank (among many others on the team, including manager Fielder Jones) skipped it. He also had to cancel an appearance on a trap shooting tour of baseball players. But there was good reason—Anna Plank gave birth to a son, Eddie Jr., on October 18 in New Oxford, where the couple resided.

Plank thought he had some more good news on the way as well—a new team to play for in 1916. The day after Plank's son was born, Brooklyn Tip-Tops owner Robert Ward, who was the Federal League's biggest backer, died. The Federal League had filed a federal lawsuit against the American and National Leagues, but Ward's death hastened peace talks between the rival circuits. No matter the outcome, Plank thought the St. Louis Terriers were doomed. "There are too many clubs there already," Plank told a Gettysburg reporter regarding St. Louis. "Both the American and Nationals have teams playing in that city and there is no room for a third club."[1]

Plank also dropped some news in his interview. Despite wide reports of him having signed a two- or three-year deal with the Federal League, his contract only was for one season. He could sign with any team he wished, he said, but those who had shown interest were waiting to find out the result of upcoming meetings between the three leagues.

A week later it became official: St. Louis Terriers owner Phil Ball would buy the St. Louis Browns, and Chicago Whales owner Charles Weeghman purchased controlling stock of the Cubs. Those who were on the St. Louis and Chicago Federal League clubs had their contracts transferred to the new teams in the same city.

As far as Plank was concerned, let the bidding begin. He wouldn't be returning to the Philadelphia Athletics, however. Once the move to shutter the Federal League became known, Athletics manager Connie Mack made it clear he had no interest in a reunion. "No, I won't claim Plank or any other Federal Leaguer, I am building up a young ball team,"[2] he said.

There were plenty of other suitors. John McGraw was coy in not answering questions about Plank, but it was widely believed the New York Giants were interested in signing the veteran left-hander. "Wild Bill" Donovan, manager of the New York Yankees, visited Gettysburg to discuss a deal with Plank, but he left with an unsigned contract. Fielder Jones, installed as manager of the St. Louis Browns, sent Plank a contract for the 1916 season. "I think we can agree on terms without much parley," Jones said. "Indeed I expect my first offer to be acceptable to Plank, who is a very keen, but reasonable business man."[3]

However, in no short order Plank's options became limited. The National Commission, a three-man ruling board of the American and National Leagues, saw to that. It was leaked to the press on February 1 and made official a week later—Plank's reserve clause rights belonged to the Browns. He was not a free agent. Plank argued that when the Athletics waived him, no team claimed him, thus he was a free agent. The National Commission ruled otherwise.

According to the commission, two National League teams had in fact claimed Plank—Boston and Cincinnati. In addition, the New York Yankees engaged in negotiations with Plank before he signed with the Federal League. But the commission said even these points didn't matter—the Philadelphia Athletics never officially gave Plank his unconditional release. In Plank's appeal to the commission, he also said that according to the agreement between the three leagues, no former Federal League player would be penalized. Also, since the Federal League and the St. Louis Terriers were defunct, no one had the right to retain his services or enact the reserve clause. The commission's response: "The player's second contention is correct to the extent that all former Federal League players have been restored in good standing, but special privileges have not been conferred on them. His transfer to the St. Louis American League club is of record, and his salary for 1916 is a matter for negotiation between him and that club. The player's request to be declared a free agent is denied."[4]

The decision of the commission, which consisted of American League president Ban Johnson, National League president John Tener, and Cincinnati Reds owner August Herrmann, was unanimous. Plank never stood a chance even with the convoluted notion that he belonged to the Browns despite the Athletics never having technically released him. That ruined Plank's chance to pitch in the National League and be Christy Mathewson's teammate, as McGraw had agreed to sign Plank if he secured his release.

Instead, as the *St. Louis Post-Dispatch* noted, "Plank must sign with the Browns or quit the game."[5] With no ability to negotiate with other teams, and no Federal League to help drive up salaries, the Browns could offer him a big pay cut from his 1915 salary—which is exactly what they did. Jones sent Plank a contract which would pay him $4,000—half his 1915 take—with an additional $1,000 to be given for "exceptional performance."[6]

Now a family man, and wanting to build a house in Gettysburg, Plank accepted the offer, sending a telegram to Jones. A couple of months later, he bought a parcel of land in Gettysburg across from the college (on Carlisle Street) for $2,500. Soon, a three-story Colonial Revival–style house would be built.

"That's the best news I've had for a long time," Jones said after learning of Plank's intention to sign. "I regard Plank as the greatest money-pitcher in baseball. Put a prize on the eventualities of one game, let the pennant or world's series devolve on its outcome, and I would know of no pitcher alive I would rather see in there for my money than Plank."[7]

Plank wouldn't sign the contract until he arrived in Palestine, Texas. It was one of the few things he actually did at spring training. He pitched in only one game down south, going four innings against Denison on March 20 while playing with a bunch of Browns backups. Not that he didn't stay busy. His time in Texas included breaking up an attempted robbery, playing "football" in the lobby of the hotel using a rolled-up towel along with fellow left-handers Earl Hamilton, Ernie Koob, and Carl Weilman, challenging passers-by to a game of checkers or dominoes, managing the team of backups and, while at games, leisurely playing catch on the side of the field.

When the season began, Jones left Plank and fellow pitchers George Baumgardner and Bill Fincher back in St. Louis as the Browns opened the season in Cleveland. The plan remained to take it slow with Plank. In fact, Jones wanted to hold him out until St. Louis' next series—at his old stomping grounds in Chicago. On a rainy day at Comiskey Park in front of 18,000 fans, the Browns had a 6–1 lead in the seventh inning when Weilman walked three batters. Dave Davenport entered, and a walk and a single produced three runs. With two out, Plank was brought in to face former Athletics teammate, and good friend, Eddie Collins. "When Collins joined the Athletics, [Connie] Mack wouldn't let him bat against me, and I never before faced Eddie as a pitcher, in practice or a game,"[8] Plank noted afterwards. Plank won the first matchup, getting Collins to fly out.

The score remained 6–4 in the ninth inning when Plank suddenly and uncharacteristically lost control. With one out, he walked George Moriarty.

18. Meet Me in St. Louis (Again)

Eddie Collins (center) receives a car before the 1914 World Series for winning the Chalmers Award, given to the league's MVP. Eddie Plank (third from left) can be seen flashing a rare on-camera smile (George Grantham Bain Collection, Library of Congress).

After striking out Happy Felsch, he issued free passes to Buck Weaver (on a 3–2 pitch) and Collins. Instead of heading directly to first, Collins veered towards Plank and the two had a brief conversation. Plank had been jawing with umpire Silk O'Loughlin when Collins told him, "He missed one on me."[9] That certainly didn't soothe Plank, who after the game seethed, "Yesterday was the first time I had spoken to O'Loughlin in five years, and if it wasn't rotten work I wouldn't have spoken to him then."[10]

It didn't get any better as he walked Jack Fournier to force in a run, making it 6 5 with the bases full and two out. Jones really wanted this win—he had been talking about it for a week—and came out to talk to Plank. "If I lose this game, I'm going to lose it with you in there," he told the pitcher. "But I think you'll win. I haven't weakened on you yet."[11] As Jones left, the White Sox fans jeered and bellowed. Plank yelled out to Jones, "Do you hear all the noise, them shouts and screams? Well, that's music to Old Man Plank's ear. The louder they holler the more I feel like winning."[12] Jones, relaying the story to reporters later at the team hotel, queried, "Can you, I ask, lose confidence in a fellow who talks like that?"[13]

The next batter up was Joe Jackson, entering his first full season with the White Sox in which he would bat .341. Plank got ahead 2–2 before

Jackson whistled a grounder past third baseman Charlie Deal. But shortstop John Lavan hustled to his right, dove, and fed the ball just in time to second baseman Del Pratt to force Fournier (and also just in time to get spiked by the sliding Chicago first baseman).

A few days later, it was revealed that Plank wasn't even supposed to pitch due to a sore elbow. Plank, though, went against doctor's orders and hurled anyway. Days later, it wasn't his elbow which was giving him trouble, it was the thought of O'Loughlin's umpiring. "There is no other such inning in my record with the American League, and that one wouldn't be there if Silk O'Loughlin gave me a square deal," he fumed. "Silk wouldn't give me the corners that inning, and whenever they take the corners off the plate, Eddie Plank will have to quit. I don't pitch much on dead center, but I have managed to nip enough of the corner to get by. That's why I'm still in the league."[14] In Plank's next game, a seven-inning relief outing in a 15-inning tie on April 22 at home vs. Cleveland, the *St. Louis Post-Dispatch* observed, "Plank had perfect control."[15]

Especially at 40 years old, control was imperative for Plank, particularly on the first pitch when he would try to hit a corner to get ahead of the batter with a quick strike. His crossfire still froze batters, and as he aged he started using his curveball and changeup more, although, as noted by the *Detroit Free Press*, "Now and then he flashed a little speed, nothing like Walter Johnson's, of course, but just fast enough to be effective when blended with his floaters."[16]

It was just another reason why Jones had confidence in him.

> I'll tell you why Eddie Plank ... is a wonderful pitcher and why he may still be a great hillman at 50. Plank has a golden asset, he has always had it—control. That has kept him up there. He wastes nothing. He cuts the corners with his strikes and gives the batter the minimum. His pitches that are "balls" are the ones that look good a couple of feet before they reach the batter. Plank can give any batter two balls and then hold his own. Few pitchers ever have had the wonderful control that Plank possesses. The old boy knows every batter in the league. If he has a lead on the opposing team and a new batter faces him, watch him experiment with that newcomer. While it's safe, Plank will test the batter and ascertain what he will hit at, what he ignores and so on. Then when the time comes and the game is close, that batter is not a gamble to Plank—he knows him. Add to this the fact that Plank has lived a careful life and you have the secret of his wonderful success. Plank is in bed at 10 o'clock, the gay white way does not interest him in the slightest. His regular habits have assisted his wonderful constitution. Show me a pitcher like him today.[17]

Plank faced a similar situation as he had in Chicago in the ninth inning at Detroit on May 5. It was just his second start, and the Browns led, 5–1, when he allowed four hits, which scored three runs, then walked pinch hitter Donie Bush on four pitches to load the bases with two down. Jones stuck with Plank, who got Oscar Vitt to ground out and end the contest. "I think Plank is the best pitcher in the American League today. You can absolutely depend on him," Jones said. "I will never take him out of the game as long as he assures me that he is all right. In Friday's battle, after he had passed Bush and been hit four times in the ninth round, when I walked out to the diamond I didn't do it to steady him or caution him. I merely asked if he felt fit to go on. When he said it was all right, that ended it. And he came through. He's the best money-pitcher in baseball."[18]

Things weren't going swimmingly for the Browns, however. They lost seven straight in late April and had two five-game skids in May. Included in that was Plank's return to Philadelphia on May 15. St. Louis had a 4–1 lead when Plank allowed four runs in the seventh inning. Wally Schang hit a two-run triple—after taking what Plank thought was strike three ("In justice to Plank it must be admitted that it looked very much as if Schang should have been called out on strikes,"[19] observed the *Philadelphia Evening Public Ledger*)—to tie the game, then scored the go-ahead run on a wild pitch. The Browns lost, 5–4.

At the season's start, knowing he had a mix of former Browns and Terriers, Jones had stated, "It will take a full month before this team attains its highest degree of efficiency. If, therefore, we are in the race by June 1, just get a bet down on us for the pennant. By that time we eight will be working together as a machine or have proved ourselves failures."[20] After the Browns split a doubleheader with Cleveland on June 1—Plank pitching the final three innings—they were 15–25, eighth out of eight teams and 9½ games out of first place. The team would reach .500—but not until August 1.

Plank was scuffling, too. After a loss in relief to Chicago on July 4, his record stood at 6–9 and his ERA a bloated—for him—3.21. On July 7 he beat Walter Johnson, 5–0, allowing five hits and, after heading to Gettysburg to attend to his ailing mother, blanked New York at home in the back end of a July 30 doubleheader, 2–0. The win was the 10th in a row for the Browns, all at home, despite a hot and humid summer in St. Louis. It was so warm at night the players took to sleeping in the grandstand at Sportsman's Park. Plank and Armando Marsans bought cots and started sleeping there; soon others followed as the heat wave—and lack of sleep—continued. "The only danger attached to this is the possibility of being blown away,"[21] Plank said.

The streak extended to 14 games on August 4 when Plank beat Boston and Babe Ruth, who wore lettuce leaves soaked every inning in ice water in his cap, 6–1. Plank went the distance, allowing only two hits while Ruth was gone after five innings, having allowed five runs on nine hits while striking out in his only at-bat (believe it or not, he was hit for by Hal Janvrin in the sixth). "They [Plank and Herb Pennock] were two of the smartest pitchers I ever saw. Both had a lot of stuff and great control," Ruth asserted years later. "Plank and Pennock knew just what they were going to do and did it—on every pitch."[22]

Plank's next start came in the second game of a doubleheader vs. Washington on August 8, and three weeks shy of his 41st birthday, he nearly got his no-hitter. It ended in a way that can't seem possible in the 21st century—in fact, it wouldn't be possible. After Plank walked the leadoff hitter, who stole second, in the ninth inning and got a pop-up for the first out, Washington third baseman Eddie Foster strode to the plate. But in his hands was not his normal piece of lumber. Foster jokingly was swinging a fungo—a thin-handled, thick-barreled bat usually used in drills for fly balls; writer W.J. O'Connor described it as "nothing more than a bloated toothpick, or a good-size walking stick."[23] But it was no laughing matter for Plank after Foster connected with the bat and hit a ball between right fielder Ward Miller and center fielder Marsans which rolled to the fence for a double. "Everybody laughed because Eddie [Foster] was giving the impression it was impossible to hit Plank," Walter Johnson recalled decades later. "Foster swung and hit a looper ... So Plank had a one-hitter, instead of a no-hitter—and all because of a prank."[24]

Plank would have been just the second 40 year old to throw a no-hitter, joining Cy Young, who did it in 1908 (only three others have done it since—Warren Spahn, 1961; Nolan Ryan 1990 and 1991; Randy Johnson, 2004), and had to settle for a one-hitter, and a 2–1 win. Plank pitched two scoreless innings to close out a win on August 11, despite Jones wanting to hold him for the next day's start—which Plank started anyway and beat Cleveland, 11–0, allowing just two hits (both by Tris Speaker) with no walks.

In his last five games, Plank had pitched 38 innings and allowed just nine hits and four walks, giving up two runs (a 0.47 ERA) with 15 strikeouts. He had won each of his four starts and saved another. In his four complete-game starts he surrendered four, two, one and two hits. Wrote Grantland Rice: "This would be a remarkable streak if spun out by Alexander or Johnson or say any star in his prime. But for a veteran of 40 years old, at least, eight years beyond the average pitching life, it is one of the most remarkable achievements in the history of sport."[25]

Rice also spoke with one of Plank's former teammates with the Athletics, Andy Coakley, who was now the head coach at Columbia. "In my opinion he is the greatest left-hander that ever lived," Coakley told Rice.

> Not as brilliant as Rube Waddell, but for an average performance his work surpasses them all. I can't recall a bad ball game that Plank pitched. Here is another

detail. Even when he broke in with the old Mackman Plank frequently complained of a sore arm. He had trouble here and there with his elbow and his shoulder. He was not an iron man in any sense of the word ... He was a pitcher you would figure might last five or six years as a star. But here he is today ... pitching more brilliantly than he ever worked in his life. I have kept close track of base ball for a long time, but I can't recall in all that time any such continued exhibition as these four games of Plank's against New York, Boston, Washington and Cleveland. Four games—two runs, nine hits—an average of 2.25 hits and one-half a run to the contest. It doesn't sound possible.[26]

Plank's good fortune ended at, of all places, Shibe Park. A single and a pair of errors loaded the bases in the 10th inning of a 3-all tie. With one out, Wally Schang, who homered earlier in the contest, was due up. This time Jones took Plank out. He received a rousing ovation from the fans. They didn't know it, but it was the last time he would pitch in Philadelphia. Dave Davenport relieved and walked Schang on a 3–2 pitch—catcher Hank Severeid was so angered at the ball four call that he threw the ball as hard as he could in the direction of left field.

Plank couldn't match that incredible pitching stretch—he lost his next two starts—and St. Louis hit its zenith on August 31, moving to four games back—as close as the Browns were to first place since April 30 and also the closest they'd get. It was also Plank's 41st birthday. Naturally, reporters were curious about his thoughts on longevity. He acquiesced and offered this advice:

Be regular in sleeping! I always make it a point to be in bed at night between the hours of 10 and 11 and out of the "hay" in the morning between 8 and 9. Don't overeat! I eat most anything and always was a lover of rich foods, plenty of meat and all kinds of vegetables. A little soup, a sandwich and a glass of milk constitute a filling luncheon. I never drank or smoked in my life as I really think tobacco and strong drink affects eyesight and nerves. Take things easy in the spring, working slowly for about two weeks. I find that I dare not throw a ball with any speed until the training has advanced that distance. Give the muscle in your arm plenty of time to get set, then start throwing a little more and harder each day. Live in the open as much as possible. I have always been a farmer when not playing baseball and think the outdoor life is the healthiest to live. Don't employ strenuous methods to develop your pitching arm. Remember you are going to be a pitcher; not a strong man. Pitching only will keep the arm in shape. Don't try to mock the delivery of some other pitcher. Pitch the way that is most natural to you. Drink coffee if you like it, but only at breakfast and dinner. I have always taken coffee twice a day and do not think it injurious. Don't try to strike out every batter who faces you. Strive to keep the batsman from reaching first base in the easiest way. Don't try to do all the work. Remember there's a team behind you. Give the fielders a chance. Save yourself for times when you need to tighten up. Keep your arm covered after a workout lest it catches cold.[27]

He added, "I don't know whether it is that I have more on the ball this season than I had in other years, but at any rate I feel that I have just as much stuff as I ever did."[28] He wasn't so far off. Plank made seven appearances in September, with six starts, of which he completed five. He won four of his six starts and also pitched two scoreless innings to finish off a one-run win, posting a 1.61 ERA over 56 innings.

But wins were harder to come for Plank on the Browns of 1916, mainly because St. Louis was largely a .500 team, something he wasn't used to from his previous stops in Philadelphia (save 1908) and the Federal League. The Browns did rally in the second half of the season yet still finished in fourth place at 79–75 (an improvement over the non–Terriers-infused team of 1915, which went 63–91; owner Ball said, "We had much quantity and not so much quality on our club during the 1916 season."[29]). Plank finished 16–15 (his final victory on October 1 vs. Detroit not only gave him a winning record but also it was his 300th career win in the American League) but did have a 2.33 ERA, which was 10th-best in the American League, in 235⅔ innings. He also was seventh in shutouts (3) and ninth in complete games (17). Not bad for the oldest pitcher in the major leagues. Only five other pitchers age 30+ threw 200 or more innings, and the next oldest after Plank was the St. Louis Cardinals' Red Ames, who turned 34 on August 2.

Manager Jones was clearly enamored of Plank and his former Terriers pitchers. In a postseason series against the St. Louis Cardinals, which the Browns won four games to one, Jones only used Dave Davenport, Bob Groom, and Plank, all Terrier carryovers. The Cardinals, who finished tied for last in the National League, had no former Federal League players on their roster. "Jones made no secret of the fact that he was pleased because Dave, Bob and Eddie had come through for him but didn't go into detail,"[30] reported the *St. Louis Star*.

Plank had no issue with Jones, either. He had always been complimentary of his manager and his mind for strategy. It was St. Louis with which he had a problem. Plank didn't want to be located there in 1917, and he made his thoughts very clear to Jones: In the upcoming off-season, Plank wanted a new home. He demanded to be traded.

♦ 19 ♦

A Disappearing Act

Eddie Plank reunited with some of his former Athletics teammates on a barnstorming tour—an illegal one, as the National Commission prohibited exhibitions after the World Series. His good friend Harry Davis played first base, Wally Schang was the catcher, and the outfield consisted of a couple of his former pitching mates, Chief Bender and Joe Bush, as well as Amos Strunk. Davis was fined $100, although the fine against Plank, and many others, was suspended.

He likely reminisced and remembered the good times while playing with some of his old teammates. But a reunion was not what he had on his mind for 1917. Before Plank headed back East and Fielder Jones to Portland following exhibition games against the St. Louis Cardinals after the conclusion of the 1916 season, the pitcher and manager held a meeting. It was there that Plank told Jones he was done playing in St. Louis. His reasoning was that he needed to be closer to his home, where he could be closer to his family as well as numerous properties he owned. Not only did Plank still have the family farm outside Gettysburg, where his parents lived, but he also had a house being built in town (which the Plank family would move into in late February) and apartments in Philadelphia he and Jack Coombs bought after the 1914 season. St. Louis was too far for Plank to make trips back to Pennsylvania to check on—and maintain—his properties.

In an interview in late October, Plank made it abundantly clear of his intention. "It's not that I have been badly treated by Fielder Jones—nothing of the sort, Jones treated me royally," he said, "I have no kick on that score, but I don't like St. Louis and will not go back, in fact I will quit unless I am traded or sold."[1]

The baseball world took notice. Plank was, of course, a big name, but even at age 41 he had shown he could still be quite effective. Washington and the New York Yankees stepped to the forefront as not only viable options, but also interested parties. "I would take Plank in a minute if the price or proposition of trade was in keeping with his value," Washington

Pitcher Jack Coombs was Eddie Plank's teammate and occasional hunting partner from 1906–1914. Coombs said Plank "was an inspiration to me" (George Grantham Bain Collection, Library of Congress)

owner Clark Griffith declared. "He still is a pitcher, when handled right, who could win a lot of games for his team."[2]

The problem for Plank was that he was not waived or a free agent. He had to rely on the Browns making a trade. St. Louis was not about to just give him away. Browns business manager Branch Rickey wanted to upgrade at third base. Jimmy Austin had been the team's starter since 1911, and even managed a few games in 1913, but he received a big bump in salary after nearly jumping to the Federal League in 1915, and then batted only .207 in 1916 and would be 37 in 1917.

The major-league winter meetings in Chicago were approaching, and the Browns had a keen interest in New York's Fritz Maisel and Washington's Eddie Foster. St. Louis reportedly was offering Plank, and maybe more, for Maisel, and Plank and Austin for Foster. "It is an absolute fact that Plank will willingly return to the Browns, although he prefers to play in the East," Rickey said as the meetings commenced. "He has explained himself in this matter in a manly way. He's not averse to returning to St. Louis, but he advised us that he would welcome a transfer to the East. We are trying to oblige him."[3]

When Rickey and owner Phil Ball left the Windy City, they did so without a new third baseman for St. Louis and with Plank still on the roster.

19. A Disappearing Act

"My colleagues all took me for Santa Claus," said Yankees owner Tillinghast L'Hommedieu Huston.

> They seemed to think Col. [Jacob] Ruppert and I were plumb full of the Christmas spirit, as they offer us all the old birds they could dig up for Fritz Maisel. We had three different offers for Maisel. St. Louis offered us Eddie Plank, aged 41, and a player who has been in the league since 1901.... Naturally we laughed at all of those offers. A year ago Maisel was considered one of the real stars of the league and then they were offering us real stars for him. I do not understand why they all seem to think Maisel is on the market. We still regard him as quite an asset, and Bill Donovan expects to start him next season at second base.[4]

The Yankees might have scoffed at St. Louis' offer, but they still wanted Plank. They made a straight cash offer for the pitcher, reportedly $10,000. "We have turned it down," owner Ball said. "We want players here more than money."[5]

Talks continued between the Browns and other teams. Detroit entered the picture in early February with third baseman Oscar Vitt being insinuated in a potential return. Vitt was a member of the Player's Fraternity, which was threatening a strike. Plank, among others, had been kicked out of the group for not paying yearly dues. Foster and Maisel remained targets as well as Ball, Jones, and Rickey prepared to head to the American League meetings in New York in mid–February, but the Browns manager let other clubs know they still weren't going to give Plank away, despite his desire to be dealt. "Plank's arm is as good as it ever was, and I wouldn't say that he was losing his head," Jones said. "I saw Eddie pitch and win games last season without using a slow ball and when you fastball any team in our league to defeat, you're pitching. Therefore, there shall be no haste in trading Plank. Pitchers of his type are not easily found."[6]

Meanwhile, it was reported that Tigers owner Frank Navin had a "sole ambition of buying the release of Eddie Plank."[7] Jones indicated he still was interested in Maisel and hoped a swap of Plank and others could net the player from the Yankees. New York manager Bill Donovan was willing to part with Maisel for Plank and Browns second baseman Del Pratt. "I'd like to get Maisel from the Yankees, but I wouldn't trade Pratt for him," Jones said. "I need Pratt to keep my infield up to the notch. But I'd give Plank for Maisel in a minute."[8]

Just as in Chicago there was a lot of talk, and just as in Chicago the Browns contingent left New York without having made a move. True to his word, Jones would not include Pratt in a deal for Maisel, and no other terms could be agreed upon. "I regard Plank today as the greatest 'money' pitcher in the game. Just put something on the game and I'd rather have Plank in there than any pitcher I know," said Jones, who also made the point known he liked having good left-handers on his staff with so many good lefty hitters in the American League. "So why should I be disappointed over the failure to get Maisel? The truth is that the success of the Plank-for-Maisel deal never greatly interested me."[9]

Rickey was infuriated at the demands of other teams and didn't hold back when asked why Plank wasn't traded and Maisel acquired.

> I have never seen anything like it in all my baseball career. Seven clubs in our league are absolutely confident of winning the pennant. They wouldn't consider any kind of a trade. Why, I believe they would hesitate about trading a second-string pitcher for George Sisler. They're wild. They're blind. They are so egotistical that it's painful. I have never before heard of a condition that parallels the present one in the American League. You can say for me that we're just as cocky as the rest. We didn't trade Eddie Plank and we didn't come away from New York in tears, either. Plank will pitch for the Browns and he'll be a big help to us. Just wait and see for yourself.[10]

Plank had insisted he wouldn't play for St. Louis in 1917. But with spring training in Palestine, Texas, just a week away, his options were to play for the Browns or not play at all. Despite all his bluster over the years about retirement, Plank wasn't ready to quit baseball just yet. Now it came to, again, compensation. The two sides dickered but Plank ended up signing after getting a raise to $5,500.

Plank was a late arrival to camp and ended up not pitching much, in part because the weather was colder than expected. "I have made many training trips, but this is the worst weather that I have ever run into with a ball club in the South,"[11] Plank said.

Before Plank began his 17th major league season, Philadelphia sportswriter and Gettysburg native Bill Duncan penned a tribute to the veteran left-hander:

> When speaking of great pitchers and the way they fall in rank,
> First place, in my opinion, goes to old friend Eddie Plank.
> Since nineteen-one he's served them up with finest kind of skill.
> And every year, for Mack or Jones, he's always filled the bill.
> Now Rube Waddell, when in his prime, was known as quite a bear.
> And he, with Eddie, on the "A's," once formed a winning pair.
> But Rube has passed; Chief Bender, too, has lost his once great rep.
> While Eddie still can buzz them through with just all kinds of pep.
> Matty, Rucker, Brown, are gone, but on this you sure can bank.
> That this year's leading southpaw may well be friend Eddie Plank.[12]

Fielder Jones had plenty of pitchers who could be vying for the top left-hander. Much to his word back in the winter meetings, Jones had armed his staff with plenty of southpaws to help the Browns combat such dangerous hitters as Ty Cobb, Eddie Collins, Tris Speaker, and Joe Jackson, among others. In addition to Plank, Jones had Earl Hamilton, Ernie Koob,

19. *A Disappearing Act* 201

and Carl Weilman at the start of the year to go with right-handers Dave Davenport and Allan Sothoron.

St. Louis opened up the season at home against Chicago, which had Collins and Jackson. Plank liked the White Sox's chances of winning the pennant. "They are going to make it hard for the pitchers," he said. "There will be no loafing for the right-handers or left-handers either, when pitching against the Sox. Every man in that lineup is dangerous and you'll have to be on the alert every minute."[13]

Plank, though, wasn't ready to pitch against the White Sox or anyone else, at least in his eyes, declaring himself not yet fit. He watched on the bench when Eddie Cicotte no-hit the Browns in the third game of the season. He also sat when the Browns took two of three at Sportsman's Park against Cleveland. Finally, he said he was "ready to go,"[14] and Jones promptly announced he would start the opener of a series in Chicago.

The United States had entered the war in Europe weeks earlier, and patriotism was in full display at Comiskey Park as Plank prepared to make his first appearance of 1917. The *Chicago Tribune*'s I.E. Sanborn wrote that the park displayed "more American flags than we supposed there were in the world … It was one circle of red, white and blue."[15] The White Sox took the field in full khaki uniforms, hats included, and did some military drills before the contest in front of the more than 27,000 fans.

Despite pitching for the first time since a March 13 scrimmage and with a light drizzle falling most of the game, Plank pitched a complete game, winning 6–2, allowing seven hits while walking none and striking out three. "Plank pitched wrong to only two batters in the entire game. He sure is a master. I would rather have him out there in the pinch than any boxman in the game," said Jones, who relished any victory over Chicago. "Considering it was Plank's first game of the season and that he was working against the chesty White Sox I consider his performance a wonderful one."[16]

Plank wouldn't make his next start until May 18, with only three short relief appearances in between. That gave Plank time to perhaps continue his tutoring of Koob, his latest left-handed pupil. "Right now Koob has more speed than any other left-hander in the league," Plank said in late April. "His speed is his best asset, though he has a good curve ball…. When he learns a better change of pace, he should be unbeatable."[17] On May 5, Koob threw a no-hitter against the White Sox.

The next day the teams played a doubleheader, and in the opener Plank came in for Sothoron with runners on second and third in the sixth inning and got out of the jam unscathed. After pitching the seventh inning, Plank went to Jones and told him his shoulder was hurting. Groom finished up the final two innings, then also started the second game—and also threw a no-hitter.

Plank tried pitching again on May 8, getting a start in St. Louis against Chicago, but after one inning again complained of shoulder pain and was done for the day. It would be 10 days before he took the hill again. He would manage seven innings vs. Washington but got pounded for 10 hits and eight runs (although each tally came after or as the direct result of one of the Browns' five errors). It was the fifth straight loss in what would be a six-game skid, dropping St. Louis to 14–17. The *St. Louis Post-Dispatch* reported, "the morale of the team is low."[18]

After pitching the ninth inning in a 4–3 loss to Boston on May 24, Plank faced the defending World Series winners three days later. He engaged in a pitching duel with Carl Mays, the contest eventually being called at 5:08 p.m. due to darkness in the 11th inning with the score tied at 1. Plank went the distance, allowing eight hits while driving in the only run for St. Louis with an RBI single in the third inning.

St. Louis had lost four games in a row before the tie and were now 15–22, in fifth place and 10 games behind first-place Chicago. Plank's performance had Jones feeling confident nonetheless. "Plank showed Sunday that he is now in form. Holding the champions to eight hits and one run in eleven innings speaks well for the condition of his left arm," he said. "That was only the third game he has started this season, but he is now ready to take his turn. That will help."[19]

Plank matched up with Washington's Walter Johnson in his next start, June 1 on the road, before leaving for a pinch hitter in the ninth inning. The Browns scored twice off Johnson in that inning and won in the 10th. While he didn't figure in the decision, the *St. Louis Post-Dispatch* ran a cartoon on its front page with the caption "One Plank is keeping the Browns afloat."[20]

Soon, Plank was adrift. The Browns headed to Philadelphia next on its road trip, and Plank had been given the nod to pitch the opener but was so sick he had to stay back at the hotel. The next day's game was rained out, but Plank was in no better shape. The *St. Louis Star* reported, "something he ate has turned his system topsy-turvy."[21]

Suddenly, Plank was no longer even at the Aldine Hotel. No one truly knew where he was. Plank packed his bags and reportedly told some teammates (likely his roommate on the road, outfielder Bill Rumler), "I guess the club is about to lose another player."[22] St. Louis had a number of players sidelined due to illness or injury. Browns players thought he was headed home to Gettysburg. Jones said that wasn't the case. Rumors circulated that he was hospitalized in Philadelphia. Both the *St. Louis Star* and the *Evening News* of Harrisburg, Pennsylvania, claimed he had a nervous breakdown. The *Evening News* also reported Plank was "preparing for a minor operation."[23] The *St. Louis Post-Dispatch* would later report that Plank wasn't happy—after all he had demanded a trade and instead was back in St.

Louis—and "twice reported as having difficulty with the management, and once he went home for several days."[24]

It's pure speculation as to what exactly happened to Plank—there's no account of him referring to this situation—but the underlying cause appears to be whatever was causing him to be ill in Philadelphia. The term "nervous breakdown" used by the papers likely didn't refer to a mental state, but a physical one. When he finally did return—Jones had expected Plank back in time for the next series in Boston but he didn't arrive until June 18 at the train station in New York—the *St. Louis Star* said that he had been "recuperating from stomach trouble."[25]

Whatever the issue, he was in shape to pitch June 20, the opener of a series in Detroit, and he tossed a complete game, allowing seven hits and just one walk in a 3–2 win, although for the second straight game he didn't strike out a single batter. The *St. Louis Star* incorrectly reported this being his 300th career win. Even taking away his time in the Federal League, it was win No. 303. He had no plans to stop now. A Detroit writer asked, likely jokingly, if he planned to pitch until he was 50. Plank, two months away from turning 42, responded, "If the old arm holds out and they are willing to pay me a salary that makes it worth my while to keep on pitching, just say that I'll be in there."[26]

Plank's next two starts, at Detroit and Cleveland, were both shortened. He lasted six innings in a loss to the Tigers and was hit for after two innings against the Indians. He struck out just one batter in those eight innings and had only eight overall on the season over 56 innings.

Plank didn't have the zip on his fastball any more, so he started developing a changeup—called a floater or slow ball back then. He had it working well enough in his June 30 start at home against Detroit, a 4–3 win. After one at-bat in which he meekly popped out on a changeup, Ty Cobb yelled at Plank as he headed back to the dugout, "I ought to have my throat cut for hitting at that stuff, Ed."[27]

Little moments like this might have made Plank chuckle, but the experience in St. Louis was becoming worse. By July 4 the team was 20 games out of first place. Plank pitched more often in July than he had in any preceding month. He made four starts with two appearances in relief—going seven innings in one stint and 3⅔ in another. Plank closed the month showing some of his old form, though.

On July 17 he went the distance in beating Boston's Dutch Leonard, 3–2, at Sportsman's Park, with the Browns scoring the winning run in the bottom of the ninth inning. Plank was allowed to bat in the inning, although he fouled out. Perhaps Jones left him in because he didn't allow a runner to reach base after Larry Gardner's triple with two outs in the third and had just four fly balls hit to the outfield all game. *This* was his

300th career victory, according to in Clarence F. Lloyd of the *St. Louis Post-Dispatch*. Record keeping was not pristine in 1917.

One certainty was when Plank blanked Washington on July 22 in the first game of a doubleheader (in just an hour and 39 minutes, at that), it was his 69th career shutout and meant he had thrown at least one in each of his 17 seasons.

That doubleheader wrapped up a long homestand in which the Browns went 12–17. Including the second game of the twin bill, St. Louis lost its next eight games. Plank suffered two of those defeats: a 3–2 loss in Boston which was lost with two outs in the bottom of the 12th, and 3–1 at New York on August 2, taken out for a pinch hitter after seven innings.

Plank's next start came in Washington, where the Browns and Senators had split the first two games of the series. It turned out to be another classic battle against Walter Johnson. Plank was in an unusually good mood throughout the contest. He and Johnson continually exchanged playful barbs, and Plank also had some "friendly repartee"[28] with Clyde Milan, Washington's speedy outfielder. In the ninth inning, Milan also was partly responsible for Plank enjoying a good laugh. Expecting a bunt with Milan at the plate, catcher Hank Severeid decided to dart out quickly from his position, ready to pounce on the ball. Severeid moved, Milan didn't offer at a changeup, and the ball continued on its path (and perhaps struck the umpire, although that was not noted). Plank doubled over and eventually laid down to try and compose himself.

The changeup was working especially well on this day, but Johnson was on his game, too, and neither team had accounted for any runs after nine innings. It remained scoreless after 10; Plank had allowed just three hits. Still scoreless in the 11th, he walked catcher Eddie Ainsmith and, after Johnson popped out on a bunt, Milan singled to left. Ainsmith was running on the pitch and made it to third. Eddie Foster, no fungo bat this time, hit one up the middle into center field, and Ainsmith trotted home with the winning run. Including World Series games, it was the 11th time in his career that Plank pitched a complete game and lost, 1–0. "He probably lost more one-run games than any pitcher of his time,"[29] said Bob Quinn, business manager of the St. Louis Browns from 1917 to 1922 and owner of the Boston Red Sox from 1923 to 1933.

A few days later back in Gettysburg, Ira Plank was going about his daily routine when his brother suddenly appeared. "I've quit baseball,"[30] Eddie said. This time he appeared to mean it.

◆ 20 ◆

Industrial Work

It was over a week after Eddie Plank pitched his final game that it was revealed he decided to retire. Twice during that span the *St. Louis Post-Dispatch* printed that Plank was scheduled to pitch. After finishing a road trip in Detroit, St. Louis manager Fielder Jones finally told reporters that Plank retired. The pitcher confirmed the news while visiting a friend in Hanover, Pennsylvania, saying, "I now admit for the first time that I am through with baseball."[1]

Plank offered no further explanation at the time, leaving the door open for speculation about why he finally quit the game. Recounting the day his brother returned home over 20 years later, Ira Plank remembered Eddie telling him, "I am tired of traveling. The farm is for me."[2] Jones told reporters the stress of the game was becoming too much for Plank and it was causing his stomach ailment. There were also reports of friction between Jones and Plank.

Others thought the losing had become just too much for Plank to bear. The *St. Louis Star* brought up one of Plank's familiar, oft-repeated retorts: "Unless I can be a winner, I don't want to be in baseball."[3] Used to being on consistent winners before coming to the Browns, after Plank's 1–0 loss to Washington and Walter Johnson, St. Louis' record was 38–65 and the team was in last place, a very distant 27½ games out of first place. The atmosphere and the morale clearly weren't good. Back in late May, the *St. Louis Post-Dispatch*'s W.J. O'Connor wrote, "They lost because they are, at present, a losing ball club. They are thinking like losers, acting like losers and they ARE losers. Even Fielder Jones is getting in the losing habit."[4] At that point the Browns were only six games under .500; one can imagine how much worse the situation was at 27 games under .500. The *New York Herald*'s Frederick Lieb wrote in 1919 that Plank "became so disgusted with the quality of support that he quit the Browns and went home."[5]

The timetable of events is not exactly clear, but there are enough pieces of the puzzle from later reports—for example, Jones gave a more detailed explanation the following January and Plank discussed his retirement with the *Philadelphia Inquirer*'s Jimmy Isaminger in 1920—to get a general feel of what occurred.

After losing August 6 against Washington, Plank was exhausted. He could barely make the walk back to his hotel. The next day, Plank headed home to Gettysburg, as he often did during the course of his career when he knew he wouldn't be needed for a few days. Retirement clearly was on his mind. He likely told his wife and family, and on August 8, he and Ira purchased from Harry Bream the Centre Square garage located on York Street in Gettysburg.

The Browns' next series, which began August 8, was in Philadelphia. The *Post-Dispatch* reported that either Plank or Ernie Koob was expected to start August 10. This could have been information from Jones or just speculation based on Plank's turn in the rotation and Koob having only pitched a few innings of relief recently. Tom Rogers got the nod instead. Plank likely had returned or was going to return to the team. Things get a little murkier here. Jones would claim that Plank tried to warm up but his shoulder hurt too much and he was shelved. The next morning, Plank asked Jones to come to his hotel room. When Jones arrived, Plank, according to the manager, was in tears. "It seems that he had been to a doctor and was advised to quit baseball for the rest of the season," Jones recalled, "that his arm was in bad shape."[6] Jones told Plank to head back home, rest, and return when ready, although he was doubtful that would occur. (Jones, speaking in early 1918, vehemently denied that he and Plank didn't get along, offering as proof that "it was only last Christmas that I received a long letter and a picture of his baby from Plank, with best wishes from himself and family."[7])

But Plank had already purchased the garage with his brother. Was he intending to finish out the season regardless? Plank didn't provide any clarity in his interview with Isaminger, but he did say pitching was taking too much out of him. "It was physical exhaustion that seized me in every hard game I pitched that caused me to retire," Plank said. "I had just as much stuff as I ever did, but a game of ball began to tax my strength too much. I soon realized that the wear and tear of baseball was taking my very blood out of me, and I decided to quit."[8]

Plank might have been exaggerating—or merely forgetting—how he pitched in 1917. He didn't have his best stuff anymore. Certainly, pitching was more taxing because he had to mix things up. He *was* still effective—pitching to a 1.79 ERA and 1.092 WHIP, but he struck out only 26 batters in 131 innings and completed just eight of 14 starts. At 41, the oldest pitcher in the league, age had finally caught up with him—and even then, no one over the age of 34 threw more innings than he did in 1917 (and the next-oldest pitcher in the majors was 37).

Still, back in 1917, some thought this was a case of a boy calling wolf—Plank had threatened retirement in the past and was known not to want to be in St. Louis, thus he was doing this just to get out of his contract and play elsewhere. With World War I under way and a draft instituted, sending ballplayers off to the armed forces, it was thought that older players would be needed to fill roster spots. At 42, Plank was not eligible for the draft at the time.

A wire report in the *San Francisco Chronicle* in November stated that Plank was getting his arm in shape in preparation for such a role. In December, the *Washington Post* said, "Eddie Plank is out with an announcement that he may be seen in action another season,"[9] even though no such declaration had been made.

That report likely emanated from St. Louis, where Browns business manager Bob Quinn told reporters he expected Plank to pitch in 1918. The team had placed the pitcher on the voluntary retired list, meaning he was still subject to the reserve clause if he were to return, thus Browns property. With a lot of unknowns due to the war and the draft, Plank suddenly became a hot topic among other ballclubs. Quinn sent a letter to the pitcher asking him if he would be willing to change his mind and pitch in 1918. The only baseball Plank seemed interested in was umpiring an exhibition game between Connie Mack's Athletics—the frost between the two seemingly having melted—and the local Seventh Infantry team at Gettysburg's Nixon Field, with 10 percent of the proceeds going to the Army Relief Fund.

Plank's name kept being bandied about among ballclubs, even the Browns. Fielder Jones included Plank among the members of his expected rotation in 1918. The New York Yankees once again were taking an interest in Plank, with Lewis A. Dougher of the *Washington Times* writing in early January that the pitcher was "destined to play with the Yankees next season."[10]

Dougher had good information. On January 22, Plank, along with second baseman Derrill Pratt—whom the Browns were now willing to deal after he and shortstop Doc Lavan sued the Browns for slander (owner Philip Ball accused them of quitting on the team) were sent to New York for pitchers Nick Cullop and Urban Shocker, second baseman Joe Gedeon, third baseman Fritz Maisel, catcher Les Nunamaker, and $15,000.

However, the Yankees made the mistake of making the deal without consulting Plank and at least gauging his plans. Plank didn't even know he had been traded until two days later, when a reporter in Gettysburg tracked the pitcher down to get his reaction. Plank made a few things clear, besides not being aware of the transaction. He never mailed Jones saying he would play. Nor did he indicate to anyone that he would pitch in 1918. Admitting that his arm felt good, he nevertheless repeated his stance on retirement. "I am not interested. I am through with baseball and do not expect to don a uniform again," Plank said. "When I quit the St. Louis team last season and came home I announced that I was through and I meant it. I will not play with the Yankees or any other team next season."

Plank repeated his claims to another reporter, which was sent out in a *United Press* wire report.

> I will not go to New York next season. I am through with baseball forever. That goes. I am not trying to hold anybody up, and I hope that my retirement will not upset the deal between New York and St. Louis, but if it does I cannot help it. When I announced last summer I was through with baseball at the end of 1917 I meant just that. Talk about doing your bit in the army, I guess I have done my bit in baseball and am entitled to a rest. I am not all in by any means. My left wing is as good as ever, but I have enough. I have my farm, my home and enough to take care of me, so why should I work and worry any longer? If the deal is dependent on my signature for its completion then I am sorry to say that will be all off.[11]

The Yankees, though, weren't ready to give up on their quest for Plank. Owner Col. Jacob Ruppert talked about visiting Gettysburg to talk to the pitcher. The team sent Plank a contract which was categorized as "liberal terms"[12] by the *St. Louis Star* upon word from Ruppert. Even after Plank sent a letter to the American League office in New York to confirm his retirement, Yankees manager Miller Huggins still was making plans to head to Gettysburg.

> I have heard informally that Plank really intends to remain retired. I sincerely hope we can induce him to change his mind. I have written him a letter telling him we will be greatly disappointed if he is not with us on our training trip. I think by the time the warm weather comes around Plank will be with us. I know how it feels. Every fall I would decide I had enough of baseball and would honestly make up my mind to retire, but each spring I would be back for more punishment. I think that is an experience which comes into the life of every veteran ball player. If Plank is with us I really expect him to win a lot of games for New York, as he pitched some fine ball for the Browns before he retired last August.[13]

While Huggins was planning his pitch to lure Plank back to the major leagues, the now-seemingly retired former pitcher was going about his new career, getting the garage he purchased with his brother ready for business. The brothers signed up to be a Firestone dealer—the company putting out a press release to newspapers to ensure they'd be connected to the well-known ballplayer—and headed to Cleveland to find automobiles to buy and ship to Gettysburg which could be sold at the garage.

Still, the subject of baseball kept coming up. He was asked about it again at the auto show. And again he said he was through with the game.

"Too much business. I have my farms at Gettysburg to look after and am interested in the automobile business. I can't very well afford to neglect either of these businesses," Plank said. "I guess I'm through with baseball. I've about served my time. It might be possible for me to go in there with New York and win my share of games. I don't know. At any rate, I don't believe I'll leave my business this year."[14]

Plank left a sliver of hope. "I don't believe" was not a definitive statement. Perhaps Huggins was correct—the closer spring training got, the more Plank was mulling over changing his mind. On March 1, the Yankees manager said he had received correspondence from Plank. "I have received a letter from Plank and he writes that he hasn't made up his mind whether or not to play another year,"[15] Huggins revealed. A report in the *Washington Herald* claimed Plank would let his brother run the business while he attended spring training in Macon, Georgia, with the Yankees.

On March 8, Huggins left New York for spring training. He was confident Plank would join on one of the stops. He didn't. Once in Macon, Huggins had a new plan: Plank wouldn't report to spring training but would eventually be on the team, and he would be worked into shape in order to pitch in the second half of 1918. Huggins was partly correct. Plank would pitch that summer but not for the Yankees, or any major league team for that matter. But he would be facing major leaguers.

With World War I ongoing and the United States instituting a selective service, a new option emerged for players. Baseball was not an essential industry, making them subject to being drafted. Working at a steel plant? That would make someone temporarily exempt since steel was very essential to the war effort. In 1917, the Bethlehem Steel League was formed. It generally consisted of locals from six steel plants playing an abbreviated baseball schedule.

But in 1918, the league started bringing aboard major league players. "I want some good wholesome games that will furnish amusement and entertainment for the Bethlehem Steel Company's employees, and don't bother me about details of expense,"[16] Charles M. Schwab, Bethlehem Steel owner and financial backer of the league, said just a few days before White Sox star Joe Jackson signed on with the Wilmington, Delaware, team.

However, weeks earlier Plank became the first big name to sign with the league. Steelton, Pennsylvania, manager George Cockill let it slip on April 17 that Plank wired the skipper that he would play for his team. Days later, while stopping off in Philadelphia, Plank insisted he was retired.

> I am through with baseball, and nothing can force me to get back into the game. The work is too hard, the strain is too great, and, anyway, I believe I have done my share. My brother and myself have a garage in Gettysburg and, as business is good I will stick to that. There is nothing in the report that I will

play independent baseball every Saturday up the state. There is nothing in it. Suppose I receive $100 a game for pitching. I will have to keep myself in condition just the same, and if I do that I might as well get some regular money in the big league. No, I will not play with anyone this year. That goes for the Yankees, too.[17]

Perhaps this was just a negotiating ploy, as when the official list of players in the Bethlehem Steel League was announced, Plank's name was on it. Cockill had traveled to Gettysburg and, unlike Huggins, had given a successful pitch. Besides being on the team, players also were given jobs—usually nothing too strenuous—to comply with having essential work. Plank had no worry about being drafted (the eligible age wouldn't be expanded to 45 years old until late September) and instead of working at the plant, he was given at least $200 a week to drive around Pennsylvania to find workers for the steel plant. "Officials say he is as good a salesman as a ball player," reported the *Reading Times*.[18]

Reports said he also received money for each start he would make for Steelton. With the season running 18 weeks, Plank would make at least $3,600. Games would be played just on Thursdays (originally Wednesdays) and Saturdays, and he was reportedly contracted to pitch only once per week. It wasn't a bad way to make a living—and he still could attend to his garage during the week.

Other teams were located in Bethlehem, Pennsylvania, Lebanon, Pennsylvania, Sparrows Point, Maryland, Wilmington, Delaware, and Fore River, Massachusetts. Several major leaguers followed Plank's lead. The May 2 player announcement included Yankees first baseman Wally Pipp (Fore River) and infielder Chick Fewster (Sparrow's Point). Days later, Brooklyn pitcher Norman Plitt, who had already been drafted, joined so he could be closer to his parents, who lived in Newark, Pennsylvania. Each team included several former and current major leaguers.

The season began May 11 and ran through early September. "I am in fine shape and feel like getting back into the game,"[19] indicated Plank. It was thought Plank would pitch in the opener but he didn't, even when starter George Pierce had to leave after three innings with chest pains. Roughly 3,000 people attended the 1-0 Steelton 10-inning win over Bethlehem. Another 3,000 showed up on May 18 when Plank lost, 4-3, to Lebanon. He was announced in advance as Steelton's pitcher for a May 30 game at Harlan, which was debuting Jackson, and 5,000 attended—and Plank didn't pitch in the 2-1 loss. Plank's name often came up when announcing the next day's starters, whether he pitched or not. It didn't take long to learn doing this helped jack up attendance.

When Plank did pitch, he was warmly greeted. "That Plank is a favorite with the fans was shown when the veteran was given applause many

20. Industrial Work

times during the game,"[20] reported the *Harrisburg Telegraph* after he beat Fore River and Al Mamaux, who left Brooklyn to play in the Steel League, 6–1, on June 1.

Plank no longer used his fastball much, but he won his next six starts as well. On June 15, he topped Lebanon's 28-year-old Jesse Buckles, who appeared in a couple of games with the Yankees in 1916, 3–1, striking out seven. "The exhibition of Saturday displayed Eddie Plank at his best, for which superb craft he bombarded the Lebanon batters with wily curves, the treacherous slow ball and now and then sent over a speeder," said the *Harrisburg Telegraph*. "It was high art in pitching and the multitude of watchful rooters could relish the entertainment."[21]

In the second game of a doubleheader on July 4, he blanked Harlan, 1–0. Jackson had one of the four hits mustered off Plank. "If I had that fellow's smoke I'd be good for twenty-five years more,"[22] said recent arrival from New Orleans Tom Phillips, who must not have had much of a fastball.

Plank beat Red Sox stalwart and Fore River ace Dutch Leonard twice, on June 29 (6–2) and July 21, a 1–0 game in which Plank allowed only three hits and Leonard, who fanned 11, four. Plank got the better of another major leaguer, the Yankees' Allan Russell, tossing a four-hit shutout while going 2-for-3 with an RBI at the plate in a 5–0 win over Sparrow's Point on July 20.

In his seven-game winning streak, Plank hurled 63 innings—going the full nine innings each time—allowing just six runs on 42 hits. Plank said three major league teams had reached out to him with offers to pitch for them down the stretch of the 1918 season, not to mention a myriad of shipyard teams (Chief Bender, for one, was at the Hog Island shipyard near Philadelphia). "Plank has everything he had fifteen years ago,"[23] stated Cockill, Plank's Steelton manager.

Plank kept pitching in the Bethlehem Steel League but limped to the finish line, losing three of his final four starts. Steelton and Bethlehem finished in a tie for first place, and it was decided that a best-of-three series would determine the league's champion. The proceeds from the first two games would go to charities (the Steelton Red Cross received the first game's, which amounted to around $1,000). Steelton won the opener, 2–1, as Pierce edged New York Giants pitcher Jeff Tesreau.

Plank was expected to pitch the second game, and potential clincher, in Bethlehem on September 14. Two days before that, he registered for the draft. He listed his present occupation as farm manager and automobile dealer. There was still the matter of finishing his contract with Steelton.

However, in the second game the pitching matchup was the same as in the first—Pierce for Steelton vs. Bethlehem's Tesreau. Perhaps the

43-year-old Plank had run out of gas, or maybe he was being saved in case there was a winner-take-all game.

Over 6,000 fans showed up to see if Bethlehem could force a Game 3. Tesreau was perfect through five innings and Steelton trailed, 2–0, when it rallied for two runs in the eighth. During that inning, Pierce was taken out for a pinch-hitter. It was Plank's time after all.

Plank set down Bethlehem in order in the eighth, and neither team scored in the ninth. In the 10th, Steelton put two men on with none out and Plank up. After hitting 10-for-32 (.313), which made him one of the leading batters in the league, during the regular season, Plank was left in to bat and bunted, but the lead runner was forced out at third. After a fly out, Joe McCarthy, future World Series manager for the Cubs and Yankees, ripped a triple to right, then scored when the relay throw was botched by the third baseman. Plank put the first two runners on in the home 10th and allowed a run on a fielder's choice. A walk put the tying run on base and the winning run at the plate. A fielder's choice to the shortstop (unassisted) and a fly to right ended the game and gave Steelton the championship.

A banquet was held in early October for the team at which each player was presented a gold watch. A bird-shooting contest was held, too—each player shot at 10 birds at a 30-yard rise—which Plank won by hitting all 10. It wasn't a bad way to bring an end to his 1918 baseball season. Now, there was the matter of whether he would play in 1919.

◆ 21 ◆

End of the Line

Eddie Plank wouldn't have helped the fortunes of either the New York Yankees or St. Louis Browns in 1918. Both teams finished under .500 in a truncated season (due to the war effort) which ended September 11—three days before Plank's relief effort helped Steelton win the Bethlehem Steel League.

After the conclusion of the American League season, Plank was placed on the ineligible list of the Yankees. Pitcher Nick Cullop, also involved in the trade which sent Plank to New York, had remained on his farm instead of signing with St. Louis and was similarly on the Browns' ineligible list.

While Yankees manager Miller Huggins hoped that Plank, even at 43, would pitch in 1919—as a reliever—there was a twist. Both Browns business manager Bob Quinn, in November, and Huggins, in December, let it be known that Plank was actually the property of St. Louis while Cullop was New York's. When neither signed nor reported, as per agreement of the trade, their rights reverted back to their original team. This would be confirmed in December when the Browns placed Plank on their reserve list.

That didn't stop the Yankees from sending Plank a contract which he returned in February, unsigned. It was official—officially official this time—he was retired and would now spend his time in Gettysburg attending to his garage and with his wife and young son. In a letter distributed to newspapers, Plank wrote, "This is not an attempt at a holdout. An old fellow like me has gotten over that stage, but it will be impossible for me to return to the American League."[1] In an interview a week later, he added, "I've played my last professional game. I might go in and take a few games, and then I might not. I've seen my day, and I did my best to make good."[2]

L.C. Davis of the *St. Louis Post-Dispatch* penned one of his poems, paying tribute to the pitcher. He titled the prose simply "Eddie Plank":

> I see our old friend Eddie Plank
> Refuses to become a Yank.
> The job he has declined;

> Regardless of the loss of kale,
> He put his contract in the mail
> And sent it back unsigned
>
> The noble southpaw has retired
> And he refuses to be hired
> For anybody's gold.
> He graced the mound for many years
> And listened to the rooters' cheers,
> But now he's growing old.
>
> With his reliable old whip,
> He captured many a championship
> Upon the diamond green.
> The stars who might be said to rank
> With rough and tough old Eddie Plank
> Are few and far between.
>
> When Eddie Plank was in his prime
> He fooled the batter every time
> Occasion might require;
> But now in Gettysburg, P-a.,
> He has decided he will stay
> And from the game retire.
>
> More power to your elbow, Ed,
>
> Although your arm is far from dead,
> You've earned a rest at that;
> The boys with whom you had to cope
> Don't wish you any harm, but hope
> You'll stay right where you're at.[3]

Plank did keep baseball in his life, in spurts. In June and July, he umpired some local games, including one between Gettysburg College and Mount St. Mary's. He created a bit of a stir in early July when, visiting Philadelphia on business, he stopped by Shibe Park and warmed up on the sidelines. It was pure nostalgia for Plank, who just wanted to see how his arm held up when throwing and also likely to get one last chance to throw a pitch, even if not off the mound, at his old stomping grounds.

The Bethlehem Steel League disbanded in 1919 but was attempting to restart in 1920. Knowing Plank would be a nice draw, and perhaps had a few innings remaining in his left arm, George Cockill made another trip to Gettysburg. He wasn't as convincing this time. Plank turned down the offer, even when Cockill tried to sell a plan in which he would only pitch on holidays.

Stopping back in Philadelphia in July 1920, Plank recommended Gettysburg College pitcher Byron Yarrison, who at the time was with Hanover of the Blue Ridge League, to Athletics business manager John Shibe.

21. End of the Line

Philadelphia swung a deal for Yarrison, who would make the majors in 1922, though he wouldn't fare well.

A rumor of Plank potentially joining the Portsmouth Truckers of the Virginia League in August 1920 never came to fruition (this also ensured Plank never pitching in the minor leagues), but he did take the mound that month, throwing four pitches—all strikes (one foul)—for a hospital fundraiser game between Gettysburg courthouse officials.

Plank continued to umpire over the years as well as help his brother, Ira, the manager of the Gettysburg College baseball team. The itch to play returned in 1922 when he formed a team of older men—naming themselves Bald and Gray—and played local Gettysburg clubs, with Plank manning third base, while also playing a little center field and even pitching an inning or two here and there.

In 1923, he pitched at a Gettysburg alumni game—allowing just one hit in five innings against the varsity squad—as well as one inning at a fundraiser in Harrisburg for a player who was beaned in the head. His last pitching appearance came in June 1924 at another alumni game, although he only went one inning. He did single and double, however, at the plate. In 1925, his participation at the annual contest was limited to umpiring.

Plank's association with baseball continued with visits from former teammates and friends. Eddie Collins went through Gettysburg while traveling, for example. In late September 1920, Yankees pitcher Carl Mays stopped at Plank's garage. This was just over a month after a Mays pitch had struck and eventually killed Cleveland shortstop Ray Chapman. That subject was not brought up, but the gambling scandal of the 1919 World Series was broached—charges had just been filed against the eight "Black Sox"— with Mays saying he believed the players were guilty of throwing the Series. Mays also talked about his teammate Babe Ruth, saying, "To the best of my knowledge, Ruth has made about $150,000 this summer. About the only thing he has left is a check for $3,000 and some of the boys of our club have bet him that he won't have enough money next spring to pay his income tax."[4]

In 1923, Plank and Chief Bender helped out their former Athletics teammate, Jack Coombs, who was the head coach at Williams College. Plank was excited about a proposed meet-up with Christy Mathewson at a Gettysburg-Bucknell football game in Altoona on November 8, 1924, with the former World Series adversaries acting as captains, however the plan didn't come to fruition.

Plank attended a few World Series, traveling to New York in 1921 and 1922 to witness the Giants and Yankees play and to Washington in 1924 and 1925 to witness the Senators host the Giants and Pirates. At Game 1 of the 1922 series at the Polo Grounds, Plank gathered with some of his former

Athletics teammates—Frank Baker, Joe Bush, Wally Schang, and Bob Shawkey, all of whom now played for the Yankees—for a pregame picture.

He also took in a couple of prize fights, most notably the heavyweight championship bout in July 1921 in Jersey City, New Jersey, between Jack Dempsey and Georges Carpentier. "It looks like Dempsey to me,"[5] Plank correctly predicted days before the bout.

While Plank was now merely a spectator, his name was kept alive through various all-time team pronouncements. In 1921, the *Chicago Tribune* placed him on its list of greats along with Walter Johnson, Nap Rucker, Ed Walsh, and Cy Young. Noted writer Damon Runyon included Plank on his list of the 10 greatest pitchers from 1911 to 1921. After the 1924 season, Walter Johnson listed his All-American team and had Plank as one of his seven pitchers along with Chief Bender, Jack Chesbro, Addie Joss, Rube Waddell, Walsh, and Smoky Joe Wood (Johnson notably left himself off). The following year in *Liberty Magazine*, umpire Billy Evans also named his All-American team, and Plank was tabbed along with Grover Cleveland Alexander, Chesbro, Johnson, Joss, Mathewson, Waddell, Walsh, and Young.

Connie Mack had a tough time choosing his all-time left-handed pitcher, and while he decided on Waddell, as a manager he favored Plank. "Waddell was the best left hander. I mean the greatest as far as actual ability was concerned. If it came to a question, though, of Rube or Eddie Plank on my club, I would have taken Plank,"[6] Mack said. Wrote the *Philadelphia Public Ledger*'s Cullen Cain in 1921: "To my mind, Plank should be named in any group of five great pitchers of the game."[7]

Plank operated the garage with his brother—now called Eddie Plank's Garage—until selling it in early 1921, although it was reported that Plank "will continue his connection with automobiles as the agent for several makes of cars, with headquarters in Gettysburg."[8] The garage maintained his name until it was sold again a year and a half later.

When not conducting his automobile business, Plank retained the competitive side of himself in hunting and shooting. He was big on the clay trap shooting circuit and often acquitted himself well in competitions.

As he did in the offseason during his playing days, Plank took more than a few hunting excursions. He even was part of a 10-person group who bought a 1,300-acre forest with the purpose of using the grounds to track game—it was a fertile area—and establish a hunting club.

In November 1922, while hunting in Lycoming County, Plank bagged a 310-pound black bear. His hunting party loaded the carcass onto a sled, where a team of horses dragged it four miles before they ran out of steam. A group of eight men then carried the bear the final mile into town. In December, Plank was fined by the gaming commission for violating deer-hunting laws. He also had a run-in with a rattlesnake in the mountains of his forest preserve. No word on how he killed the snake, which had nine rattlers, but knowing Plank's skill with a gun, that method is a safe bet.

Plank's name and connection in the automobile industry got him a spot in a promotional silent film issued by the Ford Motor Company in honor of its 10 millionth car. The auto—a Model T—made the journey from New York City to San Francisco in June 1924. It became quite the spectacle, with people turning out to see the car and communities holding parades. The film shows the car in different locales, including Trenton, New Jersey, where the mayor was featured, to Philadelphia and then to, as the movie card (or intertitle) read, "Just a short visit at Gettysburg, where history was made."[9] After the car is seen driving onto the battlefield, the next intertitle pops up—"Eddie Plank, onetime famous baseball pitcher, said 'this is the 10 millionth hit for Ford'"[10]—and then a cut to Plank, in a white-buttoned, long-sleeved shirt, shaking hands with the driver.

By this point, Plank and his family had moved into a new house on Carlisle Street. The old one had been sold to a Gettysburg College fraternity—the Druids, a 23-year-old organization, making it the oldest on campus. The house being right across the street from the school made it a good location. At some point, Plank expressed to friends that he wanted to head back to his farm, but judging from his actions and living arrangements after getting married to Anna Myers, that likely wasn't in the plans of his wife.

It was in this new domicile that Plank received a visitor on February 20, 1926. Edward Weikert was looking for signatures to get himself on the ballot for the state Congress. Weikert was a Democrat, and Plank was a well-known lifetime follower of that political party. Also, Weikert had been employed in the automobile field, so he likely knew Plank through those connections as well. Plank signed, and later that year Weikert was elected to the Pennsylvania House of Representatives.

The next day, a Sunday, he, his wife and Eddie Jr., now 10, made a trip to Biglerville to visit his sister, Grace, who recently had been sick. Plank hadn't been feeling well himself the past few months, but it was nothing he felt was that serious (one report would later say Plank, according to relatives, had "complained of pains in the neck and back of his head, and appeared nervous"[11]). However, it was serious. On the morning of February 22, back at home in Gettysburg, Plank was still in his nightgown when he collapsed.

Plank had suffered a stroke and was in bad shape. Confined to his bed, Plank's left side—including that left arm which pitched so many innings—was paralyzed. He couldn't speak, although he was conscious and his other faculties were working. When family members—many of whom congregated at the house, including brothers Ira and Luther and his sister Grace (Eddie's parents weren't there, as his mother was very ill and there was a delay in telling them the news) tried talking to him, Plank could only answer with his eyes—both with recognition and the tears which followed. Some early newspaper headlines declared that Plank was expected to recover. But by mid-afternoon that possibility seemed very unlikely. "Apparently, Eddie is steadily sinking, and I can't see how he can possibly recover,"[12] said a Dr. Dalby, who had been at the Plank household late that Monday afternoon.

By Tuesday, it was no longer a matter of if but when. Anna Plank did her best to keep her husband in comfort those final hours. Surrounded by his family and close friends, Eddie Plank died on February 24, 1926, at 2:48 p.m. He was just 50 years old.

In Fort Myers, Florida, at spring training with his Philadelphia Athletics team, Connie Mack received the news of Plank's death. A look of shock and dismay crossed his face and he stood there, silent, before telling reporters "I feel like a father must feel when he has lost a son."[13]

"Any words I can voice will not describe the shock that I have suffered," he continued, trying to put words together to describe his feelings. "It was a blow to me when I learned that Eddie had suffered a stroke. But I had hoped that he might recover from that. He was a rugged man, young enough, I was confident, to pull through and regain his health.... The world has lost a fine, clean sportsman when Eddie Plank died. I am certain he did not have a real enemy in the world. He was the salt of the earth. My heart goes out in sympathy to those of his family who survive him."[14]

Mack wasn't the only one stunned. Reactions from around the baseball world were swift and continued for days, most notably from Plank's former teammates. "I can't believe that Eddie is gone,"[15] stated his former batterymate, Ira Thomas. "Every man in baseball has lost a true friend,"[16] said Amos Strunk. Jack Coombs declared: "The way Plank was honored by his fellow players was an inspiration to me. I attempted to follow in his footsteps and to do the things which he did. Through these associations I began my athlete life as athletes should begin them. I can hardly realize that such a pal as he was to me has gone."[17]

Wired messages were sent to Anna Plank and Eddie Jr., from the likes of Frank Baker, Jack Barry, Chief Bender, Carroll Brown, Eddie Collins, Monte Cross, and Herb Pennock as well as one-time Athletics trainer Frank Newhouse and umpire Billy Evans. "A great ball player in his day and a lovable character; one of God's noble men," said Athletics president Thomas S. Shibe. "I am grieved beyond the power of expression."[18]

One of the first outsiders to arrive at the Plank household was Harry Davis, the former first baseman in whose house Plank lived in-season for a

21. End of the Line

Manager Connie Mack sits in the dugout with player-turned-coach Ira Thomas, who caught Plank in 71 of his starts (George Grantham Bain Collection, Library of Congress)

couple of years. Just as Plank was there for Davis when his son died, Davis came to Anna Plank and Eddie Jr., offering his condolences and whatever help they needed. St. Louis Cardinals pitcher Bill Sherdel, who was from former Gettysburg town team rival McSherrystown, although was too young to have played on those teams, stayed at the house for hours. Sherdel also was left-handed and was one of the many offered advice by Plank over the years. Former major league pitcher Lefty George, from York, Pennsylvania, also stopped by, as did one-time umpire Frank Nallin, who told the Plank family of Eddie's exemplary behavior on the field.

"Eddie was probably the greatest southpaw that ever stepped into the box. But more than a great artist of baseball, he was a perfect gentleman and a thorough sportsman," Connie Mack said. "No one ever accused Plank of resorting to trickery or of 'dusting.' It was always a pleasure to have him on our ball club, and he was a great influence among the younger players. I have never known a finer character associated with the game."[19]

Character was never an issue when it concerned Plank, especially in his hometown, where it meant more than any exploits on the field. It was his legacy in Gettysburg. "Eddie was regarded as a god in Gettysburg then," said Junie Bream, who worked at Plank's garage, in 2000. "He's the most modest, generous man I ever knew. When he put his arm around me and said, 'How you doin', Junie?' it meant the world to me."

Plank's baseball legacy, though, both nationally and in Gettysburg, was a bit more complicated. One of the game's greatest pitchers at the turn of the century would slowly fade into history—but, with a little fight, be brought back, at least partially.

◆ 22 ◆

Legacy

> How well do I remember
> Your great pitching, Eddie Plank,
> You were cool as mid–December
> Against Tiger, Brown or Yank,
> Revealing art and beauty
> In deliveries fast and slow,
> Supreme-like in mound duty,
> As you faced the fiercest foe.
> I remember in the pinches
> When a master batsman stood,
> You controlled your curves by inches,
> As they foiled the swinging wood;
> I recall in vivid drifting
> Back upon the spike shot trail,
> You, a sportsman rare, uplifting
> Like a guidepost to the frail.
> With the spirit of a Custer
> As a victor, or when downed,
> Diamonds shone with added luster
> When you toiled upon the mound;
> Let the worthy be rewards,
> Give the absent their just rank,
> As an ace you are recorded,
> You were all of that, Ed Plank.[1]
> —"To Eddie Plank" by George Moriarty, former
> Detroit and Yankees third baseman and American
> League umpire beginning in Plank's final season

Eddie Plank loved Gettysburg. He was born there, raised there, lived there before, during and after his playing days—even making trips to the town when he could during off-days of his professional baseball career—and he died there. In return, Gettysburg loved Eddie Plank right back.

While Plank's burial on February 26 would be a private service at

Evergreen Cemetery for family only, his funeral was not. The casket was brought to Gettysburg's First Presbyterian Church, and there the hometown hero lay in state between 1–3 p.m. Businesses around town closed for those two hours so everyone who wanted could pay one final tribute to Plank. One by one they lined up and slowly moved through the church while "throngs gathered on the outside and silently awaited their turn."[2]

At 3 p.m. the organ was played, and the pews filled up to capacity. They listened with rapt attention as the pastor, the Rev. W.C. Robinson, read his sermon, which was similar to something he had published in the *Gettysburg Times* a day earlier. He best summed up Plank's life with this passage: "Eddie contended lawfully in the great game of life, and so death is his coronation. He was true to his manhood, true to his parents, true to his wife and home, true to his God and church. What better could be spoken of any man?"[3]

Because it was February and teams were at spring training, and with the funeral just days after Plank's death, Harry Davis was the only former teammate at the funeral. The pallbearers—and honorary pallbearers—were all family and longtime friends. When the casket left the church, hundreds who couldn't get inside waited outside to see it put in the hearse. Others lined the sidewalks to the cemetery as the car made its way to Plank's final resting place. Other than the actual burial, this was a community event.

Gettysburg didn't forget about Plank quickly. A little less than a month after Plank's death, Dr. Henry W.A. Hanson, the president of Gettysburg College who also eulogized Plank at his funeral, announced that the school's new gymnasium, which was being built on campus at a cost of $125,000, would be named after Plank. Money would come in, but not a lot. Twenty-five dollars here, $15 there, and so on. An event at the Majestic Theater in mid–May raised $219.25. That brought the total to $567.25, well short of the $125,000 sought.

The gym's memorial fund committee went to Philadelphia to meet with Athletics manager Connie Mack to gain his support. "I am surprised, yes, somewhat displeased at the lack of interest in Gettysburg in the Eddie Plank memorial," Mack said.

> I was certain that Gettysburg would respond to this appeal to perpetuate the memory of Eddie, whom we all idolized, and who we can truthfully say, did more to raise the standard of American baseball to its present high position, than any other baseball player during the last 20 years.
>
> I expected to find the campaign considerably further advanced at this time and it is disappointing to learn that Gettysburg does not demonstrate its interest in this project more than it has. We in Philadelphia are proud of Eddie's record during his pitching days with the White Elephants. We all liked him, because of his clean sportsmanship and his gentlemanly conduct. In erecting

a gymnasium to his memory, Gettysburg is taking a big step in promoting and fostering conduct such as was exemplified by your Gettysburg Eddie.[4]

Mack announced the Athletics would hold a fundraising "Eddie Plank Day" (it would be rained out and held in 1927; it rained then, too, but this time was played albeit in front of a smaller-than-expected crowd). Other teams, such as Chicago, Cleveland and Detroit, followed suit, as did a myriad of minor-league clubs. "Such a project surely is deserving of the support of every fan in America," wrote Grantland Rice. "It is a testimonial to clean sportsmanship. I will do everything I can to assist you in this movement."[5]

The *St. Louis Post-Dispatch* ran a $25,000 fundraising drive, Mack and the Athletics donated autographed baseballs to be auctioned off, clay-shooting tournaments provided proceeds, local theaters made hefty contributions, taking away from their own profits, and checks arrived from all over the world—one for $2 from South Korea sent by Dr. A.I. Ludlow, a friend of Plank's, was noted in the papers.

The gym's first event was held April 28, 1927—two plays performed by a local drama club—even though the building was not yet completed. The Eddie Plank Memorial Gym, the cost of which rose to $133,337, had its formal dedication on June 7. "Here is a case of a great athlete whose work for his school and for the boys of future generations goes on and on," C.E. Billheimer, director of physical education at Gettysburg College, said just over one month later. "He helps them after death even as his living spirit and courage helped them when he held forth in the struggles of baseball and as a good citizen and friend. For the first time in its history his old school can care for all who want to take part in sport and take care of them in as fine shape as any school. He would be proud and glad of that."[6]

Plank's name would be bandied about in the years to come as more baseball luminaries, including Babe Ruth in 1931 and 1941, listed their "all-time" teams and included him among their pitchers. Ty Cobb, who had more than one run-in with Plank on the field, had nothing but nice things to say about his old adversary. He was very helpful in raising money for the memorial gymnasium and instrumental in the Tigers holding an "Eddie Plank Day" to contribute to the cause. "Plank was one of my best friends and I am pleased to cooperate in any way possible to assure the success of the $125,000 Memorial gym fund,"[7] Cobb said.

In 1928, Cobb named Plank as his left-handed starter on his 20th century all-time team (Cy Young got the nod as right-hander). "(Rube) Waddell had more stuff than Plank, but Plank was steadier and lasted longer,"[8] he reasoned. In 1948, Cobb selected five pitchers for his latest team: Grover Cleveland Alexander, Carl Hubbell, Walter Johnson, Christy Mathewson, and Plank. In 1953, Cobb went with six pitchers, Plank included (he

A tribute to a hometown hero: The Eddie Plank Memorial Gymnasium in 1930, three years after it opened (courtesy of Special Collections/Musselman Library, Gettysburg College, Gettysburg, PA).

dropped Hubbell and added Lefty Grove and Ed Walsh). He would repeat those six hurlers when asked again two years later. "Eddie was never fully appreciated but he was a ballplayer's pitcher,"[9] Cobb said.

When it came to the Hall of Fame, however, Plank had little traction among members of the Baseball Writers' Association of America (BBWAA), who voted on players gaining entry. The first balloting for the Hall—which opened in Cooperstown, New York, in 1939—occurred in 1936. Plank's name wasn't even on the ballot. In 1937, he garnered 23 votes, or 11.4 percent, well shy of the 75 percent needed for induction. Things didn't get much better the next two years. Plank got 38 votes in 1938 (14.5 percent) and 28 in 1939 (10.2 percent).

Of course, while one has to consider this was entirely new for the BBWAA, the writers were also very stingy and particular with their votes. Alexander, who won 373 games, didn't gain induction until his third time on the ballot, and it took Plank's former teammate and friend Eddie Collins, he with 3,315 hits, 741 stolen bases, 1,821 runs, and a career .333 average, four years to get enough votes, and even then he barely made it with 77.7 percent in 1939.

22. Legacy

There was no Hall of Fame voting in either in 1940 or 1941. The BBWAA voted in only Rogers Hornsby (78.1 percent) in 1942. Plank received 63 votes (27.0 percent), tied for 17th-most. There was no voting in 1943 and 1944 due to World War II, although Commissioner Kenesaw Mountain Landis was voted in via special election two weeks after his death in late November 1944.

Voting resumed in 1945—and the writers elected nobody. Plank received 33 votes (13.4 percent). The next year it was more of the same—no players were voted in, and Plank received 34 votes (16.8 percent). In 11 years (albeit with four years absent of voting), the BBWAA had elected just 13 players to the Hall of Fame. Other committees, for executives, 19th century players, and special reasons (such as the deaths of Landis and Lou Gehrig) put 15 more in the Hall until 1945, when the Old Timers Committee named 10 players who mostly appeared in the previous century. Plank was going to need some help.

Former Gettysburg resident H.C. Mitinger took up Plank's cause. In 1940, Mitinger visited the Cooperstown museum and came away with a feeling that someone was missing among the game's immortals. Mitinger, who said he knew Plank all his life, took to pen and paper and pleaded to the 300 sportswriters who made up the BBWAA, sending each a letter. In part, he wrote:

> Perhaps it is a new idea to conduct a campaign for a former pitcher's entry into the baseball Hall of Fame, but after a recent visit to Cooperstown I cannot remain silent. There can be no question of your choices which have been made and are now honored, and with them I heartily agree, but there is one outstanding athlete and gentleman who, in my opinion, shared by all who knew him, should also be honored. I refer to Pitcher Ed Plank of Gettysburg and the "Athletics." … If, as we understand it, the purpose of the shrine at Cooperstown is to mold ambition, character and ability of our youngsters who are visiting there in ever increasing numbers, as well as to perpetuate the achievements of the great players, there can be no denial of Plank's right to a place in the Hall.[10]

Mitinger also recounted Plank's statistics and a bevy of people who would support him in Plank's cause, including local businessmen and various baseball people such as Connie Mack and Branch Rickey. Mitinger's plea fell on deaf ears, partly because he wrote it in the summer of 1940 and there was no voting until 1942. Also, as noted above, the BBWAA was very selective.

There was one sportswriter who was listening, though. Bill Duncan of the *Philadelphia Inquirer* was also a Gettysburg native and Plank backer. He wrote letters to numerous well-known writers, including Grantland Rice, asking for their help in gaining Plank some publicity to help influence voters. Plank did gain a few votes over the years but was still a far cry from election.

Enter Mack. Plank's former manager with the Philadelphia Athletics was still managing, and owning, the team and was well-thought-of in the baseball world. When the BBWAA didn't vote in anyone in the 1946 election, the Hall's Old Timers Committee was set to add members later in the year. Mack impressed upon the committee that he thought Plank should be included.

On April 24, 1946, Plank was one of 11 named to the Hall of Fame by the Old Timers Committee. Among those joining him was former teammate Rube Waddell and Ed Walsh. Upon hearing the news, Ira Plank simply stated, "That's great. It makes me very happy."[11] Plank's actual induction ceremony wouldn't occur until July 21, 1947—a Monday morning—at 11 a.m., before the start of an exhibition game between the Boston Braves and New York Yankees.

Baseball Commissioner Happy Chandler wasn't in attendance, so National League president Ford Frick handled the ceremony, which was held atop the Hall's steps. Walsh, who was one of 15 being inducted (the BBWAA had voted in four players earlier in the year), was the only former player at the event. Anna Plank and Eddie Jr. (with his wife) made the trip from Gettysburg, as did nine others from the surrounding area, including Eddie's brothers Ira and Luther and, of course, Mitinger.

Plank's Hall of Fame plaque, as many were in the early days, is a bit understated. It reads:

ONE OF THE GREATEST LEFTHANDED PITCHERS OF MAJOR LEAGUES. NEVER PITCHED FOR A MINOR LEAGUE TEAM, GOING FROM GETTYSBURG COLLEGE TO THE PHILADELPHIA A.L. TEAM WITH WHICH HE SERVED FROM 1901 THROUGH 1914. MEMBER OF ST. LOUIS F.L. IN 1915 AND ST. LOUIS AL IN 1916-17. ONE OF FEW PITCHERS TO WIN MORE THAN 300 GAMES IN BIG LEAGUES. IN EIGHT OF 17 SEASONS WON 20 OR MORE GAMES.[12]

The plaque is interesting because of the inclusion of Plank's one season in the Federal League, where he won 21 games. Plank's career statistics came into question beginning in 1956. Cleveland pitcher Bob Lemon was closing in on the seventh 20-win season of his career (he would win exactly 20 in 1956), and Plank was mentioned as also having done it seven times. But that didn't include his time in the Federal League.

It turned out that official baseball statistics were spotty. We know now that Plank owned a career record of 326–194 with a 2.35 ERA, 410 complete games, 69 shutouts, and 2,246 strikeouts. In 1951, the *Little Red Book* (which published American League statistics) had Plank with 324 wins (in 1960 it would change that to 325 and still be one short). Another publication, *One-for-the-Book*, listed Plank's record as 305–181, discarding his Federal League season (and also missing two other losses). The *Encyclopedia of Baseball* was close with Plank's record as 325–194. Its revised edition corrected the wins to 326 but listed his losses at 192. *Baseball Register* had Plank at 325–190.

Plank-o-phile Bill Duncan had seen enough and wanted it straightened out. He decided to write American League president Joe Cronin to see if he could set the wheels in motion to find Plank's actual win total, and specifically whether his Federal League statistics should be included. Duncan got a reply from the AL's director of public relations, Joseph W. McKenney, who wrote that the 21 Federal League wins counted and Plank had … 325 wins.

Duncan also heard from former BBWAA president Les Biederman, who in 1961 informed him, "Our organization ruled two years ago that Federal League record do not count in major league records."[13] This sparked the American League to conduct an investigation. Charley Segar, the league's secretary-treasurer, put it all to rest—the Federal League's records should be included, and Plank's final record was 326–194.

Plank held the record for most wins by a left-hander until Warren Spahn passed him with win No. 327 on September 29, 1962. Spahn tossed seven shutouts in 1963, giving him 62, and once again calling into question Plank's career total. Nothing was more confusing than following the progression of his total via the *Little Red Book*. In 1938 the publication had Plank with 69 shutouts. But in 1959, it was 58. Then in 1964, 64. Seymour Siwoff, editor of the *Little Red Book*, said in May 1964 that while they included Plank's Federal League wins in the 1964 edition, they neglected to add his shutouts, thus he would be listed with 70 in the 1965 book. Of course, he really had 69 but Spahn never passed him, finishing with 63. Plank still holds the record for most shutouts and complete games by a left-handed pitcher, and judging by the way baseball has changed in regards to the use of starters and relievers, it's likely he'll hold those until the end of time.

In the 1970s, Plank's name emerged again—but this time among baseball card collectors. The T206 Plank card, issued by the Sweet Corporal Sweets cigarette company circa 1910, was ranked as the second-most valuable card by the *Book of Lists* in 1978 at $1,000. In 2019, a Plank card fetched over $51,000, and one in near-mint condition has been valued at $850,000. The reason isn't necessarily because of Plank but due to the fact there was a limited run of these cards and thus few are available.

Like much of Plank's career, the reasons given for the lack of cards are pure conjecture. The *New York Times* said in 1973 that it "did not get wide distribution because the engraver's plate for his card broke."[14] Another hypothesis is that Plank didn't smoke and perhaps didn't want to be associated with tobacco. *Sports Collectors Daily* noted that Plank was in a few other early card sets from tobacco companies but not in prominent ones which were issued. While Plank was not among those in a Sweet Corporal Sweets promotion from 1910 to 1912—cardboard pins which included the mug shot of individual players—he was part of the most popular Philadelphia baseball player contest run by the tobacco company in 1914. "Plank isn't in a *ton* of tobacco sets but does appear enough times that the anti-tobacco argument isn't a slam dunk,"[15] decided *Sports Collectors Daily* in 2019.

Plank was immortalized further over a half-century after his death. In 1972 he was inducted into the Pennsylvania Sports Hall of Fame, located in Harrisburg. In 2001, he was part of an inaugural class of 26 inductees for the Adams County Chapter of that Hall of Fame. In 2012, Plank and later stars Johnny Callison and Mike Piazza were part of the ninth class of the Philadelphia Sports Hall of Fame.

Eddie Plank on a 1909 Ramly Turkish Cigarettes baseball card. This same design, with a red "A" printed over his jersey breast, was also used by the Sweet Corporal Sweets cigarette company circa 1910 on a card which is now considered one of the priciest on the market due to its rarity (Library of Congress).

Most appropriately, Gettysburg gave Plank proper acknowledgment in 2000. It was long overdue. The Eddie Plank Memorial Gym had since turned more into an office building—and now is referred to simply as the Plank Gym—with newer and more modern athletic facilities built on the Gettysburg College campus. When Plank played, he was associated with that town nearly as much as the Civil War battle. If a town could be proud of an individual, such was the case. But over the years as time passed, Plank became just a name, more forgotten as those who knew him passed way. It took a 1982 graduate of Gettysburg High School, Matt Kerr, to lead the charge and finally get Plank the recognition he deserved.

On August 31, 2000—no coincidence the 125th anniversary of Plank's birth—a small group which included politicians, Eddie's great-grandson, and a 95-year-old Junie Bream gathered at the Adams County Historical Society for the dedication of an Eddie Plank historical marker. The marker originally was to be posted in Straban Township, where Eddie was born and grew up. Instead, it was more appropriately planted in Gettysburg, at the intersection of Carlisle Street and West Lincoln Avenue, where the Plank family lived, and across the street from the college where Eddie's baseball career took off.

The marker reads similarly to Plank's Hall of Fame plaque, but with a local touch:

> Eddie Plank (1875–1926). Baseball great. One of the most dominant pitchers of the twentieth century. "Gettysburg Eddie" compiled a record of 326–194 throughout his career (1901–17), mostly with the Philadelphia Athletics. He won 20 games or more eight times and helped the A's win six pennants and three world championships. Plank was born here, attended Gettysburg Academy. He retired and died in Gettysburg. Elected to the Baseball Hall of Fame, 1946.[16]

It might be off the beaten path for the Civil War enthusiasts who travel to town to see the famous battlefield and the spot where Abraham Lincoln delivered perhaps his most memorable speech months later, but for Gettysburgians who walk by and take a look, it's a reminder of a man who loved his hometown. And that love is forever returned. "Gettysburg is not just three days in 1863," said Kerr.

It's also very much the life of Eddie Plank. As the *Gettysburg Times* said in April 1926,

> There are two things that have given Gettysburg the right, if you please, to bask in the sunshine of national notoriety and fame. They are: First: The fact that the most decisive battle of the Civil War was waged around the town. Second: The fact that Eddie Plank was born within the shadow of Gettysburg, in an humble farm home, went out into the world and made a name for himself and came back to Gettysburg and die.[17]

> Farewell to rooters' repartee
> And bleachers' persiflage!
> For Eddie Plank has gone away
> To open a garage.
> No more the great left-hander will
> Disport upon the green.
> Henceforth this sport will show his skill
> In handling gasoline.
> He travels to the timbers tall,
> But still it might be worse.
> The "stuff" he once put on the ball
> He'll now put in his purse.
> Yet, barring caution and his curves,

He'll hit 'em hot and swift.
The best in life Ed Plank deserves—
To him our hats we lift.
How swiftly players make a hit,
Then disappear from sight!
They gladly come, they sadly "Git"—
First "Greetings," then "Good-night!"
And some we catch are mighty fish
And some of little rank.
But he was good! and so we wish
Good luck to Eddie Plank[18]

—by an anonymous author and purportedly Anna Plank's favorite ode to her husband, likely written after he retired from baseball and went back to Gettysburg

Chapter Notes

Preface

1. *Evening Independent*, October 14, 1943.
2. *Brooklyn Daily Eagle*, January 9, 1938.
3. https://www.youtube.com/watch?v=oQED3NY4u7E.
4. *Baseball Digest*, May 1952.

Chapter 1

1. *News Comet* (East Berlin, PA), May 25, 1934.
2. Ibid.
3. *Gettysburg Times*, February 25, 1926.
4. *Gettysburg Times*, August 31, 1985.
5. "How I Got My Start," From Plank's Baseball Hall of Fame library clippings file, copyright 1910.
6. *Adams County Independent*, August 10, 1895.
7. *Gettysburg Compiler*, August 6, 1895.
8. *Gettysburg Compiler*, August 27, 1895.
9. *Harrisburg Telegraph*, May 19, 1896.
10. *Adams Country News*, November 8, 1913.
11. *Pittsburgh Post-Gazette*, September 18, 1921.
12. Ibid.
13. Ibid.
14. *Gettysburg Compiler*, June 27, 1899.
15. *Gettysburg Compiler*, July 4, 1899.
16. Ibid.
17. *Gettysburg Compiler*, July 11, 1899.
18. *Hanover Record* via *Gettysburg Star and Sentinel*, May 8, 1900.
19. *York Gazette* via *Gettysburg Star and Sentinel*, July 25, 1899.
20. *Gettysburg Star and Sentinel*, July 11, 1899.

Chapter 2

1. Email correspondence with Amy Lucadamo, September 12, 2018.
2. *The Gettysburgian*, March 21, 1900.
3. *Gettysburg Compiler*, April 17, 1900.
4. *Richmond Times*, June 12, 1900.
5. *Richmond Times*, June 13, 1900.
6. *Richmond Times*, June 14, 1900.
7. *Gettysburg Compiler*, June 19, 1900.
8. *The Sporting News*, August 23, 1917.
9. *Chester Times*, August 16, 1900.
10. *Chester Times*, August 18, 1900.
11. *The Gettysburgian*, May 9, 1901.
12. *The Gettysburgian*, May 15, 1901.
13. "How I Got My Start," from Baseball Hall of Fame clippings file, copyright 1910.
14. *Grand Forks Evening Times*, Octpber 19, 1911.
15. *El Paso Herald*, April 1, 1911.
16. *The Sporting News*, December 1, 1921.
17. *Harrisburg Daily Independent*, August 5, 1903.
18. *Gettysburg Compiler*, September 13, 1911.
19. *The Sporting News*, November 17, 1938.
20. J. C. Kofoed, "The Crossfire King," *Baseball Magazine* (October 1914): 33–36.
21. *The Sporting News*, May 18, 1901.
22. *Baltimore Morning Herald*, May 14, 1901.
23. *The Sporting News*, May 11, 1901.
24. *Baltimore Morning Herald*, March 14, 1901.
25. *The Gettysburgian*, May 29, 1901.
26. *The Gettysburgian*, May 22, 1901.

Chapter 3

1. *Philadelphia Inquirer*, May 19, 1901.
2. *Philadelphia Record*, May 19, 1901.
3. *Philadelphia Inquirer*, May 19, 1901.
4. *Washington Post*, May 19, 1901.
5. *Washington Times*, May 19, 1901
6. *Philadelphia Inquirer*, May 19, 1901.
7. *The Sporting News*, June 8, 1901.
8. *Detroit Free-Press*, June 4, 1901.
9. Ibid.
10. *Philadelphia Times*, June 4, 1901
11. *Detroit Free-Press*, June 4, 1901.
12. *Philadelphia Bulletin* via *Gettysburg Star and Sentinel*, June 12, 1901.
13. *Philadelphia Times*, June 9, 1901.
14. *Philadelphia North American* via *Gettysburg Star and Sentinel*, June 12, 1901.
15. *Philadelphia Press* via *Gettysburg Compiler*, June 11, 1901.
16. *Detroit Free-Press*, June 12, 1901.
17. Ibid.
18. *Philadelphia Inquirer*, June 14, 1901
19. *Philadelphia Evening Telegram* via *Gettysburg Compiler*, June 18, 1901.
20. *Baltimore Morning Herald*, June 28, 1901.
21. *Baltimore Morning Herald* via *Philadelphia Inquirer*, July 9, 1901.
22. Ibid.
23. *Chicago Tribune*, July 23, 1901.
24. *Detroit Free-Press*, July 21, 1901.
25. *Philadelphia Times*, August 22, 1901.

Chapter 4

1. *Sporting Life*, April 12, 1902.
2. *Philadelphia Times*, May 3, 1902.
3. *Philadelphia Record*, May 3, 1902.
4. *Washington Times*, May 7, 1902.
5. *Detroit Free Press*, August 25, 1902.
6. *Philadelphia Inquirer*, September 2, 1902.
7. *The Sporting News*, September 20, 1902.
8. *Boston Globe*, September 16, 1902.
9. *Boston Post*, September 21, 1902.
10. *Philadelphia Record*, September 28, 1902.
11. *Philadelphia Record*, September 30, 1902.
12. *Philadelphia Record*, September 12, 1902.

Chapter 5

1. *Reach's Official American League Base Ball Guide for 1903* (Philadelphia: A. J. Reach, 1903, 46.
2. *Baltimore Evening Sun*, April 24, 1940.
3. *St. John Sun*, May 20, 1909.
4. *Washington Evening Star*, August 25, 1900.
5. *Detroit Free-Press*, June 6, 1902.
6. Baseball Daily History, "The Sudden Reappearance of 'Silver King," June 27, 2013.
7. *New York Times*, October 5, 1913.
8. *Gettysburg Times*, February 25, 1926.
9. *St. John Sun*, May 20, 1909.
10. *Gettysburg Times*, February 27, 1926.
11. *Los Angeles Evening Express*, November 5, 1909.
12. Lawrence Ritter and Donald Honig, *The 100 Greatest Baseball Players of All Time* (New York: Crown Publishers, 1981), 259.
13. Carroll Slick, "On the Mound," *Saturday Evening Post*, June 8, 1929.
14. *Pittsburgh Press*, February 17, 1926.
15. *Philadelphia Record*, March 12, 1903.
16. *Philadelphia Record*, May 7, 1903.
17. *Philadelphia Record*, May 14, 1903.
18. *Philadelphia Ledger* via *Gettysburg Star and Sentinel*, October 7, 1903.
19. Ibid.
20. Ibid.
21. *Sporting Life*, August 29, 1903.
22. *Sporting Life*, August 22, 1903.
23. *The Sporting News*, August 23, 1917.

Chapter 6

1. *The Sporting News*, January 18, 1912.
2. *Gettysburg Star and Sentinel*, November 11, 1903.
3. *The Sporting News*, March 19, 1904.
4. Ibid.
5. *Gettysburg Compiler*, September 14, 1904.
6. "50 years ago," *Gettysburg Times*, September 14, 1954.
7. *Boston Sunday Post*, September 11, 1904.
8. *Philadelphia Ledger* via *Washington Evening Star*, July 9, 1904.
9. *Boston Globe*, September 20, 1904.
10. *The Sporting News*, March 25, 1905.
11. *Mansfield Daily Shield*, September 27, 1911.

Notes—Chapters 7, 8, 9

12. *Sporting Life*, May 13, 1905.
13. *The Sporting News*, August 5, 1905.
14. *The Sporting News*, August 12, 1905.
15. *Philadelphia Inquirer*, August 27, 1905.
16. *Ibid.*
17. *Boston Globe*, September 17, 1905.
18. *Philadelphia Record*, September 29, 1905.
19. *Philadelphia Record*, September 30, 1905.
20. *The Sporting News*, October 7, 1905.
21. *Philadelphia Inquirer*, October 5, 1905.
22. *Pittsburgh Press*, August 29, 1907.
23. *New York Times*, October 8, 1905.
24. *Evening World*, October 9, 1905.
25. *Philadelphia Record*, October 10, 1905.
26. *El Paso Herald*, October 8, 1921.
27. *Philadelphia Inquirer*, October 14, 1905.
28. *Sporting Life*, October 28, 1905.
29. *Ibid.*

Chapter 7

1. *Sporting Life*, November 4, 1905.
2. *Gettysburg Compiler*, November 1, 1905.
3. *Sporting Life*, November 11, 1905.
4. *Philadelphia Record*, March 29, 1906.
5. *The Sporting News*, April 14, 1906.
6. *Philadelphia Inquirer*, April 20, 1906.
7. *Chicago Tribune*, August 9, 1906.
8. *Gettysburg Compiler*, September 13, 1911.
9. *Philadelphia Inquirer*, Aug. 9, 1906.
10. *The Sporting News*, September 15, 1906.
11. *Philadelphia Inquirer*, March 27, 1907.
12. *New York Evening World*, March 29, 1907.
13. *Detroit Free Press*, March 29, 1907.
14. *St. Louis Post-Dispatch*, March 31, 1907.
15. *Philadelphia Inquirer*, July 27, 1907.
16. *Detroit Free Press*, August 9, 1907.
17. *Philadelphia Inquirer*, August 9, 1907.
18. *Philadelphia Inquirer*, October 1, 1907.
19. *The Sporting News*, October 17, 1907.
20. *Washington Evening Star*, March 4, 1912.
21. *Saturday Evening Post*, April 13, 1912.
22. *Gettysburg Compiler*, Sept. 13, 1911.
23. *Washington Herald*, October 5, 1907.
24. *Ibid.*
25. *Washington Post*, October 23, 1907.

Chapter 8

1. *The Sporting News*, January 23, 1908.
2. *Detroit Free Press*, February 29, 1908.
3. *Pittsburgh Press*, January 22, 1908.
4. *Sporting Life*, June 6, 1903.
5. *Washington Evening Star*, August 11, 1907.
6. *Berkshire Eagle*, March 11, 1974.
7. *Williamsport Daily Gazette and Bulletin*, February 27, 1908.
8. *Philadelphia Inquirer*, February 27, 1908.
9. *Detroit Free Press*, February 29, 1908.
10. *Gettysburg Times*, April 10, 1923.
11. *The Sporting News*, February 25, 1909.
12. *New York Times*, May 23, 1954.
13. *Ibid.*
14. *Sporting Life*, April 3, 1909.
15. *The Sporting News*, April 15, 1909.
16. *The Sporting News*, March 5, 1908.
17. *Boston Post*, April 13, 1909.
18. *Philadelphia Inquirer*, April 13, 1909.
19. *Ibid.*
20. *Ibid.*

Chapter 9

1. *Philadelphia Inquirer*, April 12, 1909.
2. *Powers Day Program*, June 30, 1910, 16–17.
3. *Sporting Life*, February 2, 1907.
4. *Decatur Daily Review*, April 9, 1911.
5. *The Sporting News*, June 16, 1910.
6. *Philadelphia Inquirer*, April 13, 1909.
7. *Philadelphia Inquirer*, April 25, 1909.
8. *Philadelphia Inquirer*, April 27, 1909.
9. *Washington Herald*, April 27, 1909.
10. *Philadelphia Inquirer*, April 27, 1909.
11. *Washington Herald*, April 27, 1909.
12. *St. John Sun*, May 20, 1909.
13. J.C. Kofoed, "The Crossfire King," October 1914, from Baseball Hall of Fame clippings file.
14. *Lewiston Evening-Journal*, February 14, 1940.
15. *North American Newspaper*

Alliance article in *Anaconda* (MT) *Standard*, January 4, 1927.
16. *Philadelphia Inquirer*, June 28, 1909.
17. *Philadelphia Inquirer*, September 6, 1909.
18. *Bend* (OR) *Bulletin*, March 9, 1926.
19. *Ibid.*
20. *Ibid.*
21. *Ibid.*
22. *Ibid.*
23. *Philadelphia Inquirer*, August 8. 1909.
24. *Ibid.*
25. *The Sporting News*, August 26, 1909.
26. *Ibid.*
27. *Philadelphia Inquirer*, September 17, 1909
28. *Washington Evening Star*, September 20, 1909.
29. *Philadelphia Evening Telegram*, September 20, 1909.
30. *Ibid.*

Chapter 10

1. *The Sporting News*, August 5, 1909.
2. *Ibid.*
3. *Ibid.*
4. *Gettysburg Times*, April 5, 1910; *Adams County News*, April 9, 1910.
5. *Ibid.*
6. *Ibid.*
7. *Norwich Bulletin*, February 22, 1910.
8. *Sporting Life*, March 19, 1910.
9. *Ibid.*
10. *The Sporting News*, October 28, 1937.
11. *Ottawa Citizen*, July 29, 1952.
12. *Washington Evening Star*, April 15, 1910.
13. *Ibid.*
14. *Detroit Free Press*, June 6, 1910.
15. *The Sporting News*, August 4, 1910.
16. *Philadelphia Inquirer*, August. 20, 1910.
17. *Chicago Tribune*, August 20, 1910.
18. *Washington Evening Star*, September 5, 1910.
19. *Gettysburg Times*, April 10, 1923.
20. *The Sporting News*, September 8, 1910.
21. *Washington Evening Star*, November 1, 1910.
22. *Gettysburg Times*, October 21, 1911.
23. *Washington Evening Star*, November 1, 1910.
24. *Daily Sentinel* (Woodstock, IL), February 26, 1926.
25. *Ibid.*
26. *Washington Evening Star*, November 1, 1910.
27. *Adams County News*, November 5, 1910.
28. *Gettysburg Compiler*, February 1, 1911.
29. *Detroit Free Press*, December 4, 1910.
30. *Havana Post* via *Washington Post*, December 24, 1910.
31. *Washington Post*, December 24, 1910.
32. *St. Louis Star and Times*, March 27, 1915.

Chapter 11

1. *Washington Herald*, April 1, 1911.
2. *Grand Forks Evening Times*, October 19, 1911.
3. *Gettysburg Compiler*, March 29, 1911.
4. *Philadelphia Inquirer*, June 3, 1911.
5. *Philadelphia Inquirer*, June 5, 1911.
6. *Boston Post*, June 24, 1911.
7. *Washington Evening Star*, June 30, 1911.
8. *Philadelphia Inquirer*, June 30, 1911.
9. *The Sporting News*, August 23, 1917.
10. *Gettysburg Times*, April 10, 1923.
11. *Saturday Evening Post*, June 8, 1929.
12. *Detroit Free Press*, February 17, 1918.
13. Interview by Michael J. Birkner, Gettysburg College Oral History Collection, November 27, December 4, 2000.
14. *Washington Herald*, March 26, 1913.
15. *The Inter Ocean* (Chicago), August 20, 1911.
16. *Philadelphia Inquirer*, Aug. 20, 1911.
17. *Milwaukee Sentinel*, April 4, 1915.
18. *Philadelphia Inquirer*, June 9, 1911.
19. *The Sporting News*, Sepember 7, 1911.

Chapter 12

1. *Philadelphia Inquirer*, October 14, 1911.
2. *Sporting Life*, October 7, 1911.
3. *Philadelphia Inquirer*, October 12, 1911.
4. *Washington Herald*, October 17, 1911.
5. *New York Tribune*, October 17, 1911.
6. *Washington Herald*, October 17, 1911.
7. *Philadelphia Evening Bulletin*, January 3, 1946.

8. *The Day Book* (Chicago), November 6, 1911.
9. *Ibid.*
10. *Philadelphia Inquirer*, October 17, 1911.
11. *Boston Post*, October 17, 1911.
12. *Philadelphia Inquirer*, October 17, 1911.
13. *Washington Herald*, October 17, 1911.
14. *Ibid.*
15. *Washington Herald*, February 3, 1912.
16. *New York Sun*, October 17, 1911.
17. *Honolulu Evening Bulletin*, February 26, 1912.
18. *Gettysburg Times*, October 21, 1911.
19. *The Sporting News*, November 2, 2011.
20. *Washington Herald,* February 3, 1912.
21. *Washington Times*, December 22, 1911.
22. *St. Louis Post-Dispatch*, October 27, 1911.
23. *Gettysburg Times*, February 17, 1923.
24. *Reading Eagle*, October 28, 1911.
25. *The Sporting News*, December 28, 1911.
26. https://www.fhwa.dot.gov/ohim/summary95/mv200.pdf.
27. *Washington Times*, February 4, 1912.
28. *Calumet News*, January 22, 1912.
29. *Boston Post*, April 30, 1912.
30. *Philadelphia Evening Telegraph*, July 17, 1912.
31. Syndicated article in *Gettysburg Times*, February 10, 1927.
32. *Mansfield Daily Shield*, September 27, 1911.
33. *Detroit Free Press*, July 30, 1912.
34. *Milwaukee Journal*, September 6, 1912.
35. *Ibid.*
36. *Washington Herald*, September 28, 1912.
37. *New York Times*, November 17, 1912.
38. *Washington Times*, September 28, 1912.

Chapter 13

1. *Washington Times*, February 8, 1913.
2. *Fort Wayne Sentinel*, November 22, 1912.
3. *The Sporting News*, November 14, 1912.
4. *Sporting Life*, December 14, 1912.
5. *Muscatine Journal*, November 9, 1912.
6. www.annandalechamber.com/Difference_Century_1912.rhtml.
7. *Washington Herald*, March 26, 1913.
8. *Calumet News*, February 15, 1913.
9. *Washington Evening Star*, February 8, 1913.
10. I via *Gettysburg Times*, February 8, 1913.
11. *Ibid.*
12. *Washington Times*, May 1, 1913.
13. *Oxnard Daily Courier*, March 31, 1913.
14. Special to *Philadelphia Inquirer*, May 6, 1913.
15. *Milwaukee Journal*, May 18, 1913.
16. *The Sporting News*, June 19, 1913.
17. *Philadelphia Inquirer*, June 13, 1913.
18. The Sporting News, April 24, 1913.
19. *Ibid.*
20. *The Sporting News*, July 17, 1913.
21. *Ibid.*
22. *Times Herald* (Olean, NY), January 12, 1917.
23. *Bend* (OR) *Bulletin*, March 9, 1926.
24. *Baseball Digest*, May 1952, 30.
25. *St. Louis Globe-Democrat* via *Evening Independent*, August 1, 1914.
26. *Gettysburg Times*, February 27, 1926.
27. *Anaconda Standard*, January 4, 1927.
28. *St. Nicholas: An Illustrated Magazine for Young Folks* 41 (October 1914): 611.
29. *Sporting Life*, September 27, 1913.
30. *St. Louis Star*, July 21, 1913.
31. *Pittsburgh Press*, August 30, 1913.
32. *Washington Times*, October 7, 1913.
33. *Reading Eagle*, June 7, 1914.

Chapter 14

1. *Sporting Life*, October 11, 1913.
2. *New York Evening World*, October 6, 1913.
3. *Herald-Journal*, October 4, 1913.
4. *Washington Times*, October 7, 1913.
5. *Washington Herald*, October 8, 1913.
6. *New York Tribune*, October 7, 1913.
7. *Gettysburg Times*, February 28, 1964.
8. *The Day*, December 9, 1914.
9. *Pittsburgh Press*, October 12, 1913.
10. *Pittsburgh Press*, October 9, 1913.
11. *Ibid.*
12. Connie Mack, "Honesty in Baseball," *Saturday Evening Post*, November 29, 1913.

13. *Baseball Digest*, May 1952, 28.
14. *The Sporting News*, April 6, 1939.
15. *Sporting Life*, November 15, 1913.
16. *Washington Herald*, October 11, 1913.
17. *Washington Evening Star*, October 11, 1913.
18. *Sporting Life*, October 18, 1913.
19. *Washington Evening Star*, October 11, 1913.
20. *Anaconda Standard*, January 4, 1927.
21. *New York Evening Journal* via *Gettysburg Times*, February 24, 1934.
22. Ibid.
23. Ibid.
24. *Milwaukee Journal*, May 20, 1941
25. *Toronto Sunday World*, October 13, 1913.
26. *Philadelphia Inquirer*, October 13, 1913.
27. *Pittsburgh Press*, September 3, 1916.
28. *Boston Post*, October 12, 1913.
29. *Philadelphia Inquirer*, October 12, 1913.
30. Ibid.
31. *Sporting Life*, October 18, 1913.

Chapter 15

1. *Prescott Journal Miner*, October 15, 1913.
2. *Sporting Life*, November 8, 1913.
3. *Philadelphia Inquirer*, October 19, 1913.
4. *Philadelphia Inquirer*, October 14, 1913.
5. Ibid.
6. *Philadelphia Inquirer*, October 30, 1913.
7. *Gettysburg Times*, September 5, 1962.
8. *Gettysburg Compiler*, November 12, 1913.
9. Ibid.
10. *The Gettysburgian*, November 12, 1913.
11. *Gettysburg Compiler*, November 12, 1913.
12. *The Gettysburgian*, November 12, 1913.
13. *Adams County News*, January 31, 1914.
14. *Reading Times*, February 11, 1914.
15. *Gettysburg Times*, January 24, 1914.
16. *Lewiston Evening Journal*, February 17, 1914.
17. *Fort Wayne Sentinel*, February 21, 1914.
18. *Philadelphia Inquirer*, February 24, 1914.
19. *Philadelphia Inquirer*, July 11, 1914.
20. *Gettysburg Times*, April 6, 1914.
21. *Philadelphia Evening Ledger*, October 17, 1914.
22. *Philadelphia Inquirer*, May 3, 1914.
23. *Baseball Magazine*, January 3, 1915.
24. *The Sporting News*, October 29, 1936.
25. *St. Louis Star*, April 30, 1917.
26. *Gettysburg Star and Sentinel*, September 21, 1914.
27. *New York Times*, December 9, 1914.
28. *Oakland Tribune* via *Baseball History Daily*, July 8, 2015.
29. *Brooklyn Daily Eagle*, April 4, 1922.
30. Ibid.
31. Ibid.
32. *Baseball Magazine*, December 1914.
33. *Philadelphia Inquirer*, September 30, 1914.

Chapter 16

1. Connie Mack, *My 66 Years in the Big Leagues; The Great Sstory of America's National Game* (Philadelphia: Winston, 1950), 35.
2. *The Sporting News*, November 5, 1914.
3. Ibid.
4. *Boston Post*, October 11, 1914.
5. Carroll S. Slick, "On the Mound," *Saturday Evening Post*, June 8, 1929.
6. F. C. Lane, "Batting" *Baseball Magazine*, 1925.
7. *Toronto World*, October 12, 1914.
8. *St. Louis Post-Dispatch*, March 14, 1916.
9. *Gettysburg Times*, April 27, 1949.
10. *Youngstown Vindicator*, January 21, 1914.
11. *Washington Times*, May 20, 1914.
12. F. C. Richter, *Sporting Life*, June 27, 1914.
13. Fred Lieb, *Connie Mack, Grand Old Man of Baseball* (New York: G. B. Putnam's Sons, 1945).
14. *Washington Evening Star*, October 25, 1914.
15. *Philadelphia Inquirer*, October 25, 1914.
16. *Philadelphia Inquirer*, November 1, 1914.
17. Ibid.
18. Ibid.
19. *Philadelphia Inquirer*, November 1,

1914; *Gettysburg Times*, November 2, 1964 (addition of "fat salary" line).
20. *Gettysburg Times*, January 19, 1920.
21. *Sporting Life*, December 12, 1914.
22. *Washington Times*, November 4, 1914.
23. *Detroit Free Press*, November 3, 1914.
24. *Detroit Free Press*, November 13, 1914.
25. *The Day*, November 13, 1914.
26. *Philadelphia Inquirer*, November 28, 1914.
27. *New York Evening World*, November 30, 1914.
28. *Philadelphia Inquirer*, December 17, 1914.

Chapter 17

1. *Harrisburg Telegraph*, February 23, 1915.
2. *Ibid.*
3. *Washington Times*, February 4, 1915.
4. *New Oxford Item*, February 25, 1915.
5. *Gettysburg Star and Sentinel*, February 23, 1915.
6. *Gettysburg Times*, March 31, 1914.
7. *St. Louis Post-Dispatch*, February 19, 1915.
8. *Gettysburg Star and Sentinel*, April 3, 1915.
9. *St. Louis Star*, March 27, 1915.
10. *St. Louis Post-Dispatch*, April 5, 1915.
11. *St. Louis Post-Dispatch*, April 17, 1915.
12. *St. Louis Post-Dispatch*, April 28, 1915
13. *Sporting Life*, May 8, 1915.
14. *St. Louis Star*, June 12, 1915.
15. *St. Louis Post-Dispatch*, June 3, 1915.
16. *Chicago Tribune*, June 3, 1915.
17. *Philadelphia Evening Ledger*, June 28, 1915.
18. *Baltimore Sun*, June 27, 1915.
19. *St. Louis Post-Dispatch*, June 27, 1915.
20. *St. Louis Star*, July 14, 1915.
21. *Sporting Life*, August 14, 1915.
22. *Ibid.*
23. *St. Louis Post-Dispatch*, February 14, 1916.
24. *St. Louis Post-Dispatch*, September 20, 1915.
25. *St. Louis Post-Dispatch*, February 23, 1916.

Chapter 18

1. *Gettysburg Times*, December 16, 1915.
2. *Sporting Life*, January 18, 1916.
3. *St. Louis Post-Dispatch*, January 16, 1916.
4. *Sporting Life*, February 12, 1916.
5. *St. Louis Post-Dispatch*, February 22, 1916.
6. *St. Louis Post-Dispatch*, March 2, 1916.
7. *St. Louis Post-Dispatch*, February 23, 1916.
8. *St. Louis Post-Dispatch*, April 17, 1916.
9. *Ibid.*
10. *Ibid.*
11. *Ibid.*
12. *Ibid.*
13. *ibid.*
14. *St. Louis Post-Dispatch*, April 21, 1916.
15. *St. Louis Post-Dispatch*, April 23, 1916.
16. *Detroit Free Press*, May 6, 1916.
17. *Pittsburgh Press*, July 15, 1916.
18. *St. Louis Post-Dispatch*, May 7, 1916.
19. *Philadelphia Evening Public Ledger*, May 16, 1916.
20. *St. Louis Post-Dispatch*, April 14, 1916.
21. *St. Louis Post-Dispatch*, August 1, 1916.
22. *Decatur Herald*, January 25, 1931.
23. *St. Louis Post-Dispatch*, January 7, 1917.
24. *The Sporting News*, September 3, 1942.
25. *Sporting Life*, September 9, 1916.
26. *Ibid.*
27. *Pittsburgh Press*, September 3, 1916.
28. *Ibid.*
29. *St. Louis Star*, November 2, 1916.
30. *St. Louis Star*, October 9, 1916.

Chapter 19

1. *Dayton Daily News*, October 28, 1916.
2. *Washington Evening Star*, November 5, 1916.
3. *St. Louis Post-Dispatch*, December 15, 1916.
4. *Buffalo Commercial*, December 19, 1916.
5. *Washington Times*, January 9, 1917.
6. *St. Louis Post-Dispatch*, February 12, 1917.
7. *Washington Herald*, February 12, 1917.

8. *Philadelphia Inquirer*, February 17, 1917.
9. *St. Louis Post-Dispatch*, February 19, 1917.
10. *St. Louis Post-Dispatch*, February 18, 1917.
11. *St. Louis Star*, March 20, 1917.
12. *The Sporting News*, April 5, 1917.
13. *St. Louis Star*, April 13, 1917.
14. *St. Louis Post Dispatch*, April 19, 1917.
15. *Chicago Tribune*, April. 20, 1917.
16. *St. Louis Star*, April 20, 1917.
17. *St. Louis Star*, April 30, 1917.
18. *St. Louis Post-Dispatch*, May 19, 1917.
19. *St. Louis Star*, May 28, 1917.
20. *St. Louis Post-Dispatch*, June 2, 1917.
21. *St. Louis Star*, June 8, 1917.
22. *Evening News* (Harrisburg, PA), June 20, 1917.
23. *Ibid*.
24. *St. Louis Post-Dispatch*, August 15, 1917.
25. *St. Louis Star*, June 21, 1917.
26. *St. Louis Star*, June 25, 1917.
27. *St. Louis Post-Dispatch*, July 1, 1917.
28. *Washington Post*, August 7, 1917.
29. Baseball Hall of Fame clippings file for Eddie Plank.
30. *Hanover Evening Sun*, November 8, 1938.

Chapter 20

1. *Reading Times*, August 16, 1917.
2. *Hanover Evening Sun*, November 8, 1938.
3. *St. Louis Star*, August 15, 1917.
4. *St. Louis Post-Dispatch*, May 25, 1917.
5. *New York Herald*, April 13, 1919.
6. *St. Louis Star*, January 12, 1918.
7. *Ibid*.
8. *Gettysburg Times*, January 19, 1920.
9. *Washington Post*, December 7, 1917.
10. *Washington Times*, January 4, 1918.
11. *Harrisburg Telegraph*, January 24, 1918.
12. *St. Louis Star*, January 30, 1918.
13. *New York Herald*, February 2, 1918.
14. *Reading Times*, February 22, 1918.
15. *Washington Herald*, March 2, 1918.
16. *Harrisburg Telegraph*, May 10, 1918.
17. *Reading Times*, April 24, 1918.
18. *Reading Times*, May 15, 1918.
19. *Ibid*.
20. *Harrisburg Courier*, June 2, 1918.
21. *Harrisburg Telegraph*, June 17, 1918.
22. *Harrisburg Evening News*, July 6, 1918.
23. *Reading Times*, August 7, 1918.

Chapter 21

1. *Providence News*, February 12, 1919.
2. *Bismarck Tribune*, February 21, 1919.
3. *St. Louis Post-Dispatch*, February 27, 1919.
4. *Gettysburg Times*, October 20, 1920.
5. *Gettysburg Times*, June 30, 1921.
6. *Salisbury* (NC) *Evening Post*, May 18, 1922.
7. *Gettysburg Times*, August 10, 1921.
8. *El Paso Herald*, January 22, 1921.
9. https://www.youtube.com/watch?v=NQ9hV7X87zA.
10. *Ibid*.
11. *News Comet* (East Berlin, PA, February 26, 1926.
12. *Gettysburg Times*, February 23, 1926.
13. *Gettysburg Times*, February 25, 1926.
14. *Ibid*.
15. *Ibid*.
16. *Ibid*.
17. *Gettysburg Times*, February 27. 1926.
18. *Gettysburg Times*, February 25, 1926.
19. *Evening Independent*, February 25, 1926.

Chapter 22

1. *Harrisburg Telegraph*, March 10, 1926.
2. *Gettysburg Times*, February 27, 1926.
3. *Reading Eagle*, February 28, 1926.
4. *Gettysburg Times*, May 15, 1926.
5. *Gettysburg Times*, June 3, 1926.
6. *Gettysburg Times*, August 20, 1927.
7. *Gettysburg Times*, May 31, 1926.
8. *Salt Lake Telegram*, June 3, 1928.
9. *Salt Lake Telegram*, January 4, 1950.
10. *Gettysburg Times*, August 12, 1940.
11. *Gettysburg Times*, April 24, 1946.
12. https://baseballhall.org/hall-of-famers/plank-eddie.
13. *Gettysburg Times*, February 10, 1961.
14. *NY Times News Service*, June 4, 1973.
15. https://www.sportscollectorsdaily.com/eddie-plank-tobacco-cards-honus-wagner/.
16. *Gettysburg Times*, September 1, 2000.
17. *Gettysburg Times*, April 2, 1926.
18. *Gettysburg Times*, February 25, 1926.

Bibliography

Books

Foster, John B., editor. *Spalding's Official Baseball Record*. New York: American Sports Publishing, 1915.
Honig, Donald, and Lawrence Ritter. *The 100 Greatest Baseball Players of All Time*. New York: Crown, 1981.
Lane, F.C. *Batting*. New York: Baseball Magazine, 1925.
Lieb, Fred. *Connie Mack: Grand Old Man of Baseball*. New York: G. B. Putnam's Sons, 1945.
Macht, Norman L. *Connie Mack and the Early Years of Baseball*. Lincoln: University of Nebraska Press, 2007.
Mack, Connie. *My 66 Years in the Big Leagues: The Great Story of America's National Game*. Philadelphia: Winston, 1950.
Morris, Peter. *Game of Inches: The Stories Behind the Innovations That Shaped Baseball*. Chicago: Ivan R. Dee, 2006.
Murnane, Timothy Hayes, editor. *Wright & Ditson Base Ball Guide*. Boston: Wright & Ditson, 1910.
Nemec, David, editor. *Major League Baseball Profiles 1871–1900: The Ballplayers Who Built the Game*. Lincoln: University of Nebraska Press, 2011.
Wiggins, Robert Peyton. *The Federal League of Base Ball Clubs: The History of an Outlaw Major League*. Jefferson, NC: McFarland, 2009.

Articles

Evans, Billy. "Famous Pitchers and Their Styles: Interesting Stories About the Game's Greatest Twirlers and How They Achieve Success." *St. Nicholas: An Illustrated Magazine for Young Folks* 41 (May 1914): 607–611.
_____. "Pitchers and Pitching." *St. Nicholas: An Illustrated Magazine for Young Folks* 42 (September 1915): 1014–1018.
French, William Fleming. "The Man Who Did Not Flash." *Illustrated World*, August 1922.
"Honesty in Baseball." *Literary Digest*, May 24, 1913.
Mack, Connie. "How to Make A Winning Ball Team." *Saturday Evening Post*, April 13, 1912.
Slick, Carroll S., with Joe Bush. "On the Mound," *Saturday Evening Post*, June 8, 1929.

Newspapers

Adams County (PA) *Independent*
Adams County (PA) *News*
Altoona (PA) *Mirror*
Altoona (PA) *Tribune*
Anaconda (MT) *Standard*
Ardmore (PA) *Daily Ardmorette*
Baltimore *American*
Baltimore *Evening Sun*
Baltimore *Morning Herald*
Baltimore *Sun*

Bibliography

Bend (OR) Bulletin
Berkshire (MA) Eagle
Bismarck (ND) Tribune
Boston Daily Globe
Boston Globe
Boston Post
Boston Sunday Post
Brainerd (MN) Daily Dispatch
Bridgeport (CT) Evening Farmer
Brooklyn Daily Eagle
Brownville (TX) Herald
Buffalo Commercial
Buffalo Enquirer
Buffalo Illustrated Express
Calumet (MI) News
Calumet (IN) Times
Charlotte News
Chester (PA) Times
Chicago Tribune
Cincinnati Enquirer
Colorado Springs Telegraph
Daily Gate City (Keokuk, IA)
Daily Kennebec (ME) Journal
Daily Sentinel (Woodstock, IL)
Daily Times (Salisbury, MD)
Day Book (Chicago)
Dayton Daily News
Decatur (IL) Daily Review
Decatur (IL) Herald
Deseret (UT) Evening News
Detroit Free Press
Detroit Times
El Paso Herald
Ellensburgh (WA) Capital
Eugene (OR) Register-Guard
Evening Independent (St. Petersburg, FL)
Florence (SC) Morning News
Fort Wayne (IN) Sentinel
Frederick (MD) News
Gazette Times (Pittsburgh, PA)
Gettysburg Compiler
Gettysburg Star and Sentinel
Gettysburg Times
The Gettysburgian
Grand Forks (ND) Evening Times
Guthrie (OK) Daily Leader
Hanover (PA) Evening Sun
Harrisburg (PA) Courier
Harrisburg (PA) Evening News
Harrisburg (PA) Sunday Courier
Harrisburg (PA) Telegraph
Hart County (KY) Herald
Hartford Courant
Helena (MT) Independent Record
Honolulu Evening Bulletin
Indianapolis Star
The Inter Ocean (Chicago)

Klamath Falls (OR) Herald and News
Kokomo (IN) Daily Tribune
Lebanon (PA) Daily News
Lewiston (PA) Daily Sun
Lewiston Evening Journal
Lima (OH) News
Lincoln (NE) Journal Star
Logansport (IN) Reporter
Los Angeles Evening Express
Los Angeles Herald
Lowell (MA) Sun
Mansfield (OH) Daily Shield
Milwaukee Journal
Milwaukee Sentinel
Monroe (LA) News-Star
Muscatine (IA) Journal
Nebraska State Journal
New Castle (PA) News
New Oxford (PA) Item
New York Evening World
New York Sun
New York Times
New York Tribune
News Comet (East Berlin, PA)
Norwich (CT) Bulletin
Ogden (UT) Evening Standard
Ogden (UT) Standard
Ogden (UT) Standard-Examiner
Oregon Daily Journal
Oshkosh (WI) Daily Northwestern
Ottawa Citizen
Oxnard (CA) Daily Courier
Pensacola Journal
Philadelphia Daily Ledger
Philadelphia Evening Bulletin
Philadelphia Evening Public Ledger
Philadelphia Evening Telegraph
Philadelphia Inquirer
Philadelphia Record
Philadelphia Times
Pittsburgh Daily Post
Pittsburgh Post-Gazette
Pittsburgh Press
Prescott (AZ) Journal Miner
Providence Evening News
Reading (PA) Eagle
Reading (PA) Times
Richmond Dispatch
Richmond Times
Richmond Times-Dispatch
St. John Sun
St. Louis Globe Democrat
St. Louis Post-Dispatch
St. Louis Republic
St. Louis Star and Times
Salisbury (NC) Evening Post
Salt Lake Telegram

San Francisco Call
San Francisco Chronicle
Santa Ana (CA) Register
Santa Cruz (CA) Evening News
Sarasota (FL) Herald-Tibune
Syracuse Herald
Tampa Tribune
Times Herald (Olean, NY)
Topeka State Journal
Toronto Sunday World
Traverse City (MI) Evening Record
Trenton Evening Times
Victoria (TX) Advocate
Washington Evening Star
Washington Evening Times
Washington Herald
Washington Post
Washington Times
Waterbury (CT) Evening Democrat
Wilkes-Barre (PA) Evening News
Williamsport Daily Gazette and Bulletin
York (PA) Daily
York (PA) Gazette
Youngstown (OH) Vindicator

Periodicals

Baseball Magazine
1903 Reach Guide
1910 Reach Guide
1911 Reach Guide
Sporting Life
The Sporting News

Collections

Eddie Plank clippings file, National Baseball Hall of Fame library
Gettysburg College Oral History Collection. Charles C. "Junie" Bream, by Michael J. Birkner, November 27 and December 4, 2000; Ralph Mahaffie, by Michael J. Birkner, June 4, 1994.

Correspondence

Amy Lucademo, Gettysburg College College Archivist, September 11–12, 2018
Steve Slaughter, Association of Licensed Battlefield Guide, October 2, 2016

Online Resources

Ancestry.com
Annandale, Virginia, Chamber of Commerce
Ballparks.com
Baseball History Daily
Baseball-Reference.com
BaseballAlmanac.com
Censusrecords.com
Chronicling America, Library of Congress
CooperstownExpert.com
LA84 Foundation digital library
Fultonhistory.com
Hunterstown-Thenandnow.com
National Baseball Hall of Fame
New York Times Online archive
Newspapers.com
PaperofRecord.com
Retrosheet.org
RootsWeb.com
SABR Bio Project
Seanlahman.com
Sports Collectors Daily
U.S. Department of Transportation, Federal Highway Administration

Index

Numbers in *bold italics* indicate pages with illustrations

Adams, Babe 186
advertisements 97, 135
age 9, 18–19, 24, 98, 108, 125, 132, 141, 160, 186, 192, 194, 195, 203, 206
Ainsmith, Eddie 204
Alexander, Grover Cleveland 1, 162, 194, 216, 223
all-star teams 97, 132, 165, 216, 223–224
all-time lists *see* statistics
all-time teams *see* all-star teams
Almendares 106, 133
Altrock, Nick 121
American League 5, 21, 30–31, 32, 40, 166
American League Park 25, *46*
Ames, Red 124, 196
Anson, Adrian "Cap" 97
Atkins, Tommy 103
Austin, Jimmy 198

Baker, Charles "Bock" 6, 7, 22, 23, 24
Baker, Frank "Home Run" *52*, 80, 84, 91, 92, 93, 95, 96, 100, 103, 106, 114, 115, 116, 120, 122, 133, 135, 143, 146, 147, 148, 149, 152, 156, 162, 171, 216, 218
Ball, Phil 175, 178, 180, 188, 195, 198, 199, 207
Baltimore Orioles 5, 6, 7, 22, 23, 28, 29, 33, 35, 38, 160
Baltimore Terrapins 183, 185–186, 187
banquet 40, 61, 125, 156–158, 188
barnstorming 41, 60, 66, 79, 98, 132, 197
Barrett, Jimmy 26
Barry, Hardin 128
Barry, Jack 78, 80, 95, 96, 98, 103, 114, 116, 130, 133, 135, 148, 153, 156, 164, 167, 218
Barton, Harry 20
baseball card *107*, 227–228, *228*
battlefield guide *see* Gettysburg battlefield
Baumgardner, George 190

Beck, Erve 30
Bell, George 108
Bender, Charles Albert "Chief" 19, 20, 45, 49, 51, 52, 54, 56, 58, 61, 64, 65, 67, 68, 70, 73, 77, 78, *78*, 79–80, 81, 86, 94, 96, 99, 100, 101, 102, 103, 104, 105, 108, 116, 117, 118, 119, 124, 125–126, 128, 130, 132, 133, 134, 136, 142, 143, 144, 145, 146, 150, 156, 161, 162, 165, 166, 169, 172–173, 174–175, *175*, 176, 182, 183, 185, 197, 211, 215, 216, 218
Bennett Park 94
Bernhard, Bill 6, 22, 32
Bethlehem 211–212
Bethlehem Steel League 209–212, 213, 214
Biederman, Les 227
Birmingham, Joe 133, 141–142
Bliss, Jack 98
Bodie, Ping 129
Bonner, Frank 36
Borton, Babe 179, 184
Boston Braves 33, 165, 166–168
Boston Red Sox 6, 21, 22, 29, 30, 34, 36, 38, 45, 46, 49–50, 51, 54, 55, 63, 64, 70, 71, 85–86, 90, 101, 110, 111, 114, 116, 127, 128, 129–130, 139, 141, 161–162, 164, 173, 193–194, 202, 204
Bowerman, Frank 66
bowling 48, 79, 125
Bradley, Bill 35, 46
Bream, Charles C. "Junie" 113, 219–220, 229
Brennan, Bill 185
Bresnahan, Roger 35, 66
Bressler, Rube 163–164, *163*
Bridwell, Al 118
Brooklyn Dodgers 30, 37
Brooklyn Royal Giants 65
Brooklyn Tip-Tops 2, 160, 170–171, 182, 186

243

Index

Brown, Carroll "Boardwalk" 126, 143, 144, 151, 161, 218
Brown, Mordecai 158, 178, 180
Bruce, Louis 20
Brush, John T. 30, 51
Buckles, Jesse 211
Bucknell 16, 18, 27, 150
Buffalo Blues 186
Burns, George 152
Bush, Donie 88–89, 92, 94, 110, 128, 169, 192
Bush, Joe 44, 143, 144, 150, 155, 161, 165, 167, 197, 216

Callahan, Jimmy 173
Callison, Johnny 228
Cambridge 18
Cantillon, Joe 40, 73
Carlisle 12, 16, 18, 19, 24
Carr, Charlie 22
Carrick, Bill 33, 34
Carrigan, Bill 139, 173
Casey, James "Doc" 27
Cassidy, Joe 20
Castro, Luis *34*, 36
celebration *see* banquet
Chambersburg 17
Chance, Frank 102, 124, 138
Chandler, Happy 226
Chapman, Harry *184*
Chapman, Ray 215
Chase, Hal 138
Chesbro, Jack 52, 216
Chester 17, 18
Chicago Cubs 102, 104–105, 188
Chicago Whales 171, 174, 182, 184, 185, 186, 187, 188
Chicago White Sox 6, 26, 28, 29, 35, 36, 37, 45, 50, 53, 55–56, 63, 68, 69, 70, 71, 75, 88, 91, 112, 114, 127, 141, 173, 190–192, 193, 201, 202
Cicotte, Eddie 125, 201
Cincinnati Reds 37, 179
city series 48, 62, 67, 83, 100, 132, 196
Clarke, Bill "Boileryard" 29, 60
Clay, William 18
clean living 28, 47, 49, 112–113, 157, 161, 195, 222
Clemens, Rogers 132
Cleveland Blues/Indians/Naps 2, 6, 26, 28, 30, 32, 33, 35, 36, 37, 53, 54, 55, 63, 68, 69, 70, 73, 91, 102, 111, 112, 114, 129, 138, 141, 162, 193, 194, 201, 203
Coakley, Andy 51, 54, 56, 59, 61, 64, 65, 194–195
Cobb, Ty 44, 69, 70–71, 88–89, *89*, 90, 92, 93, 94, 95, 97, 101, 104, 110, 114–116, 128, 129, 135, 168, 200, 203, 223

Cockill, George 209–210, 211, 214
Collins, Eddie 1–2, 52, *52*, 65, 78, 80, 84, 85, 89, 91, 95, 96, 97, 103, 105, 106, 110, 116, 120, 125, 127, 128–129, 130, 133, 135, 140, 143, 148, 149, 151, 153, 156, 157, 162, 164, 167, 169, 171, 172, 176, 190–191, *191*, 200, 201, 215, 218, 224
Collins, Jimmy 67, 70, 77
Collins, Ray 139
Columbia Park 21, 22, 26, 28, 55, *58*, 58, *59*, 81
Comiskey, Charles 173
Comiskey Park 190, 201
Connolly, Tommy 71, 88, 121, 139, 148
contract 31, 48, 65, 75–76, 77, 98, 125, 134–135, 158–160, 170, 174–175, 188, 190, 200, 213
Coombs, Jack 43, 62, 64, 65, 67, 68, 74, 77, 78, 79, 87, 100, 102, 103, 104, 105, 108, 109, 110, 111, 112, 116, 118, 119, 122, 123, 124, 125, 126, 128, 130, 132, 133, 134, 136, 140, 143, 149, 151, 160, 161, 169, 170, 172–173, 176, 197, *198*, 215, 218
Crandall, Doc 123, 144, 179, 186
Crawford, Sam 71–72, 88–89, 92, 94, 95, 110–111, 129
Cree, Birdie 127
Crisham, Pat 22
Cronin, Joe 227
Cross, Lave 5, 30, 33, 39, 46, 47, 48, 51, 52, 57, *58*, 58, 59, 62, 76, 103
Cross, Monte 32, 33, *34*, 40, 48, 49, 59, 65, 66, 69, 71, 74, 77, 218
crossfire 3, 42–44, 62, 121, 128, 192
Cuba 105–107, 133, 178, 180
Cullop, Nick 186–187, 207, 213
Cuppy, George "Nig" 25, 26

Dahlen, Bill 66
Danforth, Dave 164
Davenport, Dave 164, 179, 186–187, 190, 195, 196, 201
Davis, George 17, 29, 63
Davis, Harry 26–27, *34*, 36, 39, 40, 46, 48, 49, 56, *59*, 64, 66, 69, 70, 71–72, 74, 77, 80, 84, 88, 91, 94, 96, 97, 100, 103, 108, 114, *115*, 117, 118, 119, 123, 125, 133, 141, 155–156, 157, 169, 171, 197, 218–219, 222
Davis, Harry, Jr. 156
Davis, Tom 174
Deal, Charlie 166–167, 179, 192
death 217–219
debut *see* major-league debut
Delahanty, Ed 30, 33
Delahanty, Jim 110–111
delivery *see* crossfire and/or slow pitching
Derrick, Claud 106

Index 245

Detroit Tigers 2, 5, 26, 27, 29, 35, 36, 37, 51, 54, 55, 63, 67, 68, 69–70, 71–73, 88–89, 90–96, 99, 101, 102, 110, 111–112, 114–116, 127, 128–129, 138, 163, 173, 192–193, 199, 203
Devlin, Art 66, 122, 123
Devore. Josh 118, 120, 121
Dickinson College 16, 18, 19, 24
Dill, William F. 14
discussing retirement 98–99, 109, 124, 134, 155, 158, 197, 204, 205–209, 213
Dolan, Joe 29
Donlin, Mike 23, 60, 66
Donovan, Bill 71, 189, 199
Donovan, Patsy 111
Dooin, Charley 137
Doolin, Mickey 183
Dougherty, Pat 63, 113
Doyle, Larry 118, 123, 148, 153
Drake, Delos 179
Dreyfuss, Barney 40
Dubuc, Jean 128
Duggleby, Bill 30, 32
Duncan, Bill 148, 200, 225, 227
Dygert, Jimmy 55, 62, 64, 67, 70, 71, 73–74, 77, 78, 86

Easton 18
Ebling, Doc 99
Eddie Plank Memorial Gymnasium 222–223, **224**, 228
Egan, Ben 127
Egan, Rip 88
Elberfeld, Kid 35, 160
endorsements *see* advertisements
Engel, Joe 113
Evans, Billy 90–91, 100, 106, 140, 216, 218
Evers, Johnny 104, 168, **168**
Ewing, Bob 108
exhibitions 51, 67, 79, 98, 104, 118, 197

Fairfield 11
farm 8, 12, 13, 19, 79, 98, 125, 197, 209
Farrell, Frank 174
Farrell, John 29
father *see* Plank, David L.
Federal League 2, 158, 160, 166, 169–175, 178, 179, 182, 187, 188–189, 198, 226–227
Felsch, Happy 191
Fewster, Chick 210
Fincher, Bill 190
Finneran, Bill 184
Fletcher, Art 149
Flick, Elmer 32, 34, 35, 36
Fore River 210, 211
Foreman, Frank 2–3, 14–15, 17, 20–21, 42
Foster, Eddie 130, 194, 198, 199, 204
Fournier, Jack 191–192

Foutz, Frank 23
Foy, Eddie 135
Franklin & Marshall 15
Fraser, Chick 6, 22, 32, 42
Frick, Ford 226
Frysinger, Jess 17, 18, 19–20
Fultz, Dave 5, 22, 25, **34**, 36, 39
funeral 222

garage *see* Plank garage
Gardner, Larry 104, 203
Gates, E.E. 171
Gedeon, Joe 207
Gehrig, Lou 225
Geier, Phil 5
George, Lefty 219
Gessler, Doc 100
Gettysburg, Pennsylvania 7, 9, 13, 25, 31, 41, 48, 51, 61, 77, 125, 141, 142, 156, 177, 185, 189, 190, 193, 197, 204, 206, 217, 221–222, 228–229
Gettysburg Academy 14, 15
Gettysburg battlefield 76–77, 156–157
Gettysburg College 14; baseball team 7, 11, 12, **15**, 17, 18, 19, 23, 24, 48, 77, 150, 214
Gettysburg town team **8**, 11, 12, 13
Gilbert, Billy 59
Gilmore, James 171, 178
Goldman, Harry 174, 178
Gomez, Jose Miguel 106
good behavior *see* clean living
Good Intent baseball team 9, 10, 11, 49
Good Intent school 9
Gowdy, Hank 168
Grant, Eddie 149
Green, Danny 30
Grenoble, W.S. 12
Griffith, Clark 122, 130, 131, 132, 146, 160, 186, 198
Groom, Bob 130, 180, 181, 196, 201
Grove, Lefty 1, 223

Habana Reds 106, 133, 180
Hall of Fame 224–226
Hamilton, Earl 190, 200
Hanlon, Ned 30
Harlan 210, 211
Hartsel, Topsy 30, 32, 33, **34**, 39, 48, 64, 74, 84, 108, 117, 125
Hayden, Jack 22, 27
Hendrix, Claude 180, 183, 184, 185
Henley, Weldon 45, 49, 51, 55, 56, 62
Herrmann, August 189
Herzog, Buck 120, 148, 153
Hickman, Charlie 46
Hill, Hunter 52
Hilltop Park 68

Hoffman, Danny 49, 51
Hoffman, Izzy 158
Holtzworth, Allie 19
home run allowed 35, 46, 90
home run hit 45, 68, 92
Hornsby, Rogers 225
Houck, Byron 127, 132, 141, 143, 144, 170–171
Hubbell, Carl 223
Huggins, Miller 208–209, 213
Hunterstown 10
hunting 48, 79, 125, 216–217
Hurst, Tim 69
Husting, Bert 33, 34, *34*, 37, 42
Huston, Tillinghast L'Hommedieu 199

Idaville 11
injury 31, 54, 63, 101, 151, 181, 192, 201–202, 206
Irwin, Arthur 174

Jackson, Bill 184
Jackson, Joe 191–192, 200, 201, 209, 211
James, Bill 166–167
Janvrin, Hal 193
Jennings, Hughie 99, 101, 111, 115, 138, 172
Johnson, Ban 21, 35, 38, *39*, 40, 60, 61, 69, 83, 119, 125, 128, 139, 174, 189
Johnson, Chief 187
Johnson, Ernie 179
Johnson, Jack 180
Johnson, Randy 132, 194
Johnson, Russell "Jing" 162
Johnson, Walter 1, 70, 73, 100–101, 104, 128, 130, 135, 137, 146, 175, 192, 193, 194, 202, 204, 205, 216, 223
Johnson, Willis 112
Jones, Fielder 63, 68, 178, 180, *181*, 182, 184, 185, 186–187, 188, 189, 190, 191, 192–193, 194, 195, 196, 197, 199–200, 201, 202, 203, 205–206, 207
Joss, Addie 55, 216

Kansas City Packers 181, 182, 183, 186–187
Keister, Bill 23
Kenna, Edward B. *34*, 35
Ketchum, Fred 22
Killefer, Red 101
Killian, Ed 68
Kilroy, Matt 42–43
King, Silver 43
Klem, Bill 123, 152
Knabe, Otto 183, 185
Knight, Jack 64, 67
Koob, Ernie 190, 200, 201, 206
Krause, Harry 81, 86, 90, 91, 92, 94, 95, 96, 99, 108, 116, 126, *126*, 164

Lajoie, Nap 5, 22, 25, 29, 32, 33–34, 35, 36, 46, 145, 160, 162
Lake, Joe 169
Lancaster Actives 16, 17
Landis, Commissioner Kenesaw Mountain 225
Lantz, Harry 14, 16
Lapp, Jack 86, 103, 104, 110, 127, 128–129, 137, 148, 149, 151
Lavan, John "Doc" 192, 207
Lebanon 210, 211
Lee, Watty 33
Lemon, Bob 226
Lennox, Ed 63
Leonard, Dutch 203, 211
Lewisburg 18
lifestyle *see* clean living
Livingston, Paddy 85, 98, 104, 105
Lochhead, Harry 5
London, Jack 135
Loos, Pete 6, 22
Lord, Bris 20, 51, 116, 120

Mack, Connie 1, 2, 5, 6, 7, 19–21, 22, 23, 24, 26, 27, 28, 29, 30, 32–33, 34–36, 37, 38, 39, 40, 43, 44, 48, 49, 50, 51, 53, 54, 55, 56, 57, 60, 61, 62, 63, 64, 65, 67–68, 72–73, 74, 75, 77, 80–81, 83, 84, 85, 87, 88, 92, 93, 94–95, 97, 98, 99, 101, 104, 105, 109, *109*, 113–114, 116–117, 118–119, 123–124, 125, 126, 129–130, 133, 134–135, 141, 142, 143, 144–145, 146, 148–149, 151, 156–157, 158–160, 163, 166, 169, 171–172, 173–174, 178, 180, 182, 188, 189, 190, 207, 216, 218, *219*, 219, 222–223, 225–226
Mack, Earle 149
Magee, Sherry 20
Maisel, Fritz 198–200, 207
Major, Richard King 9, 10, 11
major-league debut 6, 23
Mamaux, Al 211
Mann, Les 167, 184
Mannassau, Al 28
Maranville, Rabbit 167
Marquard, Rube 119, 120, 123, 138, 144, 146
Marsans, Armando 179, 193, 194
Mathewson, Christy 1, 22, 27, 28, 30, 44, 57, 58, 59, 60, 73, 119, 121, 135, *136*, 144, 146, *146*, 147–153, 161, 190, 215, 216, 223
Mathewson, Jane 150
Mays, Carl 202, 215
McAleer, Jimmy 37, 53, 100
McBride, George 93, 130
McCarthy, Joe 212
McCreary, Martha *see* Plank, Martha
McGann, Joe 35, 60
McGinnity, Joe 23, 35, 58–59

Index

McGraw, John 23, 35, **58**, 58, **59**, 60, 66, 119, 122, 123, **136**, **146**, 148–149, 150, 152, 189, 190
McInnis, Albert 159
McInnis, John "Stuffy" **52**, 81, 84, 103, 110, 114, 116, 117, 118, 127, 129, 131, 135, 147, 148, 152, 153, 156, 168, 171
McIntyre, Marty 88–89
McLean, Larry 148, 152
McSherrystown 12, 13, 16
Mendez, Jose 106, 180
Merkle, Fred 121, 152
Mertes, Sam 59
Meyers, Chief 118, 120–121, 150–151
Milan, Clyde 104, 204
Miller, Ward 179, 185, 194
Milligan, Billy 6, 22
Milwaukee Brewers 26, 28, 29
Moore, Earl 30
Morgan, Cy 96, 102, 104, 108, 112, 116, 125, 126, 129, 132
Moriarty, George 90, 91, 94, 95, 105, 190, 221
mother *see* Plank, Martha
Mullin, George 53, 68, 69, 97
Murphy, Danny 36, 39, 50, **52**, 64, 65, 72, 79, 84, 88, 92, 93, 96, 98, 103, 111, 116, 117, 125, 127, 128, 130, 151, 160, 170–171, 172
Murphy, Eddie 134, 148, 152, 153, 154, 164, 167
Murphy, Morgan 22, 23, 25, 66
Murray, Red 118, 120, 123, 148, 152
Musselman, Morris "Doc" 12, 17, 19
Myers, Anna Cora *see* Plank, Anna
Myers, Charley 19

Nallin, Frank 219
National Commission 120, 189, 197
National League 5, 30–31, 33
Navin, Frank 75, 173–174, 199
Needham, Tom 20
New Oxford, Pennsylvania 177–178, 188
New Oxford baseball team 11
New York Giants 17, 22, 27, 35, 36, 51, 57–60, 61, 66–67, 110, 116, 118–124, 142, 143–153, 189, 190, 215
New York Highlanders/Yankees 45, 51, 52, 55, 63, 68, 70, 90, 102, 111, 116, 125, 127, 137, 138, 142, 161, 174, 189, 193, 197, 204, 207–209, 213, 215–216
Newark Peppers 2, 182, 186
Newhouse, Frank 218
Nicholls, Simon 77, 84, 85, 88, 99
nicknames 7, 11, 12, 76–77, 103–104
Nixon Field 12, 15, 17, 18, 207
Nunamaker, Les 207

O'Brien, Buck 139
O'Brien, Joe 133–134
O'Connor, Jack 40
O'Day, Hank 165
O'Laughlin, Silk 72–73, 128, 191–192
Oldring, Rube 70, 84, 103, **103**, 105, 114, 116, 120, 123, 130, 135, 148, 162, 169
Orr, Billy 155
Orth, Al 33
Overall, Orval 73
Owen, Frank 53

Packard, Gene 187
parade 40, 61, 156
Parker, Dr. Harley 113
Patterson, Roy 63
Paxtang Club 13
Pennock, Herb 127, 135, 142, 161, 169, 194, 218
Perrine, Bull 91, 116
Pfiester, Jack 121
Philadelphia Athletics 5, 6, 7, 19, 21–26, 30, 33–34, 35, 36–37, 38, 40, 42–43, 44, 45–46, 47, 49, 51–60, 61, 62–65, 66–70, 71–74, 75, 77, 85–86, 87–96, 100–105, 106, 110–116, 118–124, 125–131, 133, 135–139, 141–142, 143–154, 161–165, 166–168, 172, 189, 193, 195, 197, 207
Philadelphia Giants 65
Philadelphia Park 132
Philadelphia Phillies 5, 6, 32, 33, 38, 48, 62, 67, 83, 100, 132, 180
Phillips, Lawrence 119–120
Phillips, Tom 211
Piatt, Wiley 6, 22, 27
Piazza, Mike 228
Pickering, Ollie 49, 51
Pierce, George 210, 211–212
Pinnance, Ed 20
Pipp, Wally 210
pitching delivery *see* slow pitching
Pittsburgh Pirates 30, 40, 215
Pittsburgh Stogies 181, 185, 186, 187
Plank, Anna 177–178, 180, 188, 217, 218, 219, 226, 230
Plank, David L. 7, 8, 9, 10, 12, 14, 104, 122, 183
Plank, Eddie, Jr. 188, 217, 219, 226
Plank, Grace 9, 218
Plank, Howard 9, 10, 183
Plank, Ira 9, 14, 51, 180, 204, 205, 206, 215, 226
Plank, Luther 9, 10, 11, 77, 218, 226
Plank, Martha 7, 9, 183, 193, 218
Plank, Mattie 9
Plank farm *see* farm
Plank garage 206, 208–209, 215, 216

248 Index

Plank gymnasium *see* Eddie Plank Memorial Gym
playing outfield 17, 18, 66, 215
Plitt, Norman 210
Polo Grounds 59, 119, 123, 150, 152–153
Portsmouth Truckers 216
Postal, Fred 39
Powell, Jack 108
Powers, Mike "Doc" 5, 25, 30, *34*, 42, 46, 49, 60, **65**, 69, 71, 73, 76, 84–87
praise 10, 11, 13, 23–24, 26, 27, 28, 29, 34, 45, 47, 50, 63, 111, 121–122, 130, 137–138, 141–142, 157, 167, 179, 182, 185, 190, 192–193, 194, 199, 200, 201, 211, 216, 218–219
Pratt, Del 192, 199, 207
Prendergast, Mike 182
Pulliam, Harry 40–41

Quinn, Bob 204, 207, 213

Rawlings, Johnny 187
Raymond, Bugs 161
Reading Pretzels 158–159
Reisling, Doc 101
retirement talk *see* discussing retirement
Rhoads, Bob 55
Richmond Bluebirds 16
Rickert, Joe 66–67
Rickey, Branch 173, 198, 200, 225
Robinson, Wilbert 23
Rogers, James 32
Rogers, Tom 206
Roosevelt, Alice 52
Rossman, Claude 71, 88–89
Rucker, Nap 138, 216
Rudolph, Dick 168
Rumler, Bill 202
Ruppert, Col. Jacob 199, 208
Russell, Alan 211
Russell, Lefty 127
Russell, Reb 173
Ruth, Babe 193–194, 215, 223
Ryan, Nolan 194

St. Louis Browns 35, 37, 46–47, 54, 56, 63, 68, 70, 75, 88, 91, 110, 111, 112, 114, 127, 141, 162, 173, 180, 182, 188, 189–196, 198, 201–204, 205, 207, 213
St. Louis Cardinals 182, 196, 197
St. Louis Terriers 2, 175, 178, 179–187, 188, 193, 196
salary 11, 65, 75, 77, 134, 159–160, 174–175, 190, 200, 210
Salisbury 18
Salmon, Roger 127
Schaefer, Germany 69, **69**, 72, 90–91, 100, 101

Schang, Wally 149, 151–152, 155, 167, 193, 195, 197, 216
Schrecongost, Ossee 33, 39, 40, 49, 54, 71, 77, 161
Schrek *see* Schrecongost, Ossee
Schulte, Frank 104
Schwab, Charles M. 209
Scott, Jim 171
Segar, Charlie 227
Severeid, Hank 195, 204
Seybold, Socks 5, 39, 49, 64, 65, 74
Seymour, Cy 23, 66
Shafer, Tillie 148, 152
Shawkey, Bob 143, 144, 151, 159, 161, 165, 216
Sheckard, Jimmy 104, 158
Sherdel, Bill 219
Sheridan, Jack 58
Shibe, Ben 35, 79, 128
Shibe, John 60, 61, 79, 102, 214
Shibe Park 81–83, *81*, *82*, 85, 91, 94, 95, 104, 105, 112, 119, 122–123, 130, 132, 137, 141, 142, *144*, *145*, *147*, 150, *153*, 155–156, 162, 163, 166, *179*, 195, 214
Shocker, Urban 207
Shotton, Burt 162
sign stealing 168–169
Simmons, Hack 127
Sisler, George 200
slow pitching 2, 25, 26, 139–140
Smith, Harry 40
Smith, Jimmy 185
Smoot, Homer 20
Snodgrass, Chappie 22
Snodgrass, Fred 118, 120–121, 123, 147
Somers, Charles 40
Sothoron, Allan 201
Spahn, Warren 194, 227
Sparrow's Point 210, 211
Speaker, Tris 85, 104, 194, 200
spitball 52, 128–129
Sportsman's Park 193, 201, 203
spring training 44, 48, 51, 62, 66–67, 109–110, 159–161, 190, 200, 209
Stahl, Jake 50, 53, 90, 104, 130
Stallings, George 27, 165, 167, 168
Stanage, Oscar 91–92, 94, 95
statistics 1, 2, 25, 31, 39, 45, 49, 57, 65, 66, 73–74, 78–79, 96, 99, 108, 116, 132, 134, 137, 143, 165, 185–186, 188, 196, 206, 226–227
Steelman, Morris "Farmer" 30, *34*
Steelton 209–212, 213
Stimmel, "Speed" 12
Straban Township 9
Street, Gabby 100, 101
Stroud, Ralph 101

Index

Strunk, Amos 84, 85, 103, 105, 135, 148, 149, 166–167, 197, 218
Sullivan, Billy 56
Summers, Ed 91, 92, 101
Sunday, Billy 112, 161
Susquehanna 16
Syracuse 15

Taft, William H. 100
Tener, John 189
Terrapin Park 183
Tesreau, Jeff 144, 150, 211–212
Thomas, Ira 86, 88, 90–91, 95, 104, 110, 111, 127, 151, 158, 160, 163–164, 218, *219*
Thoney, Jack 46
Tinker, Joe 158, 174
Tobin, Johnny "Jack" 179, 181
Townsend, Happy 20
trap shooting 79, 216
Tri-State League 158–159, 170
Triple League 18

Unglaub, Bob 101

Van Zelst, Louis 155
Vaughn, Bobby 179, 185
Vickers, Rube 73, 77, 78
Vinson, Rube 20
Virginia League 16, 215
Vitt, Oscar 193, 199

Waddell, Rube 36, 37, 39, 40, 45, 47, 48, 49, 51, 54, 55, 56, 57, 61, 64, 67, 70, 71, 73, 74, 75, 76, 88, 161, 194, 216, 223, 226
Wagner, Hans 97, 160
Wagner, Heinie 85
Wagner, Honus *see* Wagner, Hans
waivers 172–174
Walker, William 171
Wallace, Bobby 160
Walsh, Ed 68, 97, 129, 141, 162, 216, 223, 226
Walsh, Jimmy 183
Ward, George 171
Ward, John Montgomery 170

Ward, Robert 188
Washington Nationals/Senators 22, 25, 29, 30, 33–34, 38, 50, 52, 56, 62, 67, 70, 73, *78*, 86–87, 88, 91, 93, 100, 101, 128, 129, 130–131, 138, 194, 197–198, 202, 204, 205, 215
Watson, Doc 179–180
Weaver, Buck 191
Weeghman, Charlie 171, 174, 175, 188
Weeghman Park 180–181
Weikert, Edwards 217
Weilman, Carl 190, 201
Welch, Jimmy 167
White, Doc 50, 121
white elephant 35, 38, 40, 47, 56, *58*, 58
Willard, Jess 180
Willett, Ed 92, 179–180, 186
Williams, Jimmy 23
Wills, Nat 135
Wilmington 210
Wilmington AA 20, 39
Wilson, Art 118, 184
Wiltse, Hooks 124, 148
Wiltse, Snake 34
Winter, George *15*, 17, 18, 20–21, 29, 31, 45
Wolf, Robin 12
Wolverton, Harry 30, 33
Wood, Smoky Joe 44, 128, 216
World Series 57–60, *58*, 104–105, 116, 118–124, *136*, *137*, 143–154, *144*, *145*, *146*, *147*, *153*, 166–168, *168*, *179*, *191*, 215–216
Wright, George 83
Wycoff, Weldon 159

Yarrison, Byron 214–215
Yeager, Joe 35
York Athletics 13
York Penn Park 17
York White Roses 11
Young, Cy 1, 34, 45, 49, 108–109, 118, 186, 194, 216, 223

Zimmer, Charles 67
Zinn, George 183

www.ingramcontent.com/pod-product-compliance
Ingram Content Group UK Ltd.
Pitfield, Milton Keynes, MK11 3LW, UK
UKHW041935140426
5217IPUK00014B/498